GREAT DAMES

GREAT DAMES

WHAT I LEARNED FROM
OLDER WOMEN

Marie Brenner

Crown Publishers, New York

Some of the essays contained in this book were previously published in *Vogue, The New Yorker,* and *Vanity Fair.*

Published by Crown Publishers, New York, New York. Member of Random House, Inc.

Random House, Inc. New York, Toronto, London, Sydney, Auckland
www.randomhouse.com

CROWN is a trademark and the Crown colophon is a registered trademark of Random House, Inc.

Printed in the United States of America

Design by Lauren Dong

Library of Congress Cataloging-in-Publication Data
Brenner, Marie.
    Great dames : what I learned from older women / by Marie Brenner-1st ed.
    1. Women—United States—Biography. 2. Women in public life—United States—Biography.
    3. Women—Conduct of life—Case studies. I. Title.
HQ1412.B734   2000
305.4'092'273—dc21   99-045585

ISBN 0-609-60612-3

10 9 8 7 6 5

for Casey and Annie and Thelma

Contents

They Were Outstanding

My mother and her friends were the first great dames I ever knew. I was a child of the South Texas suburbs, eavesdropping as my mother sat surrounded by her circle. I can see them so clearly: my mother is curled up on a white love seat in the game room decorated with my father's hunting trophies—cape buffalo and kudu, a lion skin. Her auburn hair is perfectly arranged, her makeup impeccable. As a young woman, she was occasionally mistaken for the actress Deanna Durbin. Looks matter to her and to the other women in the room. There are low voices trading information and intimacies, conversation as soothing as my mother's mango mold. They share an unknowing bond with the more famous personalities of this book—they are women, hardwired communicators, Olympic listeners. I learned a large lesson in that room: women learn from the life stories of other women. Our narratives are not always told in linear, declarative sentences; we revel in the indirect. We take in the experience of others, absorb information and secrets, a hidden code.

The great dames in this book were part of the twentieth century. They lived through the Great Depression and then the war. Circumstances did not defeat them. They were brave and intelligent, and they tried to figure out how to live. As a young girl, my mother skipped lunches for weeks to buy a cashmere sweater; she wore her hair in a

Veronica Lake pageboy and used the word "snag" to describe the pursuit of a man. As a high school girl, she spent Saturdays watching Katharine Hepburn in *The Philadelphia Story* and anything with Irene Dunne. She was out of high school when penicillin was invented; she had slumber parties and wore oversized pajamas and set her hair with rags. She went to bond rallies, rationed hairpins, and followed the progress of her brother and boyfriends through the daily headlines. My mother was in Washington working at an Office of Strategic Services typing pool. I imagine her reading the newspapers: IWO JIMA AND CORREGIDOR INVADED, JAPANESE REPORT, ENEMY PLANES REPORTED TWO HOURS FROM NEW YORK, INVASION IS ON, PRESIDENT ROOSEVELT IS DEAD, TRUMAN SWORN IN AS SUCCESSOR.

She lived in a world of limited expectations and tightly drawn borders. Many graduate schools were closed to women as were entire careers. In 1943, women were discouraged from dining at "21" without a man. As a young married, my mother watched newsreels of Edith Mae Irby becoming the first Negro to be be admitted to the University of Arkansas Medical School. It was 1949. The Senate's resident racist Theodore Bilbo of Mississippi called on "every red-blooded white man to use any means to keep the niggers away from the polls." Clubwomen in lacy hats poured tea and served canapés and read *Forever Amber* on the sly.

Now, in the Kennedy years, mother and her friends bought Adolfo knockoffs, skimmer dresses, and white slacks. My mother wore a string of pearls, a garnet pin. She read *The Second Sex* but expressed contempt for "women's libbers." My mother never needed to defend her elaborate dressing rituals. She used a phrase which has passed out of common usage—"put together." As she worked her way through her closet, she fretted over wardrobe choices: racks of silk blouses in a rainbow of pastels to match her suits. "I like to look put together," she would say. Like the term "great dames," "put together" is a phrase with implication. Loretta Young twirling into our living rooms wearing chiffon and an actressey smile. Rosalind Russell and Audrey Hepburn. "Put together" was a metaphor of a entire generation that believed in beating back the demons by whistling in the dark. Years later, I would spend an afternoon touring New York arts programs at schools with Kitty Carlisle Hart. At age eighty-seven, she was New York State Commissioner of the Arts. Mrs. Hart, a generic great dame, is always put together. That day there was a massive storm. Mrs. Hart greeted me in a lavender Ultrasuede coat trimmed with fox and an expression of a delighted child. "I always dress up. I feel that if I don't people will not give me compliments," she said. I thought instantly of my mother, a few months before she died, applying full makeup at Mt. Sinai Hospital. "Get me my round brush that curls my hair," she ordered me briskly. "They treat you better if you look good. I have to be put together."

The term Great Dames mostly shows up today as a punning headline for a story about someone being knighted by the queen. But great dames were real. The great dames advanced their ambitions with a smile. They did not whine. Kitty Carlisle Hart's daughter Catherine, a physician, used a phrase to describe her mother's particular gift: "the machinery of my mother's discipline." Dr. Hart was underscoring the essence of all these women: there was nothing frivolous behind the facade. The great dames meant business; they were determined to move up in the world. Before she walked into the segregated courtroom of Jackson, Mississippi, in 1949, another great dame, Constance Baker Motley, spent a day at Lord & Taylor searching for exactly the right dress. She knew the role she was there to play—she was one of the first Negro lawyers to ever appear in a court in the deep South. If black people needed a lawyer, she told me, they found a white man to go in for them. When she arrived in Jackson, the reporters commented on her clothes; but entering the courtroom, Motley used her chic to rebuke the mural which decorated the walls: the glories of lost Dixie. Darkies hoisting cotton bales on one side; white girls in crinolines and hoopskirts on another.

My mother began dressing over an hour before she had to leave the house. She wore pale stockings, a one-piece foundation garment. She was carefully powdered and was scented with Mitsouko. Her clothes were organized by color in her closet; she assembled them on the bed before she dressed. I was oblivious to the larger meaning of the scene. I only saw her pillbox hats. I wore cutoffs and thong sandals and made fun of her elaborate grooming, the pale shoes and matching hose in the summer heat, the Mitsouko bottles lined up neatly on a porcelain tray. The truth was I loved watching my mother dress; I learned plenty from listening to her with her friends. Like Mrs. Hart and Judge Constance Baker Motley, they were women with an aura, a gift for self-presentation. They understood the rules of the game. If they had a mantra, it would be "Project grace notes, no matter what."

The great dames understood the power of mystique, of setting yourself apart. Rapt attention was their art. They broke barriers, they had fierce ambitions and egos, a sense of destiny. They seemed to share childhood moments when they saw the possibility of their journeys, snapshots of their futures. Maybe a shiver: *I will be great.* Each woman put her finger in the warm clay of her era and helped to shape it. Constance Baker Motley, who argued *Brown* v. *Board of Education,* is a profile in courage, enduring and indefatigable in her good wool suit and hat, fighting race hate, against all odds. The ethereal and unpredictable Luise Rainer, who had won two Academy Awards by the age of thirty, then fled Hollywood by 1940, determined to rebel against any form of domination. The sunniest of the women, Kitty Carlisle Hart, who mugged with the Marx brothers and went on to be a tireless advocate for the arts, starts her morning by smiling at herself in the mirror: "Kitty, I forgive you."

I began to search out life stories of singular older women a few months before my mother's death. I was not yet forty; she would not live to be seventy. I think I wanted to hear stories that evoked the context of my mother's life. I was a noisy rebel, a member of the class of '71 with the sharp and unforgiving view of my generation of young feminists. For years, I was oblivious to the mores of my mother's generation. I saw the smoke screen and did not understand the endurance or the urgency it masked.

With the exceptions of Diana Trilling and Thelma Brenner, most of the chapters in this book started out as magazine assignments. There is a common and deceptively simple trait that links these mighty warriors—they persevered. The great dames kept their blades on the ice. Yes, these women were aided and abetted in most cases by fame and money and powerful men. But Constance Baker Motley, Luise Rainer, and the late Kay Thompson were stand-alones, women who accomplished on their own. They lived and continue to live in the present tense. Learning who they were and how they lived, I began to see hints of fears and conflicts, a human side. They were women of aspirations. They knew to try to stay on the floor until the last dance.

I started with Clare Boothe Luce. The talk of Franklin D. Roosevelt and Washington during the war, dinners with the "Gimo" and Madame Chiang Kai-shek echoed my mother's vivid memories of the secretarial pool at the OSS. In 1988, writing about Mrs. Luce's long and accomplished career, I viewed her through the lens of a younger woman filled with my own oats, not getting the larger grandeur of her rise. I saw the brass, now I see the endurance. I attended her funeral at St. Patrick's Cathedral; I flew to her South Carolina plantation, Mepkin, now owned by Trappist monks. It was to Mepkin that Luce retreated after the car crash which killed her only daughter, Ann. At Mepkin, I began to have a glimmer of the tenderness and contradictions of her history. Luce was smart and gorgeous and thought up the idea for *Life* magazine. She was twenty-seven years old when she wrote the play *The Women*—and, according to the lore, it took her just three days. Clare Boothe Luce had the internal power of creativity; she did not allow envy to slow her down. I delighted in Luce's foibles, uncovering the lies that propelled her along. She was a glamorous blonde fabulist who invented her background, schemed against her writers when she was a young editor at *Vanity Fair,* and took credit for giving Roosevelt the phrase "a new deal" and Winston Churchill "blood, sweat and tears." "A woman's best protection is the right man," a character says in *The Women,* and so it was with Clare and for that matter the other Becky Sharp of this book, Pamela Harriman.

Some of the great dames were born not long after the last frontier closed in America. When Diana Trilling and Kitty Carlisle Hart were girls, Marie Dressler was on Broadway and there were eight and a half million women working, but the underpinning of the society was still Victorian. Clare Boothe Luce came of age at about the time that neon began to light up Broadway. Lillian and Dorothy Gish, Theda Bara, and Mary Pickford were names in these women's cultural vocabulary; the new career woman was a phenomenon romanticized by H.L. Mencken in *Smart Set*: "There is something trim and twig about her. She is easy in her manners. There is music in her laugh. She is youth, hope, she is romance—she is wisdom!" In New Haven, Constance Baker Motley was a child discovering the work of W.E.B. DuBois; her father supported the family as the cook at Yale's Skull & Bones. Thirty years later, she would be working with Thurgood Marshall on the legal strategy that became *Brown* v. *Board of Education*. These great dames were never trained to be custodians of their fate, as Diana Trilling would later note. At Radcliffe in the 1920s, Trilling was served dinner by Irish maids in black uniforms and marveled at her friends' engraved calling cards to thank professors for dinner invitations. It was then as much a part of a Radcliffe education to understand the obligations of a hostess as to read Henry James.

In 1927, two years out of college, Trilling had not yet heard of Proust or Yeats or T.S. Eliot. She would later describe in a memoir the afternoon a young man named Alfred Barr, one day to become the head of the Museum of Modern Art in New York, lectured to the art history students. His presentation was silent; the audience sat and watched as he flashed slides of Picasso and Matisse, Braque, Derain, Cézanne, Duchamp, Léger.

I like to think about those great dames who were young girls in the 1920s as the vanguard of a forward march of ambition through the century. The future Kitty Carlisle Hart was then Catherine Conn in New Orleans. Her mother was eager to push her into Gentile society. Catherine's clothes were copies of Paris frocks; her mother played the violin at the interval of the Petit Théâtre du Vieux Carré. Kitty's father, a doctor, died when she was ten. Soon she and her mother were embarked on the Grand Tour of Europe, "staying at the worst rooms at the best hotels," she said. Her mother posed in front of Rolls-Royces at the George V and took flats with grand public rooms and a miserable tiny bedroom—a Potemkin village to further the image. In Hamburg, Luise Rainer was being reared in the world of the assimilated Jewish *haute bourgeoisie* with lady's maids and seaside holidays. She would argue with her father and leave home, eventually to join Max Reinhardt's bold new theater company. In England, young Pamela Digby was undaunted when she was first introduced to Randolph Churchill as "a red-haired whore." He proposed immediately, as he did to every woman, but Pamela accepted his marriage bid and traded festively on her new name for the next fifty years. Pamela

Digby's course would soon cross that of Catherine Conn and another racy beauty, the future Marietta Tree, who throughout her life liked to dress as if she were a torch singer, sporting gold shoes under her ball gown when she was in her seventies. Her grandfather, Endicott Peabody, was both a bishop and the founder of the Groton School, yet he was unable to tamp down her spirit. She would become a drawing room diplomat, captivating John Huston and Adlai Stevenson; powerful men would vie for invitations to her table. Her Sutton Place apartment overlooked the Queensboro Bridge. She lived her life with a flourish. It had been her inspiration to light the bridges of the city, and New York City mayor John Lindsay took her suggestion and did.

In Boston, my own mother, Thelma Long, wore saddle shoes and tweed skirts, shopped at Filene's Basement, and had her dates pick her up at the house of her rich cousin, Franny Cream. Her ambition was to win a scholarship to the University of Chicago. Instead, she got pneumonia her senior year of high school and after graduation moved to Washington where she was able to convince the OSS employment office to let her work for James Donovan, the handsome brother of Wild Bill. At the same time, Jacqueline Bouvier, six years younger than my mother, was learning to smoke at the Normandie Theatre in New York from a girl who pressed a Longfellow into her hand, then led her out the door when an usher told them that all the coughing was preventing people in the theater from enjoying the film.

The women of this sisterhood use words delivered in arpeggios; never declarative pronouncements, except for the noisy Clare Boothe Luce. They all respected language and deployed it well. They could be "down home"—this one had been "not watching her knitting" and her husband left her; that one's marriage "bestowed legitimacy" and "réclame." They turned the notion of confession on its ear. Facade was important to them, gallantry was important to them. They were never weighed down with the dreary language of twelve-step programs. Evasion was an art. "Denial is a marvelous thing!" Kitty Carlisle Hart said.

In New York, we are sometimes treated to glimpses of remarkable women getting on with it. Here is Brooke Astor, a close friend of most of the women in this book, entering a party at the Four Seasons in the last summer of the century. She is a tiny woman in a large pastel hat, wearing gloves, nude hose, a Bill Blass suit. Moving slowly through a glittering Manhattan room of lights, she is the largest light of all. People in the room look toward her with a flutter of excitement, pretending not to notice. She is a fixture on the A-list circuit. It is known that when Mrs. Astor comes to a dinner she expects her scotch and soda to be in place at the table. The photographers have learned to keep a respectful distance. It may have taken her all afternoon to get that hat and suit on; it may have been the Normandy Invasion, but she is a splendid sight. And her hunger for a public life continues unabated.

If a theme runs through these interviews, perhaps it is the theater of self. The great dames were women who kept themselves going by maintaining a public life. They are performers. They propel themselves along with buoyancy and suffer in silence. Unlike the poet May Sarton, they cherished neither solitude nor simplicity. They were social creatures. They were also warriors, sometimes fractious, often snappy if they felt under attack. In London in her elegant Eaton Square flat, during our interviews Luise Rainer was fanned to rage by what she perceived as the lack of respect in the voice of the twenty-five-year-old who was dutifully reading her back her quotes. "Your boots are on my aura!" the eighty-nine-year-old snapped at a researcher trying to check facts. All of these great dames were—and some still are—zealous guardians of their image. And part of the challenge for an interviewer, and even for their friends, was getting past the psychic walls they had set up around themselves.

The flamboyantly eccentric Kay Thompson identified herself not through a man but through her own creation, Eloise, a literary invention who gave my generation the first permission to rebel. Kitty Carlisle Hart's chosen persona was that of a professional charmer; Diana Trilling wore her brains on the outside. Trilling defined herself through her writing and published her final riveting memoir at the age of ninety-one. Mrs. Trilling was by then legally blind.

I type out and tape their remarks on my office wall. A toss-off from Kitty Hart: "Who were we to start with? We were a circle of friends. We understood each other. We knew that in life it all comes down to discipline. We were all very disciplined. We made time for each other. We showed up when we said we were going to show up. We made a point of remembering to call when things were not so good in each other's lives. We never said anything harsh that could be repeated. We were very careful."

A woman speaking to a biographer of the Kennedys during the war years was speaking of Kathleen "Kick" Kennedy, but she could have been describing most great dames when she said: "Gaiety, like honesty, is a kind of social courage. It is not easy to be unfailingly charming, lively, and original. It requires energy and generosity always to make the effort to be on one's best form."

And something deeper, a deeper virtue: Courage, the courage to be who you are in spite of the cost. Diana Trilling in an interview with Lis Harris of *The New Yorker*: "The great question now and forever is, 'What do you stand for? What kind of price are you willing to pay to stand there?'"

The era was a gentler one: Their world was the Alsops' Georgetown dinners, evenings with "Dick and Oscar," Rodgers and Hammerstein. "Thurgood" was the distinguished jurist Thurgood Marshall; "Clifford" was the playwright of the American theater of protest, Clifford Odets. Like corporate raiders, they had no qualms about fudging the facts. Clare Boothe Luce's biographer Sylvia Morris would reveal to the world that Clare had not only lied about her age but was illegitimate. Luce, like Pamela Harriman, had the heart of an adventuress. Harriman once accepted money from three different lovers for the same operation, according to her biographer, Sally Bedell Smith.

The fact is, we may be running out of great dames. We are told that the twenty-first century belongs to women—our skills as communicators will change politics and public-interest law, the day-to-day of government. We are ascending to leadership in every field. My generation threw off a great deal as we grew up. For years, we shut out the gentle voices of the beautiful swans; we were convinced that their ways were phony and did not apply to us. But we should pause and consider their example of style and civility, their show of gaiety, the respect the great dames had for the world around them. They were strange, rare birds with strong emotions, love and jealousy, generosity and deception. But, always, they had a patina—they were grand and they were gallant. They dressed up the world.

Kitty
Carlisle Hart

It has always been Kitty Carlisle Hart's intention not to be defeated by circumstances. The day of our interview, when the weather forecast involves Homeric gales, she has called for her fellow board members at the New York State Council on the Arts to be outside her New York apartment at "eight A.M. sharp." She has been brisk with me on the telephone: "You can't ever let the weather slow you down. We have eight arts groups to visit in Brooklyn. We always leave on time." As chairman of the Council—a post she held for almost two decades—Mrs. Hart often roams the state, checking on the Frederic Chopin Singing Society of Buffalo, the Iroquois Indian Museum in Schoharie County, the New York Latvian Concert Choir, Poughkeepsie's Bardavon 1869 Opera House, the Billie Holiday Theatre in Bedford-Stuyvesant, the Man Fa Center and the Cucaracha Theatre, among thirteen hundred other groups that receive money through the Council. However enervating her rounds might seem to many people, she revels in dank rehearsal halls, watching "glorious" jazz groups that spring up in crack neighborhoods. "I can't bear to be left out of a thing," she says.

When I arrive at her building, on the East Side, a few moments early for the arts trip, the doorman takes me upstairs to her apartment. The elevator opens directly onto her foyer, a small space with walls covered in red velvet flocked paper, Victorian in its formality. Her apartment is oddly silent; there is no early-morning bustle. Waiting for Mrs. Hart to appear, I look into her living room, an elegant jumble of books, curios, awards, and faded pastel brocade furniture in some need of repair. It is one of those rooms where time appears to have stopped. A celadon-green carpet covers the floor, a grand piano stands beside a far window, and in a bookcase are Meissen and silver pieces, CDs of many operettas she once recorded, and a youthful portrait of Mrs. Hart, her glistening dark hair in a pageboy. As one gazes at her empty living room, it is not difficult to conjure the voices and music of another era: her husband, the playwright and director Moss Hart, trading epigrams and smart remarks with Edna Ferber; Dick Rodgers playing her piano; Mrs. Hart herself rehearsing for her appearances in *Die Fledermaus*—the women speaking in sculpted and perfect diction which sometimes hid their modest origins.

And then, from another room, I hear Mrs. Hart: "Halloo, darling! I'll be right there! Oh, you are such a dear to come out on such a day!" Her voice is like a chime, the operetta singer's voice, actressy yet not artificial, a voice that seeks to charm. For twenty-one years, from 1956 to 1977, Mrs. Hart appeared every week on *To Tell the Truth*, where her persona was that of a cultivated person who deigned to be on television without seeming to be a snob; she was always set apart by a certain kindness.

Mrs. Hart has a performer's sense of timing; she walks into a room as if the Act II curtain has just gone up. Her spine is straight; her double strand of pearls is still in place; so is her hair, which is the same raven color as in her living-room portrait. Mrs. Hart has a classic oval face and a smile that gives her the expression of a delighted child. She is slim, and still has a showgirl's beautiful legs, which she often shows off in pale hose, whatever the season. For the arts tour, she is wearing a lavender Ultrasuede coat trimmed with fox; on her feet are tiny brown suede boots, also trimmed with fur. "I always dress up. I feel that if I don't people will not give me compliments," she says.

She pauses a moment in the foyer. "Let me read where we are going today—it is so interesting! We are going to Weeksville to see a restoration done of an early black community. We are going to Crown Heights to see an arts group that works with Hasidic boys and girls together. Highly unusual! Then the Brooklyn Children's Museum—a wonderful place! An African-American art gallery that serves a marginal neighborhood. A fast—I repeat, fast—lunch, which is Dutch treat. These are hard times at the Council, and we wouldn't waste money on lunch. The experimental glass blowers. The Brooklyn Historical Society. And then Red Hook, where that marvelous principal was killed." In the light, her face is grande damey, but underneath the mettle is a certain fragility, even pathos.

I follow her down the elevator, into the street, and into a van. "There are no frills here. My dear, we go over a six-hundred-dollar grant like you never saw. Governor Cuomo always tells me that we get more money than any other arts group in the country. We have been cut from fifty-four million dollars to twenty million. I was so angry! But this year we are back to twenty-six million dollars. There was a three-part series in the *Times* on arts in education, and they don't even mention us—and we give away two million dollars a year for arts in education. This is such a terrible time for the arts! I had lunch with Joe Papp's organization. They need millions just to survive. Well, we can't give it to them! I told them that they should think about getting famous stars who have been trained at the Public Theatre to support them—give fellowships in their name. But this generation is not trained in philanthropy. They will give their time but not their money. They'll come to a benefit, but they won't give you ten thousand dollars. They're not used to that kind of generosity." The van crosses the Brooklyn Bridge and turns toward Bedford-Stuyvesant. "Has anyone seen *Saint Joan* at the Roundabout? It is to die! The ideas are profound."

When we stop at the Weeksville restoration, a collection of restored nineteenth-century frame houses in Bedford-Stuyvesant, Mrs. Hart skitters through a torrential downpour into a small house. There the executive director, Joan Maynard—she is the daughter of the great ventriloquist John Cooper, whose career began in Negro vaudeville—mentions the black child and the young Hasidic scholar who were killed in Crown Heights in August of 1991, saying passionately, "Mrs. Hart, kids here need to know who they are! You wouldn't have Gavin Cato's and Yankel Rosenbaum's deaths if you had pride in your history. Hundreds of schoolchildren went to the Landmarks Commission to affect our status. We can't afford another generation who are not using their energies. Mrs. Hart—you dear, dear lady—if we don't get funded again, I will just die!"

All day long, making her way in and out of lofts, studios, and museums, Mrs. Hart tries to soothe desperate curators and theater directors. On several occasions, she is recognized by admirers who remember her trilling "Alone, Alone" from the deck of an ocean liner in the Marx Brothers movie *A Night at the Opera*. At the end of the afternoon, we are in Red Hook, in a surprisingly upbeat school in the middle of a desolate area. By now, gales and rain have made navigating the streets a challenge, but she hardly notices, rushing into P.S. 15 in time to watch a dozen elementary school students rehearse a jazz routine to the nerve-racking pounding of an African drum. "Oh, you are too marvelous!" she says to the dancers, clapping for them, and smiling. Then she is picked up by a special car, so she can be at her apartment in time to greet seventy New York State legislators whom she has invited to a reception with a group of arts administrators, the better to persuade them to pass an increased budget for the arts. "You wonder where I get my energy? My dear, it was an absolute necessity." She no longer smiles. "I had to survive."

Is it unkind to report that on her next birthday Kitty Carlisle Hart will be eighty-eight years old? If she suffers the normal private despair of the human condition or physical deterioration, it rarely occurs to anyone who meets her. An almost impenetrable bloom of optimism has made her a beloved figure in the city. Her conversation is filled with enthusiasm, French phrases, and an infectious hyperbole. "Darling, I'm still in a glow!" "Too wonderful!" "We were dining *à quatre.*" She appears to have a nature that is permanently sunny and filled with hope. "Who wants to be around anyone who complains?" she asks. "It is so unpleasant." Mrs. Hart came of age at a time when such resolute behavior reflected the highest standards. "I believe in denial," she says. "Denial is a marvelous thing." Each morning, very purposefully, Mrs. Hart dresses herself in ebullience. She gazes into her bathroom mirror—a Hollywood-style mirror surrounded by light bulbs, which is propped against a wall covered in the same red velvet flocked wallpaper as her foyer—and she thinks about any subtle indiscretions or cavalier behavior she might have perpetrated the day before. Then, in the silence of the bathroom, she smiles at herself and says out loud, "Kitty, I forgive you!"

Like most people who have ever encountered Mrs. Hart, I was immediately drawn to her cheerful demeanor, her way of whistling in the dark. She often speaks about her past in anecdotes, as if she had firmly shaped her memories into amusing stories, as a performer would. It is clearly her belief that her inordinate charm has enabled her to survive a complicated childhood and a complicated marriage; she relies on it in the most difficult circumstances. A few years ago, just after Marietta Tree died, I went to have tea with her. Mrs. Hart was unusually subdued. We sat in her pale-green living room. She said that she felt "betrayed" by Marietta, who had never told her that she had cancer. She was trying to reconcile their long relationship with Marietta's intention to disguise the truth about her health. At the request of Marietta's daughter, Frances FitzGerald, Mrs. Hart had gone to see Mrs. Tree at her apartment not long before her death. The moment she walked in, she knew that her friend was dying, but she behaved as they had always behaved with each other, pretending that nothing was amiss. Sitting by her bed, Mrs. Hart regaled Mrs. Tree with the story of how she had saved a community of a hundred houses near Jones Beach by appealing to the state attorney general and the governor. "It was the performance of a lifetime," Frances FitzGerald told me later.

"Who were we to start with?" Mrs. Hart said to me one day. "We were a circle of friends. We understood each other. We knew that in life it all comes down to discipline. We were all very disciplined. We made time for each other. We showed up when we said we were going to show up. We made a point of remembering to call when things were not so good in each other's lives. We never said anything harsh that could be repeated. We were very careful."

Mrs. Hart is famously intrepid. At thirteen, on being instructed by letter to leave her Swiss boarding school and take three trains, a ferry, and several taxis across the Continent, the Channel, and England to meet her neurotic and indomitable mother in London, Kitty did so unaccompanied, unquestioningly and without complaint. "I made it," she announced to her mother as she strolled into the lobby of the Savoy Hotel exactly on time.

Her buoyancy does not encourage introspection, and she propels herself forward with a belief in the need to contribute to the commonweal. Most people who know her resort to stock phrases to describe her: she "lights up a room," or "exudes radiance." She is a woman who suffers blows in silence, who leaves unsaid much of what she is really about, who hides from the outside world any signs of family conflict. Facade takes precedence over inner feelings; in talking about the past, Mrs. Hart glides over her mother's sulks and rages, and over Moss Hart's manic-depressive torments. Like many women of her generation, she unquestioningly assumes that such deceptions about her life are benign. They are intended to make her world easier. Yet each September, near her birthday, she sinks into a private melancholy, as if the energy she expends maintaining her exuberance does take a toll. "I'm depressed," she will matter-of-factly tell her daughter, Catherine Hart, who is a physician. The malaise will last some days, and then, as if she were facing a new season in the theater, what Catherine calls "the machinery of my mother's discipline" grinds into place, and her spirits lift.

For years, Kitty Carlisle Hart was a professional charmer, a woman, like many of her era, with a figure, a show business career, several houses, many parties, and a famous and accomplished husband to propel everything along. Her true strength did not show itself until after Moss Hart died, in 1961, fifteen years after their marriage. Although one of her roles is the keeper of the flame, it was only after his death that she transformed herself through the force of her personality into a culture czar. Ever since, she has worked tirelessly in service to tough issues in an atmosphere where money is so tight that the New York State Council on the Arts cannot afford to serve even coffee and doughnuts at its panel sessions discussing which of thousands of worthy applicants should receive state funding.

Mrs. Hart's skill as an arts administrator is based on her impressive understanding of the infinite problems of the various groups around the state. After assuming her post with the legislature she worked out an innovative decentralization budget which gave each of the state's sixty-two counties fifty-five cents per citizen from the annual budget allotted to the arts. She then traveled by plane, car, and train through rural upstate New York, assisting each county to create its own "re-grant" mechanism, through which funds could be channeled to the smaller arts groups. "We had to change everything," she says. "To get money was like Rube Goldberg before. If Onondaga County wanted a hundred and fifty dollars for costumes for a local theater production, it would have to spend months filling out the forms. We made it so they could just apply to their local council to get the whole thing going."

Mrs. Hart's ability to enchant the rural legislators in Albany has perhaps preserved the New York State Council on the Arts. "She flies to the dinkiest places. If she falls down and breaks a leg, she goes there wearing the cast!" Linda LeRoy Janklow, the chairman of Lincoln Center Theater, says. When her arts budget was cut in half several years ago, she cried, threatened to quit, then began to work the offices of the Albany legislators. "You have to realize, here comes an extremely attractive woman into an office that is about as dour as an office could be," says Peter Duchin, the Arts Council's vice chairman. "And there is Kitty, and she suddenly crosses her legs and the whole office smiles. The minute she opens her mouth, the legislator knows that she knows what she's talking about. She'll say, in effect, 'You may think that your highway budget is important, but nothing is more important than money for the arts—this is a matter of the soul.'" Mrs. Hart has fought for funding for unknown talents who have gone on to great careers, such as Spike Lee, Nam June

Paik, and Barbara Kopple. She is never afraid to call in favors. When Michael Bennett's dance and theatrical rehearsal space at 890 Broadway was threatened after his death, she appealed to the real estate man Lawrence Wien, a former beau, to save it. After weeks of meetings, phone calls, and feasibility studies organized by Mrs. Hart, Wien contributed fifteen million dollars, and the rehearsal studios are still intact.

Like the National Endowment for the Arts, the New York State Council has been involved in the ongoing debate about arts funding. Mrs. Hart questions her role frequently: Which is more important—the vision of the artists, no matter how potentially offensive, or the politics of Albany? "So far, we have been able to navigate it," she says. One morning in 1986, she awakened to headlines reading, STATE SPENDS MONEY ON MEN IN DRAG. Conservative legislators in Albany were outraged that the state was funding an exhibition of photographs of gay writers, featuring James Baldwin. "We had given an artist's residency grant to someone who was doing a photo essay on cross-dressing," Mary Hays, the executive director of the Council, says. "We were very nervous about the hearing after this headline, because, depending on how we did, five or six million dollars was at stake." Of course, Mrs. Hart prevailed.

"What would your life have turned out like if you had remained Catherine Conn in New Orleans?" I asked Mrs. Hart one afternoon, pronouncing the name with a long *o*.

"Conn—C-o-n-n," she corrected, quickly and coldly, as if it were an involuntary reflex.

"After all these years, you're still trying to pass," I suggested.

"Yes," she said seriously. "I suppose I am."

Catherine Conn grew up in a world whose underpinnings were Victorian. She was of a time and a state of mind when it was believed possible to jump into American society through the free pass of stardom, as if such enchantment would automatically rob the world of its prejudices. Re-invention was often a necessary tool for advancement, even in the theater: names were changed, accents Anglicized. The composer

Arthur Schwartz, who spoke with a distinctly British accent, told his son, Jonathan, "We're not Jewish, we're in show business." Getting out of a taxi once, Kitty Carlisle's mother was asked by a curious driver, "Is your daughter Jewish?" "She may be, but I'm not" was the reply.

In the world of Southern Jewry, Catherine Conn came from a successful family. Her maternal grandfather, an immigrant from Germany, had been a gunner on the *Merrimack* during the Civil War, and became the first Jewish mayor of Shreveport, but her mother, Hortense ("God, how she hated that name!"), was eager to advance into the sugar-plantation society of New Orleans—daring behavior for a Jewish woman of that era. Hortense Conn was an accomplished violinist, and she had exacting standards of intellectual probity; at the same time, she was grasping, and she made harsh judgments of her only child. She hardly ever showed affection. "The moments of physical closeness were so rare that when I was fifty years old, I was still trying to crawl into her lap," her daughter wrote in her memoir, *Kitty*, published in 1988. Mrs. Moss Hart, living a luxe Park Avenue life, often began her day in tears brought on by a phone call from her mother. Her son, Chris, remembers going in to tell his mother goodbye as he left for school and discovering her in a satin bedjacket, breakfast tray in front of her, crying, "Yes, Mommy. Yes, Mommy," into the telephone.

Mrs. Conn obviously saw her daughter as one means of advancement. She rapped the child's knuckles if she made a mistake in her daily piano practice, and offered bromides like "Furnish your mind." She was also deeply concerned with appearances, going to such extremes as having her only child's clothes copied from the Paris frocks brought back by New Orleans society ladies. "We lived on St. Charles Avenue and had a cook, a maid, and a governess," Mrs. Hart recalls. "My governess was so beautiful she wound up at Henri Bendel's as a model. Years later, I asked Lillian Hellman—who also grew up in New Orleans—if she had been invited to go to Mardi Gras, and Lillian said, 'Mardi Gras? They don't take Jews.' And that was the world I grew up in. My mother was eager to move me into Gentile society. I went to Miss McGehee's, and I must have been the only Jewish girl there. I guess that's why I was ignored. But my mother's entrée was through the arts. She had a foot in the Gentile world because of her music. She played the violin in the interval at the Petit Théâtre du Vieux Carré." Kitty's father, a doctor, died when she was ten. Her mother startled the locals by selling her house and taking her daughter to Europe, with the intention of marrying her off to nobility, as if she were a character in a Henry James novel.

Beginning in 1921, the imperious Mrs. Conn roamed the Continent with her daughter, using her modest amount of money to stay "in the worst room at the best hotel," as the daughter once wrote. The mother had been determined to go to Europe because she knew "that to marry me into Jewish society, the Schiffs, the Warburgs, and the Lehmans, would be impossible," Mrs. Hart says. "They were such terrible snobs and only married each other. But to marry European royalty was not nearly so difficult for a Jewish girl." As Mrs. Hart describes it, she was a juvenile Sancho Panza to her mother—as an eleven-year-old, she carried her mother's heavy luggage off trains, so her mother could pretend to be an empress in exile with servants behind her; Kitty called for porters in five languages; she spot-cleaned and pressed her mother's clothes. She mothered her mother, and never once questioned these pretenses. Arriving in Paris, her mother would pose outside the Hôtel George V in front of a line of Rolls-Royces, "pretending that one of the cars was ours," Mrs. Hart told me. "Our life in Paris was like a Potemkin village—it was all facade. We had a beautiful apartment with two or three awfully large public rooms and a dreadful little bedroom in the back with a miserable bathroom. My identity was called into question for so long because we didn't have any money. And we were always pushing our way into places where we didn't belong."

Her mother did, however, provide her with an excellent education, the finest singing lessons, and a model for her toughness. The daughter dropped Catherine for Kitty at the Swiss boarding school that her mother had gotten her into by sheer force of will; she later picked the name Carlisle from the New York phone book, rejecting Vere de Vere. As Kitty perfected her languages, her mother wrote her affectionate letters describing her visits to Sigmund Freud in Vienna, the opening of King Tut's tomb, her temper tantrums in the Sahara. During the holidays, they traveled together. "Before I went into a room, my mother would pinch me in the back and hiss, 'Be gracious!' And I always was." (In Paris, she was introduced as "Mademoiselle Conn" at a ball given by the Duchess of Albufera.) She was frightened that someone would discover the modesty of her mother's rooms. She was often treated as a "nobody," she wrote, and later, by one Italian family, as the adventuress that perhaps she was.

By the time she was a teenager, she had been thoroughly prepared to achieve her mother's desires. Sent to Rome to spend a season with a wealthy family, she arrived with a collection of copies of Chanel and Lanvin *robes de style.* "I hope you'll take good care of these clothes," her mother told her peevishly. In a rare moment of rebellion, Kitty answered testily, "I should know how. I've been taking care of your clothes long enough." In her memoir she wrote, "She treated me to theme and variations on being an ingrate, ending up with, 'You're a cold fish.' Mother probably never remembered it, but I did, for a very long time," but just before the book went to press she cut that passage out, believing it in some way unduly harsh.

If Hortense Conn implanted in her daughter a certain resilience and confidence by making her the sole object of her interest and her aims, she also frightened her through mood swings and sulks, during which Kitty struggled to placate her. Kitty was "a rather unattractive, withdrawn child" who had to learn to tell amusing stories to "turn away my mother's wrath," she now says. "My mother would go into moods where she would lock me out of our room—this when we were staying at resorts where it was imperative that you change your clothes several times a day. I would have to push pleading little notes under her door or offer her little bouquets of flowers to get her to forgive me." Once, when Kitty was fifteen, her mother flew into a rage just before fifty people were to arrive at their hotel for a cocktail party. "She slammed the door," Kitty says, "and I was left to do everything and entertain her guests, forced to make excuses for her."

"I am desperately afraid of any kind of rupture," she says. "If a housekeeper leaves me, I will take to bed. Everything came from my mother. I think it was my fear of losing her. I was convinced that every time we quarreled she would leave me. It has affected every area of my life."

When Kitty Carlisle married Moss Hart, in 1946, she was suddenly brought into a world of ideas and excitement, where people gave toasts in doggerel and signed guest books as Edna Ferber once did at Hart's estate in Bucks County: "You know I love you, don't you Mouse, but I would kill you for your house!" The marriage was an odd alliance. "We saved each other," Mrs. Hart says. Moss Hart's childhood had been as lonely and as desperate with longing as hers. He had grown up in the Bronx "in an atmosphere of unrelieved poverty," he wrote in his 1959 autobiography, *Act One,* with "the grim smell of actual want always at the end of my nose." In the 1920s, while Kitty was studying drama and singing in Paris and in London in an attempt to find a noble husband by appearing on the stage, Hart was withdrawing into the theater from his own unpleasant family circumstances. "Certainly the first retreat a child makes to alleviate his unhappiness is to contrive a world of his own," Hart wrote. When Hart's father, a cigar maker, lost his job in 1911 because of the automation of the craft, the family was forced to take in boarders. Hart dropped out of school after the seventh grade to earn money. When he was asked later where he had attended college, he would say, "Hebrew Tech." Mrs. Hart says, "I don't know which is worse, being poor when everyone around you is poor, the way Moss was, or being poor the way I was, when everyone around you is rich and you have to keep up with the Joneses."

Hart's passionate ambitions, inspired by his eccentric Aunt Kate, who took him to theater as a child, led him to take menial jobs working as an office boy, a floorwalker at Macy's, and a camp social director in the Catskills until, in 1929, at the age of twenty-five, he was able to inter-est George S. Kaufman in collaborating on his first play, a Hollywood satire called *Once in a Lifetime.* Their success eventually led to the moment of euphoria described in *Act One* when, on a high from an all-night celebration, he arrived back at his family's apartment in Brooklyn, gave them forty-five minutes to pack their bags, and moved them all to Manhattan.

By the age of twenty-six, Moss Hart was "the prince of Broadway," according to the columnist Leonard Lyons, and over the next three decades he was acclaimed for the plays *You Can't Take It with You* and *The Man Who Came to Dinner* he wrote with Kaufman and, later, for his direction of such shows as *My Fair Lady* and *Camelot*. "For years, I heard about the brilliant Moss Hart in his apartment on the twenty-sixth floor of the Waldorf Towers, blocked in his writing and threatening suicide," Mrs. Hart told me.

Moss Hart could command a room with his physical presence: he was a tall man with dark hair and Mephistophelian arched brows. His neuroses and extravagances provided his famous new friends, such as Edna Ferber and Alexander Woollcott, with plenty to tease him about. His speech, perhaps because his father was born in England, was vaguely British. Known for his wit and his sense of drama, he was "the kind of person who if he came to your party it was made," Bennett Cerf said. However, Hart's relationships with women had never endured. Although *Act One* provides a haunting evocation of a boy's coming of age, romance is noticeably absent. It was thought that he was epicene, a bit of a dandy, writing hit after hit, taken care of by George and Beatrice Kaufman and Cole and Linda Porter, with whom he often traveled. His first encounter with his future bride came on the movie set of *A Night at the Opera* where he and Porter were looking for a leading lady for their upcoming Broadway show, *Jubilee*. When Kitty Carlisle was told that Moss Hart wanted to meet her, she ran toward him and fell directly at his feet—perhaps an omen of their relationship to come. He didn't cast her for the show, and hardly encountered her over the next ten years. Meanwhile, she made her way as a middle-range singer, introducing such songs as "June in January," in *Here Is My Heart*, and "Love in Bloom," in *She Loves Me Not*, both with Bing Crosby. She starred in a Broadway adaptation of *Die Fledermaus* called *Champagne, Sec* and an Austrian operetta, *White Horse Inn*, but true stardom eluded her. During the war, her stage career faltered, and she supported her mother and herself as a night-club chanteuse, making an occasional movie and once in a while christening a warship.

Her career setbacks may have contributed to her becoming more serious and politically aware. Although she had returned to America in 1932 as a pan-European, she grew tired of camouflaging her religion. One night at a dinner party, she recalls, "they were saying dreadful things about the Jews, and in the middle of the fish course I got up and I said,

'I cannot sit here another minute and listen to this kind of talk.'" The night F.D.R. died, she was working at the Versailles, in New York City. "All these people came to the Versailles to celebrate! I was singing 'The House I Live In' with tears streaming down my face."

Meanwhile, Moss Hart, compulsively introspective, who had had one hit play after another, for almost a decade retreated into a lengthy psychoanalysis. It was said by his contemporaries that Hart, who was then in his thirties, was seeking help for his depression and for his inability to maintain satisfactory relationships with women. Later, in a letter to Kitty, Edna Ferber referred to these years euphemistically as the time of Hart's "illness." Hart's psychoanalysis inspired *Lady in the Dark,* but in 1941, when it opened, he was thirty-six and he was still alone. A girlfriend, the actress Edith Atwater, inspired a Kaufman quip: "Have you met the future Miss Atwater?" One night near the end of the war, Hart ran into Kitty Carlisle at a bond rally party at Lillian Hellman's. To him she revealed an ability to listen so carefully that it seemed as if no one else were in the room. "I knew I had riveted his attention," she recalls, and when she got home that night she wrote in a journal, "Quite an evening . . . snatched [Henry] Wallace out from under Sylvia Fine's nose . . . Moss Hart, after his trip to the Pacific, stopped going to his analyst . . . Edna Ferber perfectly delightful. Moss ditto."

"I had the best training for Moss's wife that any woman could ever have," Mrs. Hart told me. "The first time we really talked a great deal is when I was playing at the Brook Club, in Miami, in 1946. He told me all about his childhood, his mother, his poverty, and his analysis. I remember saying to myself, 'I am like Elsa von Brabant in *Lohengrin.* I must never ask what his name is.' I swore I would never ask him about his analysis, and I never did. He once said to me, 'You are the most incurious woman I know. A package could stay on the hall table for a week and you would never try to find out what was in it.' I'd learned my lesson from *Lohengrin.* "

Almost immediately, he began to talk to Kitty about a new psychiatrist, Dr. Lawrence Kubie, who was a strict Freudian, and whom he saw regularly. All through their courtship and throughout their marriage, she was able to talk to Moss without a moment of boredom or discontent, bestowing upon him the rapt attention, the sympathetic nod, the implicit understanding of every nuance—all qualities that still are at the very center of her charm—but what went on in the session with Kubie was taboo. "Until much later, I never figured out that Moss had periods of mania and depressions," she told me.

It quickly became clear to Hart's friends that he was serious about this relationship. George Kaufman wrote to his daughter, Anne, "This afternoon I am having Barberry drinks with Mossie, and it seems that romance is really in the air between him and Kitty. . . . It would not surprise me if it were marriage this time." Kitty recalls, "I had absolutely given up ever finding anyone! I used to say to my mother, 'I'm not married. I don't have any children. I'm going to wind up like Sophie Tucker singing "Some of These Days" in a café in Montana.'" Instead, when she married Moss Hart, a year after the war, she was at first so afraid of boring him that she "acted like a houseguest—Moss did everything," Phyllis Cerf Wagner recalls. "He hired the servants, he decorated the apartment," her friend Leonora Hornblow says.

As if directing a play, Hart liked to cast family members in roles he devised for them. Kitty's mother was renamed Hydrangea—which is Hortensia in French—by Moss, who found it hilarious that she called Beach Haven, their summer house on the New Jersey shore, "Bèche Hahven." Moss's father, who had once rolled cigars in a store window under the El, was given a sailor's jaunty cap and called the Commodore. Kitty was reinvented as well: she was no longer a full-time singer but, rather, a glamorous socialite, managed and dressed by her husband. Once, while Kitty was playing cards with George S. Kaufman, she lapsed into baby talk. Kaufman slapped her and said, "Stop that." Hart defended Kitty, saying, "She can talk any way she wants." She later wrote, "Whatever réclame I'd had as Kitty Carlisle was as nothing compared to being Mrs. Moss Hart." He was instrumental in helping her develop her persona, partly through extravagant outfits of feather and chiffon, but which made her famous when she began to appear on *To Tell the Truth*. On those weekly shows, a group of New York bon vivants—among them Polly Bergen and Hy Gardner—made quips as they attempted to unmask frauds and poseurs.

As a couple, the Harts were at the very center of the hilarious, hob-nobbing world of the Broadway theater at a time when it still defined American popular culture. They lived in a grand duplex on Park Avenue which had a soundproof solarium, so Hart could work at home. At his insistence, he and Kitty ate lunch together almost every day. "We lived in each other's pockets," she says. "Moss hated to let me out of his sight. We slept in a double bed, and he wouldn't even let me leave the bed to go in to the children when they were sick. It used to drive me crazy!" At night, suffering from chronic insomnia, he would turn to Kitty and say, "Tell me the story of your life again," and uncomplainingly, she would regale him until he fell asleep with anecdotes of Princess Mestchersky's finishing school in Paris and tales of her adventures while she was play-ing a thousand performances on tour in *Rio Rita* or performing with Danny Kaye at the Chez Paree in Chicago. "My parents had a mystical marriage," Chris Hart recalls. "They were both very high-strung and cre-ative. They fought with everyone—the servants, the children, their friends. But they never fought with each other."

In 1951, on their fifth wedding anniversary, Hart wrote to her, "Is there a way of saying 'Thank you' for the greatest gift one human being can give to another? In these five years you have given me the purest hap-piness I have ever known—and my love for you has grown and deepened with each year. How can I find words to thank you or even tell you how much you mean to me? . . . Perhaps I can only go on loving you more—though that does not seem possible."

At the height of their happiness, it was "delicious beyond dreams" to observe them, Leonora Hornblow recalls. In the winter of 1959, the Harts went to Jamaica with Phyllis and Bennett Cerf, and Leonora and her hus-band, Arthur Hornblow, the producer of *Witness for the Prosecution*. It was a golden trip. As a lark, Hart was nicknamed "the leader." Lolling around on the beach at the Round Hill Club, he made up a series of songs about their trip: "We are 22A/The only house with no view of the bay!" As they strolled by the water singing, they noticed that "everyone at the Round Hill Club had *Act One* at their chaise," Mrs. Hart recalls. Although *Act One* was No. 1 on the *Times* best-seller list, Hart was nettled that Cerf and Random

House were not taking out enough ads. This led to another ditty: "On the road to Doubleday/Where the happy authors play." That winter, the six friends knew that this time in their life was supremely happy. "We were all talking so much with each other that we felt we needed an appointment to speak!" Leonora Hornblow says.

The Harts were out at parties "every night of the week, or so it seemed," Chris Hart says. "My memory is of zipping my mother up into her ball gowns and watching her put on the diamond necklace supposedly given to my grandmother by the King of Bulgaria after a romantic weekend." For their own dinner parties, Kitty would descend her curved staircase wearing a long velvet gown. Moss would cast the party and plan every detail except the food. Like Kitty, he was concerned with presentation; in front of his bathroom mirror while he shaved he would often practice lines he wanted to use at the table. At the Harts' dinners, the guests might perform their signature songs, Florence and Harold Rome doing "Lucky Lindy!," Kay and Arthur Schwartz "Alone Together," the Harts "Me and Marie." Despite the gaiety, the Harts' lives were not unaffected by McCarthyism; dinners often broke up over politics. Moss Hart spent days watching the McCarthy hearings on television and recorded his rage in his diary. Once, Mrs. Hart recalls, Bernard Baruch came to her and said, "I have to warn you. There are friends of Moss's that you must never see again!" At that, she says, "I ran to Moss. Moss said, 'That is out of the question. We don't behave that way.' He called me Mrs. Antrobus, the character in *Skin of Our Teeth*. 'Any time anything goes wrong, Kitty runs for the umbrellas,' he said. Mrs. Antrobus was always trying to save everyone."

Lawrence Kubie, Hart's psychiatrist, was a continuing problem for Kitty, according to Leonora Hornblow. He insinuated himself into their social life, often attending their dinner parties and visiting them at their summer house. On one occasion, Leonora and Arthur Hornblow were invited to a dinner along with Dr. Kubie. "Moss made me crazy," she recalls. "He called me twice to see what I was going to wear. He wanted to make sure that I would mind my manners and that I didn't talk too much." Both she and Kitty had disliked Dr. Kubie "instantly," and were always repelled by his "terrible condescending quality." Dr. Kubie also treated Vladimir Horowitz and Tennessee Williams. He attempted to "cure" Horowitz of homosexuality, which he considered an illness, and he advised Williams to stop writing. Mrs. Hart says, "I knew that Moss sensed my displeasure. I always believed Moss's depressions could be cured by a pill. And I blamed Kubie for that, because there were pills that they were experimenting with. It was not my role to tell Kubie that he was doing a terrible job. All I knew was that Moss depended on him. I was not going to destroy that."

When Chris Hart was growing up, he often saw his mother walking up and down the beach with his father, trying to pull him out of his melancholy. "He would go into a depression in four days, and it would take months for him to come out," Mrs. Hart says. Often it was after his greatest successes that he would plunge into despair. As she had once been forced to soothe her distraught mother, she did everything possible to help. "He would say that success was no anodyne, because he had hoped that success would change him, and would wake up the next morning and be 'the same shit' who had gone to bed."

When Hart was depressed, he would try to tough it out, locking himself in his study and attempting to write. For the children's sake, he would try to camouflage his mood by a show of manners, but sometimes "the sadness in his eyes" would send Mrs. Hart walking alone up and down Madison Avenue to escape. "Moss was tormented about everything," she recalls. "He had problems with his mother, then he tried to understand her. He had hated being poor. He couldn't stand the boredom of it. He was particularly angry at his father, whom he could not forgive for not having provided him with an education."

Often, to combat his increasing bouts of depression, Hart would take a directing job. Early in the rehearsals for *My Fair Lady*, in 1955, it became clear that Julie Andrews was having trouble with the role of Eliza Doolittle. "We got into a taxi one day after rehearsal and I said, 'Moss, she is so awful! What are you going to do?'" Mrs. Hart recalls. "And Moss said, 'If I were David Belasco'—the theatrical impresario—'I would lock her into a room and paste the part on her.' And I said, 'Why don't you?'" Hart shut down rehearsals for two days and worked alone with Julie

Andrews until she had mastered the part. The intensity of rehearsal lifted his depression, but then he became manic. Mrs. Hart says, "Moss conceived the great black-and-white scene at Ascot on a manic high. He told me later that he could never have visualized that scene except in a mania."

Mrs. Hart is a few minutes late for our appointment today, having been detained at a lunch where she was being honored for her contribution to the arts. At this stage of her life, every month brings tributes. I sit waiting for her on the sofa where I once talked with her about Marietta Tree. When Mrs. Hart arrives, she is slightly out of breath and says she is famished, explaining, "In all the excitement, I didn't have time to eat." Her maid, Pilar, brings her sliced chicken and salad on a tray. "What a week I've had!" she says. "I am too old to be a movie star." During the first days of the week, she was playing the role of a hostess at a lunch party in the film adaptation of John Guare's *Six Degrees of Separation.* "On Monday and Tuesday, I was up at five each morning to be at the studio, and I did not get to bed until late at night! I had flowers from everyone. From Stockard Channing, from Donald Sutherland, from John Guare."

While she is eating her lunch, I ask, "Why have you never allowed anyone to write a biography of your husband?"

"He wrote his own," she answers quickly, and repeats a remark of her husband's that she has quoted in the past. "Moss always said that beginnings were the most fun and the most interesting. And he said that in later life it became 'And then I met and then I wrote.'" Mrs. Hart seems suddenly on her guard. However outgoing she may appear to the outside world, there are areas of her life she will never talk about to anyone, including her own children.

Mrs. Hart has donated lots of Moss Hart's correspondence and scrapbooks to the theater archives of the State Historical Society of Wisconsin, but a good part of the collection is to remain sealed until after her death. For years, the conditions of her gift have generated speculation among theater historians. It was commonly believed by Hart's contemporaries that he was sexually conflicted, perhaps as a side effect of manic depression. Although Mrs. Hart has discouraged several potential biographers from exploring his life, she did give the archives a diary he kept in 1953 and 1954. The diary, according to the catalog description, "was undertaken by Hart as self-therapy during a period when he was apparently depressed and experiencing difficulty with his writing." It includes "frank comments about theatrical friends and associates, his theatrical work, and the Harts' social activities." Because Mrs. Hart is of a generation that shrouded such matters, I was surprised that she had given the material to a library, despite the restriction on its use.

The subject of how Hart's manic-depression and years of bachelorhood affected their marriage enters the conversation. Mrs. Hart's voice remains steady, and she looks at me coolly. "I asked him about it. I said, 'Are you homosexual?' This was before we got married. And he said, 'Absolutely not.' He said there had been a couple of people who had made passes at him. And that was it. I never gave it another thought. His love letters were so obvious and so tender. When he wrote *Act One*, he signed it to me, 'Whatever I am, whatever I may be belongs to you.'"

When I ask if she'll permit me to see the diary, she says, "Darling, I can't let you have it. Moss wrote in an entry that the diary was for his eyes only, and I have to respect that."

As it happened, her son had a copy of the diary; he considered it harmless, and read it to me. I then realized that I had been misled by Mrs. Hart's refusal of my request. The diary details Hart's happiness in marriage and his increasing melancholia through the final stages of the writing and directing of, respectively, *A Star Is Born* and *Anniversary Waltz*, which was written by Jerome Chodorov and Joseph Fields; it was produced by Hart's brother Bernie and Joe Hyman, and Mrs. Hart was to star in it. In November of 1953, Hart wrote:

> *Awoke in a foul humor which did not lift . . . Lunch with Chodorov and Fields. Joe and Bernie in all day casting session in the office. I was in a terrible mood and I was constantly aware of my hostility towards Joe . . . Mood of enormous antagonism and rage which fastened itself onto Joe. However, being aware of it I behaved extremely*

well and let no aspect of it show. I noticed as I left the office there was an enormous compulsion to buy something which apparently goes side by side with both rage and elation ... The mood lifted completely in some magical way as I came into the house and saw Kitty.

Although I was puzzled at first by Mrs. Hart's secretiveness about a document that most readers would see as a monument to her marriage, I gradually came to see that her rare moments of anger are directed mostly at anyone who she believes has either questioned her control of Hart's image or, more understandably, has diminished Hart in any way. "Moss was everything to me," she says. "And even to discuss him in any way that I find unattractive makes me feel as if I had betrayed him." (After Hart's death, she was seriously courted by several suitors, including Thomas Dewey; she rejected them all.) When I asked Dr. Catherine Hart about her mother's angry moments, she answered quickly, "Anything to do with my father. She is very tough. There is a don't-mess-with-me quality about my mother. When she gets a grudge, it is hard to move her." Mrs. Hart once told me, "At the closing night of *My Fair Lady*, Alan Jay Lerner did not thank Moss. I called him up the next day, and I called him every name in the book. And I refused to speak to him for years."

One afternoon, I walked along Amsterdam Avenue with Dr. Hart. She has the same slim, dark good looks as her mother, but she is very much a woman of her generation, serious and without facade. Mrs. Hart resolved when her children were born that they would never have the same cold relationship with her that she had endured with her mother. She and Chris, who is now a theater producer and a director in Los Angeles, have sustained an affectionate relationship, but Mrs. Hart is particularly close to Cathy. "I knew what children of famous parents can turn out like, and I was determined that my children would have a normal life," she told me. When Moss Hart died, Cathy was eleven and Chris was thirteen. Chris later went to boarding school, but Cathy remained at home. She told me, "I don't know what my mother and her friends talk about. They are so different from my friends. I think it is generational. We can talk about anything with each other. Our marriages. Our lives. We can be free to complain. My mother is not introspective at all. There are so many things we just never discuss." As we walked together, she added, "So much of my mother's memories are mythology. But isn't it wonderful how she has made it all work for her? I really admire her for that."

On another afternoon, I have tea with Mrs. Hart. Again arriving a few moments late, she says that the morning was "a triumph." She had been asked by the governor to give a speech at the Shubert Theatre to launch a year-long national centennial celebration of Broadway. "I was onstage with the dancers from *Crazy for You* and got out of the Rolls-Royce in that marvelous scene in the first act. And then I gave my speech and got back in the Rolls-Royce."

The new ambassador designate to France, Pamela Harriman, was staying with Mrs. Hart for several days. Suddenly, she appeared in the living room. The two women had been close friends for forty years. Both of them radiated a youthful quality, as if passing their seventieth birthdays had given them full possession of their vitality.

"I've been all the way down to the World Trade Center to be drug-proofed!" Mrs. Harriman said, in a smoky voice. "It's like either going to prison or going back to school. There are all these things! Then, at four-thirty, I had to call the White House and be interviewed for forty-five minutes on God knows what."

"Oh, my dear!" Mrs. Hart said.

"It never ends! That was Ambassador Dobrynin who just called. I asked him if he was glad to be out of Moscow, and he said, 'I certainly am.'"

"My dear!"

"He said, 'I think you have a hands-on president, the first you've had in many decades.'"

"Have you had many calls?"

"My secretary is going mad!"

Some years ago, Mrs. Hart was approached about heading the controversial National Endowment for the Arts. It was Pamela Harriman, Mrs. Hart later told me, who persuaded her to "withdraw my name from consideration," on the ground that the agency was absurdly overpoliticized and not something she should be attempting to take on. As always with Mrs. Hart, it was difficult to reconcile her level of enthusiasm with her age. "I do wish that I had had my turn at the National Endowment," she added. "I just know that I could have done something to make it better."

In the style of their era, both Mrs. Harriman and Mrs. Hart spent years in the shadow of complicated and demanding men, acting the part of hostesses and biding their time, as if they were tortoises waiting to emerge from their shells. Both women understood the necessity of discipline.

One morning, I asked Mrs. Hart to do her spine exercises for me. She did so without hesitation. "Martha Graham said, 'Your spine is your tree of life,'" she told me, and then she was on the carpet in her sitting room, her legs stretched out, as supple as a dancer's, her head touching the floor. "First, the stretch!" she said. "And then I do this thirty times." With that, her legs were in the air moving up and down as, counting to thirty, she executed a series of perfect leg lifts for the stomach. As her pink-and-white ruffled dressing gown fell away, I noticed that Mrs. Hart's legs do not have a curd of cellulite or any mark that would indicate her age. "I got these exercises from Marjorie Craig forty years ago, and I do them four times a week," she told me. "It's eight minutes from start to finish."

On a warm afternoon, Mrs. Hart takes me to see another school that the New York State Council on the Arts helps to fund. "I hope you agree that the circus is an art," she says as we drive to the Harbor Junior High School for the Performing Arts, on East 109th Street in Harlem, whose faculty includes four performers from the Big Apple Circus. At the school door, Mrs. Hart is greeted by the director, Victor Lopez, as if she were royalty. Her belief in the rightness of her cause has helped hundreds of his students. As we walk down a hall toward the gymnasium, a young boy on a unicycle careens dangerously close to Mrs. Hart, but she just laughs. "Our attendance figures are way up," Lopez says. "The logic here is to understand how important the arts are for kids to stay in school. You have to figure that if these kids can break down a circus step it gives them confidence to try a math problem, and it works!"

In the gym, dozens of children tumble, cannonballing onto mats, hanging perilously from a Spanish web. Several more unicycles carom near Mrs. Hart. "Isn't this marvelous!" she exclaims. "Oh, I am so glad we came today!"

Back in the car, Mrs. Hart says she is "positively vivified" at seeing the practical application of the money from the council's grant. "You know, you can do so much! I think I've figured out a way to light the ruins of the Smallpox Hospital"—on Roosevelt Island, in the East River across from Beekman Place. "It would only cost two hundred thousand dollars, and wouldn't it be glorious illuminated? We've sent a letter to every resident of Beekman Place." Driving down Fifth Avenue, she takes out her datebook to check on an appointment. Each page is dense with her handwriting, detailing coming arts trips, dinners in her honor, meetings, parties, benefits, lunches. Mrs. Hart sees me looking at the list of the activities of her daily life. "My dear, it's madness, isn't it? I never say no to anything! It has made such a good life for me."

JULY 1993

Constance Baker Motley

rom time to time when Constance Baker Motley is invited to recall her days as an NAACP lawyer in the 1950s and '60s, she is challenged by law students who think of her as an anachronism, a holdover from a time when it was believed that the pathology between the races could be undone largely through the courts. This was the treatment she got in October 1993 when Motley, a New York federal judge, spent a week as jurist-in-residence at the law school of the University of Indiana in Bloomington. Motley is popular on the law school circuit; she and her former colleagues at the NAACP's Legal Defense and Educational Fund ride a crest of civil-rights-era nostalgia.

On May 17, 1954, when the Supreme Court issued its unanimous ruling in *Brown* v. *Board of Education* which overturned school segregation, Motley, then a Legal Defense Fund trial lawyer, was thirty-two years old. She was "the girl in the office" then, the drudge, but over the next ten years she became the only woman at the plaintiff's table in the Jim

Crow South as she and other lawyers tried case after case to enforce the *Brown* decision; she helped to desegregate lunch counters, schools, and buses, and in those years she also argued ten cases in front of the Supreme Court. In Montgomery, Alabama, she argued five different appeals in one day as the school boards tried to put off the evil moment of desegregation. In Jackson, Mississippi, a local paper referred to her as "the Motley woman." Her presence in court often brought dozens of spectators, simply to marvel at the fact that a Negro woman could actually be a lawyer. She was chided for her fashionable clothes. But the majority of the law students who gathered to hear her at Indiana were only vaguely aware of her importance. They weren't yet born when she traveled from courtroom to courtroom through Mississippi, Alabama, and Georgia.

A few days before Motley arrived in Indiana, Alfred Aman, the law school dean, arranged a display to show the NAACP Legal Defense Fund's achievements in the foyer of the law school building; among other items, news clips of Charlayne Hunter entering the University of Georgia in 1961 and James Meredith desegregating the University of Mississippi the same year were visible in a glass case. The moot court room at the law school was filled to capacity on the afternoon Motley delivered her lecture. That night, she spoke at a dinner given by the Black Law Students Association. She recalled the many school desegregation cases that had led to and followed *Brown,* but after she spoke she was kept busy by members of the BLSA answering sharp questions about her own experiences, posed by several: the narrative of Constance Motley's life seemed to contradict the reality of modern racial politics. "Shouldn't you have fought for equal schools?" one student asked her, and went on to cite the breakdown in black communities, the black-on-black crime; the miserable test scores, and the loss of pride among black men. "Your generation always used the word 'mainstream,'" another student said, and asked, "What is wrong with *black* culture?" Motley was brisk with the students. "I don't know what black culture is," she said, as if attempting to camouflage her irritation. When Motley returned to New York, she told me that she had been startled at being asked to defend herself. At this point in her life, she has come to expect, at the very least, a certain degree of respect for what she and the Legal Defense Fund accomplished.

A mistake to fight for integration? The guiding principle of Constance Baker Motley's life has been her belief that the law is the primary instrument of social reform. "In my early days at the NAACP, I could never have imagined this situation at the colleges today," she told me.

A few weeks later, I went to visit Judge Motley at the United States Court House in downtown Manhattan. I took the elevator to the twentieth floor, but Motley was not yet in her chambers; she was in court, hearing pretrial motions on a case that involved the alleged mistreatment of a Black Muslim by prison officials.

The décor of Motley's chambers was very feminine, with floral chintz curtains and pink walls. Judge Motley's law clerk had left a stack of faded newspapers for me on the conference table. A headline on the top paper, a copy of the September 11, 1963, *Times,* read, WALLACE ENDS RESISTANCE AS GUARD IS FEDERALIZED; MORE SCHOOLS INTEGRATE. The news story described the events of the previous day when, after months of resistance by Governor George Wallace, the schools in Birmingham and two other Alabama cities were integrated. It told of a blond high school girl in Birmingham who had cried when she learned that black children were enrolled in her school. "I hope my momma heard, so she'll come get me," she said. The *Times* correspondent in Birmingham related that seventy-five youths had shouted, "Keep the niggers out!" "Go home!" and "Two, four, six, eight, we don't want to integrate!" I flipped through the stack of newspapers. In one, I saw a photograph, snapped in the hallway of the federal courthouse in Birmingham in 1962, that showed Motley wearing a fashionable black coat and matching hat and an elegant printed scarf. She was looking down at the floor, as if to distance herself from the mob, but she did not look particularly afraid; in fact, she appeared oddly serene.

There was also an envelope of documents referring to Constance Motley that went back as far as fifty years. They included the expected awards letters and banquet menus, and some unexpected examples of the way she handled her anger: Motley had kept a copy of every complaint she filed with the Taxi and Limousine Commission about drivers who failed to pick her up. ("Complainant, who is a Negro, charged that respondent discriminated against her . . . because of complainant's color.") Then I came to a single-spaced letter signed "Anthropologist":

> *Mrs. Motley:*
>
> *When you made your plea before Judge Tuttle, how many windows did you raise to let your stinking body odor escape? How much cologne did you use to saturate your clothing with to prevent others from smelling your stinking body? . . . It is hard to see how any person with an ounce of brains would get up and argue that the nigger is equal to other races. It just is not so.*

As I finished the letter, Judge Motley walked into the room. I asked her about the letter, and she told me she could hardly remember receiving it. "I used to get letters like that all the time. I wonder why I even kept it," she said.

Constance Baker Motley was born in 1924. When she was admitted to Columbia Law School in 1943, her photograph ran in a rotogravure for African-Americans, and she was held up as a role model. "She's one of the few Negro women enrolled in Columbia University's famous School of Law," the caption noted. As time passed, she became the first African-American woman to be a New York state senator, a borough president (Manhattan), a federal judge. Judge Motley is tall and large-boned, but she has delicate features and dainty hands and feet. She is judicial, formal, precise. Unlike many of the civil rights activists of her generation, she is far more comfortable discoursing on the history of the Fourteenth Amendment than delivering an impassioned speech. Given what she has been through, her dry, legalistic demeanor may be her most remarkable achievement. She has been in jail cells with Martin Luther King, Jr., where the air was so foul that she became faint; she spent long nights in Birmingham churches singing freedom songs; she stayed with Medgar Evers, and, under armed guard, in the Birmingham home of a Legal Defense Fund attorney whose house was repeatedly bombed during the 1950s and '60s; for years racist insults were hurled at her by white lawyers. Yet, for all this, her memories tend to be of legal niceties. She focuses on the method by which school integration was actually achieved, the litigation strategies, the motions and sustaining orders, the quashing of subpoenas, the emergency appeals. It was her knowledge of the law that enabled her to transcend the emotionalism of the Jim Crow courts. In her 1992 memoir, *In My Place,* Charlayne Hunter-Gault recalls sitting with Constance Motley at the plaintiff's table in a Georgia courtroom during her attempt to enter the University of Georgia: "She barely acknowledged my presence. . . . I never, for example, heard her laugh in the presence of any state or university officials, except as a barely masked form of sarcasm. It seemed as if this was the most important mission in her life. In fact, she often talked about the South in those days as if it were a war zone and she was fighting in a revolution. No one—be it defendant or plaintiff—was going to distract her from carrying her task to a successful conclusion."

Until she was a teenager, Connie Baker had never heard of Harriet Tubman or Sojourner Truth. She attended a New Haven school where she was one of the few Negro students. Her parents, originally from the tiny Caribbean island of Nevis, moved to New Haven, Connecticut, at the turn of the century and became part of the clannish West Indian community there. Connie Baker had eleven brothers and sisters. Although the family was poor, the children had an air of superiority, from their parents' years at British schools. The Bakers lived on the outskirts of the Yale campus, and Connie's father was a cook at Skull & Bones; in fact, most of the Baker family was involved with Yale—her uncles also worked in the university's clubs. "They told all the little white Yalies what to do," Judge Motley's niece and namesake Connie Royster told me.

Nevertheless, she learned about black heroes and heroines and discovered the writings of W.E.B. DuBois at church lectures.

In 1993, Judge Motley was inducted into the National Women's Hall of Fame in Seneca Falls, New York. The list of women inducted with her included the physicist Rosalyn Yalow, who had won a Nobel Prize; the civil rights leader and founder of the Children's Defense Fund Marian Wright Edelman; the labor organizer Dolores Huerta; and Wilma Mankiller, the chief of the Cherokee Nation. The mother of Emmett Till, a black teenager who was murdered in Mississippi in 1955, accepted an award for Rosa Parks, who had inspired the 1955–56 bus boycott in Montgomery when she refused to give up a front seat. "Rosa Parks was willing to pay the cost to save the lost," Emmett Till's mother said. Most of the women used the occasion to make political speeches, but Judge Motley spoke about a white man named Clarence Blakeslee. "There was no money for me to go to college," she said. "I went to work at the National Youth Administration, and one day I gave a speech at a black community house. Clarence Blakeslee had built the community house. He was a contractor who had done a lot of work at Yale. He had made millions of dollars, and what he did with those millions was to help educate black Americans." Blakeslee had been impressed by the teenager's speech and had asked her where she would attend college. When Connie Baker told him that her parents could not afford to send her, he offered to pay for her entire education. "Clarence Blakeslee was a white man responsible for my being here today," she said.

Connie Baker, who was once turned away from a Connecticut beach near New Haven and from some restaurants in New Haven which wouldn't serve blacks, traveled to Fisk University in Nashville, Tennessee, by train, riding in a Jim Crow car; she was eager to experience segregation. Her parents were frightened for her; they themselves refused to cross the Mason-Dixon Line. On her first trip home, she brought them back a "Colored Only" sign. At Fisk, she met, for the first time, black students from middle-class families in the South, who were ensconced in black communities, with their own clubs and churches. "It was my first experience in a black institution with black people who were just like white people, as we used to say," Judge Motley said of Fisk. "Their parents were college educated, they had wealth. For the first time, I met blacks who were doing something other than cooking and waiting on tables. They intended to go back into the black community." White people, however, were the standard, and Connie Baker could not understand why the Fisk students were not interested in advancing in the white world. It was, she told me, the enigma of her college days. "All of our lives, we had to be like white people. We had to dress, think, and act like white people," she recalled; yet her classmates did not want to become part of the white community.

At Columbia Law School in New York, she began to work as a volunteer at the NAACP's Legal Defense and Educational Fund, Inc., a subsidiary that Thurgood Marshall and his mentor, Charles Houston, had created in 1939. It was usually called the Inc. Fund. It didn't seem to make any difference to Marshall that Baker was a woman, and he took her on as a clerk. After she graduated, in 1946, she began working full-time. Her salary was fifty dollars a week. Besides Motley, the entire staff consisted of Marshall and three other lawyers, one of whom worked part-time. At first, Motley worked on housing cases, challenging the restrictive covenants that excluded blacks from buying real estate in white neighborhoods. Marshall was then involved in several cases to integrate universities at the graduate school level, such as the ones in which Ada Sipuel sought admission to the University of Oklahoma College of Law and Heman Sweatt to the University of Texas School of Law. It was Marshall's strategy to argue the graduate school cases under *Plessy* v. *Ferguson,* the onerous 1896 Supreme Court decision that upheld existing separate-but-equal doctrine and set up the legal framework for segregation. Marshall argued that since there were no black law schools in Oklahoma and Texas, Sipuel and Sweatt should be admitted to the white institutions. Ultimately, of course, in *Brown,* the Supreme Court ruled against separate facilities, arguing that even where they were equal, segregation per se had a negative effect.

In 1949, when Connie Motley tried her first case, in Jackson, Mississippi, the people there had hardly ever seen a Negro lawyer before, and had never seen one who was a woman. She was married by then and her husband worried about her. Joel Motley was a New York real estate broker whom she had met when they were living at the Harlem YMCA and YWCA, respectively. They had gotten married in August of 1946. Her only experience in a courtroom had been observing the meticulous style of Charles Houston in a University of Maryland nursing school case. Motley found it impressive that Houston wrote down every one of his exhibits and questions in advance and never deviated from his text.

Motley and her colleague Robert Carter, who is now also a federal judge, booked a Pullman to Jackson. This was her first trip to the Deep South ever. (She had bought a new dress at Lord & Taylor for the trial.)

The case was an equalization-of-salary suit originally brought by a teacher, Gladys Noel Bates. When Connie Motley walked into the courtroom in Jackson for the first time, she was appalled by a WPA mural which covered an entire wall, depicting the glories of lost Dixie. She had never imagined that on her first big case, when she needed all the poise she could muster, she would have to interrogate witnesses and offer arguments while being confronted with such a spectacle of white women in their crinolines and hoopskirts on one side and the darkies hoisting cotton bales on the other. She recalls that trial as one of the few occasions when she was almost overcome with rage.

Other memories of the trial also remain vivid. "When we got to court on the first day, we saw that all the seats were taken by whites, because the black people believed that they had to sit in the balcony," she told me. "But this court did not have a balcony, so the blacks stood along the walls. After the first session, Bob Carter told the people that, unlike in state court, in a federal court you could sit anywhere you wanted. The next morning, we got there at nine o'clock, and all the seats were taken by blacks."

She went on to say, "In those days, no black lawyers ever went to court. If they had a case, they got a white lawyer to go for them. Bob and I needed a local lawyer to appear and sign the complaint. This was the first case since Reconstruction where blacks had appeared as lawyers in a courtroom in Mississippi. We found a black lawyer who lived in Meridian, Mississippi—James Burns. He owned a little grocery store, and he was scared to death. When we were in court, he sat with his back to us. He was making notes. He wanted to give the impression that he was just local counsel. He wanted to convey that he was not the lawyer bringing the suit. On the second day of the trial, Bob Carter said to him, 'Go out and see if our witnesses are out there.' He went out bent over completely—again, showing that he knew his place as a black man. When we went to have dinner, he would disappear; he did not want to take the chance of being killed with us.

"From time to time, the judge would rule in our favor, and once Bob spoke to the judge about a witness who was speaking very softly. He said, 'Could you ask that witness to speak up, please?' The black people in Jackson had never seen that before, and when Bob went to get his hair cut at the barbershop that evening everyone was reenacting this white man being made to speak up so a black man could hear. The final day, the judge was very polite. He addressed me as Mrs. Motley. The judge was from the Mississippi coast, and had no hostility toward black people. So, on the last day, when Bob told our lawyer to go out and get our witnesses, Burns for the first time in the entire trial walked out erect. I said to Bob, 'At least we have accomplished something in this case.'"

In the several TV movies made about the drama leading up to the *Brown* decision, the Inc. Fund is commonly portrayed as resembling a tabloid newsroom, filled with bantering black lawyers. The office jokes have become standards; one had it that Marshall called himself "HNIC"—"head nigger in charge." In Jack Greenberg's book *Crusaders in the Courts,* a history of the Inc. Fund, a different portrait emerges. Greenberg, now a Columbia Law School professor, started at the Inc. Fund several years after Connie Motley. For a while, they shared the same office. (When Greenberg, as a naive young white lawyer, first met Motley, according to his new book, he was startled when she quickly corrected his use of the term "Negress," then in common use. "Negress," she said, "was like using the word 'tigress' or 'lioness,' and was offensive to women.") In one TV miniseries, *Separate but Equal,* the actor Ron Silver portrayed Greenberg and Sidney Poitier portrayed Thurgood Marshall. Greenberg recently told me that he was nettled by the histrionics. "The idea that Thurgood was waving his arms around in court yelling and screaming and grimacing!" Greenberg said. "Thurgood didn't do that. In fact, no lawyer does that. Except William Kunstler." The real atmosphere was "lawyers at work," Greenberg recalled, the pedestrian stuff of "following precedents and filing motions for preliminary injunctions." It was difficult to tell the difference between the Inc. Fund office and any other office, except that its occupants talked about race all the time.

"What do you remember about the day of the Supreme Court's decision in *Brown* v. *Board of Education?"* I asked Judge Motley once when we were on a train on our way to Washington. It was the morning of the Supreme

Court's memorial service for Thurgood Marshall, and Motley had been asked to speak. At first, her memories were atmospheric—the pandemonium in the office, the joyous ringing of the telephones. That night, she recalled, she went home to her apartment on West End Avenue. She was proud of that apartment; the Motleys were the first black family to move into the building. Motley had big plans then for her two-year-old son, Joel—and, indeed, he ultimately graduated from Harvard Law School and became a partner in an investment banking firm. Motley's memory of the day of the *Brown* decision focused on Joel in his high chair. She had already realized, she told me, that the effect of *Brown* was going to be primarily psychological, and she informed her toddler that the Supreme Court had, that very day, undone segregation. She made no effort to explain it in terms a two-year-old might begin to comprehend, but she was convinced that Joel understood her.

When she got to the office the next morning, she learned that Walter White, the head of the NAACP, had had to cancel a lecture date in Selma, Alabama. "Thurgood called me and said, 'You go, Connie,'— very terse. He did not say, 'I will help you with your speech,' or give me any ideas. You were supposed to do it on your own. If you made a mess, you made a mess. That was the way Thurgood was. So I went to Selma that Sunday. And the place was jammed. It was a small church, and one man had even come in an oxcart."

It was Connie Motley's first real exposure to Southern black rural poverty. She recalled the drive from the airport in Birmingham to Selma, during which she looked out the window at tarpaper shacks and outhouses. She was not prepared for the starkness. "It sort of knocked me over," she said. The church was filled with people from all over Alabama, many of whom had saved their money to travel to hear Walter White. Thinking of that day in Alabama, she recalled that she knew immediately that the white people would fight *Brown* all the way. She saw her future in terms of a vast tapestry of court cases and problems, and worried about how the tiny Inc. Fund, with its minimal budget, could afford the years of litigation. On the flight back to New York, she recalled, her euphoria over the *Brown* decision faded and she felt lost, with no idea what lay ahead.

As each *Brown* v. *Board of Education* milestone occurs, civil rights legal scholars—Randall Kennedy among others—inevitably comment on the obliqueness of the Court's language, which led to years of legal maneuvers and the continued de facto segregation that plagues inner-city schools. When the *Brown* decision came down, Motley recalls, it was initially viewed as a decision that prohibited segregation but not as one that required affirmative action from state officials. Connie Motley prepared many of the hundreds of court papers and arguments necessary to enforce *Brown,* yet she never became a darling of the civil rights movement, perhaps because her skill as a litigator lay in her very thorough preparation and understanding of the arcana of the law.

Connie Motley first met Martin Luther King, Jr., in the Fifth Circuit Court of Appeals, in Atlanta. King was seen as a nuisance by the Inc. Fund, because his demonstrations had strained their ability to pursue school cases. In 1962, King had been enjoined by a court order from leading a march in Albany, Georgia. Motley arrived in Atlanta at one in the morning, in order to be in Judge Elbert Tuttle's court that day. Tuttle, an Eisenhower appointee, held relatively liberal views on race. He was born in California, and had once seen his mother leave her porch and stand at a bus stop with a black woman so the bus would stop to pick her up. At the airport, Motley was met by the Legal Defense Fund's local counsel and, to her surprise, by William Kunstler, who was a private attorney at that time and had flown in from New York a few days before, claiming to represent Martin Luther King. Kunstler arranged with Motley and the other lawyers that he would make the first argument. "First of all, Judge Tuttle, let me introduce Mrs. Motley," Motley remembers him saying in court later that morning. Tuttle then said, "Mr. Kunstler, Mrs. Motley has been here so often that she could be a member of the court." The question at hand—whether the injunction against King's march was a preliminary one, and could be appealed—was a tricky point to argue. As Motley recalls it, Kunstler told Judge Tuttle, "Well, Mrs. Motley will argue that." With little preparation, Motley stood up and spoke. Tuttle overturned the injunction. "As I was walking out," she said, "who should be sitting in the front row but Martin Luther King!" Not long afterward, the Inc. Fund became King's primary counsel.

The envelope of papers that Connie Motley keeps in her chambers includes a copy of a letter written by James Meredith on January 29, 1961, to Thurgood Marshall:

> *I am submitting an application for admission to the University of Mississippi. I am seeking entrance for the second semester which begins the 8th of February. I am anticipating encountering some type of difficulty with the various agencies here in the State which are against my gaining entrance into the school. . . . I am making this move in, what I consider, the interest of and for the benefit of (1) my country, (2) my race, (3) my family, and (4) myself.*

Connie Motley is convinced that she was assigned the Meredith case because she was a woman. "Thurgood knew they treated black men a whole lot differently in Mississippi from the way they treated black women," she told Alfred Aman, the dean of the Indiana University–Bloomington School of Law, during an interview he conducted in 1988. "This is the last place in the world we wanted to hear from," she added, explaining that Marshall was worried about being in Mississippi at that point, because the state seemed to be nearing an explosion, with Freedom Riders being arrested by the hundreds. Although by 1961 the Inc. Fund had grown to seven lawyers, and some of them were before the Supreme Court every couple of months, the office was already strained by its caseload. But Marshall knew that he had to make his ultimate stand in Mississippi.

By then, Motley was well-known in the Jackson federal court. She recalled that when she appeared to file her motion for Meredith, the judge, Sidney Mize, called to her from the bench, "Hi, Miz Motley!" "This was in the middle of another trial," she said. "He was very informal. When he took his recess, I told him I wanted to file my complaint against the University of Mississippi. Knowing there would be resistance, he said to me, 'Why did you have to come now?'"

Motley was brisk with Meredith. She told him to get decent clothes and to shave his beard. He was a meticulous record keeper, Motley recalled. At one point, she subpoenaed his files from the university. The registrar, in an attempt to stall, said, "We didn't bring the records," whereupon Meredith said, "I have a copy of everything I sent." Motley had a vivid memory of the moment: "They were floored. They had never expected that here was this student who would have a copy of all their correspondence!" One of the many tactics that were used to keep Meredith out of the university was to threaten to arrest him for having registered to vote in Jackson, where he had gone to college, rather than in his home town, Kosciusko, Mississippi. Immediately, Motley flew to New Orleans, where the court of appeals judge on Meredith's case was sitting. "They are about to arrest Meredith," she told Judge John Minor Wisdom, and then suggested, "You could issue an injunction under the all-writs statute," a statute that permits a court to take whatever action is necessary to preserve its jurisdiction. Wisdom did so. Motley met Medgar Evers, the Mississippi field secretary of the NAACP, in New Orleans and with him drove straight to Jackson. "We got there at five minutes to six to prevent Meredith's arrest for registering in the wrong town," she recalled.

For months, the Justice Department avoided weighing in on Meredith, because the new attorney general, Robert F. Kennedy, did not want a confrontation with Governor Ross Barnett. The litigation dragged on for a year and a half; Motley made twenty-two trips to Mississippi. For Joel Motley, then in grade school at Dalton, his mother's travel was part of a great crusade. "There was no question in our house that history was being made," he told me. "One day during the Meredith trial, Burke Marshall [an assistant United States attorney general] called. I remember he told my mother that he wanted her to do X, Y, and Z. She hung up the phone on him. She told us that she was happy to have his help, but he wasn't going to tell her how to run her case." On the day when Connie Motley decided that she would file a motion in federal district court to hold Governor Barnett in contempt, she drove to the Meridian, Mississippi, courthouse with Meredith and her secretary, in Medgar Evers's car. "While we were driving," she recalled, "Meredith said to me, 'Put those papers inside the *Times*. We are being followed. We don't want them to know who you are.' There we were, frightened to death, driving to Meridian. This occurred going through a wooded area.

The state police just followed us all the way. They knew it was Medgar's car, because they had been following him for years." (Within a year, of course, Evers was murdered.) "When we got to court, my secretary, in her haste, wrote 'motion' instead of 'order.' Judge Mize was presiding over the court with Harold Cox, another judge, who was the most anti-black human being I ever met. Judge Cox looked at our document and threw it at us. He said, 'Look at this, it says "motion"!' Judge Mize put his hand on Judge Cox's hand and said, 'Judge Cox, it is all over.' Mize was saying, in effect, 'You are a federal judge. You cannot take sides.'"

A few weeks before the fortieth anniversary of *Brown* v. *Board of Education,* I went to visit Jack Greenberg at Columbia University. Greenberg had been on sabbatical that year, finishing *Crusaders in the Courts,* and I wondered whether the years he spent analyzing the Inc. Fund cases had given him a larger perspective on what he and Connie Motley and their colleagues accomplished. Greenberg, who was then sixty-nine, is slightly built and appears younger than he is. I had noticed many black students on the campus; Greenberg recalled that when he entered Columbia Law School, in the nineteen-forties, there was only one black in his class and she was from the Virgin Islands. Greenberg talked about Thurgood Marshall and his legacy, and that conversation led inevitably to the subject of Clarence Thomas. Greenberg simply shook his head sadly, as if he could hardly tolerate the fact that Thomas had taken Marshall's place on the Supreme Court.

I asked Greenberg about the many celebrations that I had been told he planned to speak at for the fortieth anniversary of *Brown.* He said, "I'll tell you exactly," and pulled out a small calendar and read off a list: it included forums at Princeton, the College of William and Mary, and Texas Southern University, and an event that the Legal Defense Fund, which by then had a staff of twenty-five lawyers, would be holding in Washington on May 16th, at which the President would also speak. I told Greenberg about Connie Motley's trip to Indiana and how she was confronted by BLSA members who seemed to be trying to hold the Inc. Fund responsible for the breakdown in black communities.

"None of these things are simple," Greenberg said. "We can't do any-thing about the pathologies of the ghetto: drugs, guns, single-parent households, and housing that has collapsed. But Brown has been an important factor in producing a large black middle class."

As Judge Motley and I arrived in Washington for Thurgood Marshall's memorial service and walked through Union Station, she said, "When I first came to Washington, on that restrictive-covenants case, this was the only place Thurgood and I could eat." Motley and I had talked about some of her cases since she became a judge. In 1969, she had been vigorous in her decision to protect prisoners' rights to due process in the *Sostre* case; in 1978, it was her ruling that allowed women to enter the locker rooms of professional sports. But she said it was her time at the Legal Defense Fund that was "lasting and significant." She later remarked that she was annoyed when the Indiana law students expected her to be an architect of social policy. "We were trying to eke out a legal victory. If you want to win a legal case, you had to win a legal argument," she said. It was a warm day in November—freakishly warm—and Judge Motley decided to take a taxi the short distance to the Court. In the taxi, she again brought up the subject of what had happened to her in Indiana. "Don't those students realize that they would not even be at Indiana if it weren't for Thurgood Marshall and the *Brown* decision?" she said.

I was sitting in the front seat of the taxi with our black driver. When he heard the name Thurgood Marshall, he suddenly became attentive. He looked carefully in the rearview mirror at the Judge. When we pulled up at the Supreme Court Building, it took Judge Motley a few moments to organize her papers in her briefcase and comb her hair. I noticed a sea of gray heads moving toward the entrance of the building, and she began to tell me which lawyer had helped with each case. They were the titans of the civil rights movement—a checkerboard of leadership; a poignant image of what might have been. The unpleasant questions posed by the Indiana students were forgotten. As we got out of the car, the taxi driver asked her, "Ma'am, did you really know Thurgood Marshall?"

"Yes," she said matter-of-factly.

"My God," he said.

MAY 1994

Marietta Tree

Everyone dressed up to go to Marietta Tree's dinners. The men in their dark suits were like glamorous black shadows, as if they expected Jock Whitney to burst through the door at any moment to set the standard. It was that kind of room: the library gleamed, the lighting illuminated her shelves of good books lining the west wall, her portrait by the English society painter Molly Bishop, her porcelains, antique mirrors, worn brocade sofas, and stacks of leather albums filled with the clippings of her accomplishments over the decades.

Tree was a sensualist with the interests of a bluestocking, determined to lived in the largest arena possible. She often dressed like a torch singer; she told one of her brothers that her real career desire had been to belt out "Mr. Sandman" at El Morocco. Even in her seventies, she wore gold shoes under her ball gown, or a plunging neckline or fishnet hose. It was known she had had love affairs with John Huston and Adlai Stevenson, but her relationships were mysterious, as was the way she lived. People thought she was rich, but that was an illusion. Oxford dons, bankers from Abu Dhabi, playwrights, and politicians attended her dinners, as

did journalists and editors, for she had an able and impatient mind and liked serious talk. "It is time for 'gen con,'" she inevitably said during the main course. She meant general conversation. She would turn to a guest such as Arthur Schlesinger, Jr., and say, "Arthur is just back from Washington, where he had a fascinating conversation with the President." Her guests did not resent being made to perform; the atmosphere resembled Washington when great hostesses held court, entertained presidents, and affected policy. "There is no music more beautiful than a lot of *informed* people shouting over public affairs past and present," she wrote to a friend.

For years, Marietta Tree managed to have a drawing-room diplomat's power in New York without anyone's being quite sure where her power actually came from. She was a Peabody, a Boston Brahmin, the daughter of Puritans and rectors, an exemplar with perfect manners who had been imbued with the notion of public service. Her grandfather Endicott Peabody had been Franklin Roosevelt's mentor. All her life, Tree was a Roosevelt Democrat. At fifteen, she was at Hyde Park with the Roosevelt family on Election Night in 1932. Her devotion to fairness was honed during the Depression.

During World War II, she once sat next to the Duke of Windsor at a dinner. She was barely twenty-five years old, working as a researcher for the editorial page of *Life* magazine. In her spare time, she was working to integrate Sydenham Hospital, on the border of Harlem. At dinner, Marietta bombarded the Duke with questions. "Sir, could you describe to me the process of the Salic Law?" "Did the laws of British royal succession start with the Empress Sofia of Hanover?" Windsor gave her, she wrote, "a piercing look," told her to wire his mother at the palace, and then asked, "Why are you asking me these extraordinary questions?" "Because, sir, we are doing a story on the rise of British democracy in connection with the British general election next week." "Well," said he, "if the Socialists win, that is the end of democracy in Britain." Marietta later wrote to her parents:

> *I can say without boasting that I gave him a lot of information, as I think him a stupid as well as a prejudiced man. He is psychotically*

anti-Communist and also anti-Semitic. He has got good manners and therefore a certain charm and on the whole it was an interesting evening to examine the fabric of his mind and how it got that way.

Once, her brother George Peabody asked her to explain power. "Always tell the truth, but not all of it," she told him. She combined gravity with gaiety. In the 1950s she was a passionate advocate of civil rights. Marietta ran for state committeewoman of the Democratic Party, a seat formerly held by Dorothy Schiff, owner of the *New York Post,* and won. Her congressional district in New York was then controlled by a Republican reactionary named Frederick Coudert. She worked tirelessly to defeat Coudert by giving progressive speeches condemning his isolationism. She was also a standard-bearer in *Brown* v. *Board of Education,* the 1954 Supreme Court ruling on school integration, and spoke at length against "apartheid in America," as she later called it. She helped to write the plank on civil rights for John Kennedy's 1960 campaign.

Kennedy rewarded her by naming her to the Human Rights Commission at the United Nations. Eleanor Roosevelt had drafted the Universal Declaration of Human Rights, a document covering a whole range of covenants, from asylum to unjust imprisonment to the treatment of refugees. It fell to Marietta Tree to persuade dozens of emerging nations in Africa to adopt these principles and incorporate them into legal treaties. She traveled through Africa and America giving speeches and persuading obstinate caucuses to see another way.

For Tree, the frustrating work of the United Nations was never dreary or beside the point. She even found a strange glamour in the endless diplomatic receptions. She fought a move by the Ukrainians to gain power on the Human Rights Commission. Her State Department advisor Marten van Heuven described her combination of "girlishness and feistiness," which was perhaps the key to her success in extending the human rights agenda into the Third World. She never lost her feminine appeal. In Geneva, assisting in negotiating a treaty, Tree told her State Department aides laughingly that a Swedish diplomat had been so overcome that he had lunged for her, and knocked a gold earring into the elevator shaft. Van Heuven recalled that Marietta "thought nothing of having us get her earring back."

At times Marietta Tree seemed as flawless as a painted set. She was social, and had mastered the gracious entrance, the witty aside, the admiring word. Like Kitty Hart, she lived in a disciplined manner—rigorous about her weight and appearance. She preserved friendships by ignoring feuds and feigning optimism at all times. She was irritable when she was called a great lady or a grande dame, for she believed it implied that she was frivolous. "What do I have to do not to be called a socialite?" she once asked me.

Tree became a member of the Trusteeship Council at the United Nations overseeing territories such as Micronesia. She also became a factor in American political life, picking up honorary degrees and trusteeships at colleges and on councils. She worked for six months in Albany in 1967, helping to draft a possible new constitution for New York State. When she was in her fifties, she returned to college and took a degree in city planning. She became a partner in an international design firm and fell in love with its senior partner, Lord Llewelyn-Davies, a city planner "who thought twenty years ahead," according to one of his associates. Outside Adelaide, Australia, she guided the firm's plans for a model city and, near Melbourne, its plans for a teaching hospital that would service the working class. She traveled often to Tehran, before the fall of the Shah, to oversee the development of a two-thousand-acre model city with the national library in the center of town. She worked on a rehabilitation strategy for Times Square and helped on urban development projects in Pittsburgh and San Antonio. Privately, she helped support African students in this country and often sent checks to people in trouble who asked for her help.

She was intuitive, a fast study who knew how to captivate powerful men, but she was less a careerist than Clare Boothe Luce and Pamela Harriman. Marietta was flirty; her approach was light-hearted. As one of the first women to belong to the Century Association, she attended a black-tie dinner for members. There was only one other woman in a sea of two hundred men. "Don't you find this ratio deplorable?" the other woman asked Marietta. "I find it perfect," Tree said.

She had an elongated torso, a tiny waist, and an enormous bosom. When she put on a Madame Grès draped chiffon gown, she resembled Athena, but her face had small, perfect features. She radiated intelligence as well as inaccessibility. In 1960, John Huston cast her in *The Misfits* to do a sexy goodbye scene with Clark Gable at a train station in Reno, but Huston's camera failed to capture her sexual magnetism.

Marietta Tree was active in New York at a time when Democrats were often elitists who argued about integration, the Cold War, and McCarthyism. She lived in a large house on East 79th Street provided by her second husband, Ronald Tree, an Anglo-American investment banker who was a grandson of Marshall Field and who had once been a British M.P. Tree was often mystified by Marietta, who used her house "as an extension of the Lexington Democratic Club," recalled Russell Hemenway, an officer of the club. "There were receptions and fund-raisers several nights a week, and Ronnie never knew what he would walk into." "Who *are* all these rotters?" Ronnie Tree once demanded when he saw his house filled with strangers.

Marietta's personal maid, Alice Butler, would enter her room early and open the silk curtains; then she would draw her bath. Marietta would wake up in her canopy bed in the beautiful third-floor bedroom with French doors that overlooked her garden. Tree had her breakfast in bed and then took care of dictating her morning correspondence, to go out on her fragile blue tissue stationery from Smythson's, with an old-fashioned telephone and her number engraved in the upper-left corner. She used it to carry on extensive correspondence with senators and presidents and wrote frequent charming notes to her friends, who included Evangeline Bruce, Jacqueline Kennedy, Susan Mary Alsop, Mary Warburg, Polly Fritchey, and Kitty Carlisle Hart.

At the height of her career, Marietta would leave her house by nine A.M. to be briefed at the U.N. She was a dogged student of diplomacy and could talk for hours about the question of Chinese representation or banning the bomb. Arriving at the U.N. in her black wool suit and triple strand of pearls, she would race to the delegates' lounge and carry on two conversations simultaneously, in French and Italian. If U.S. ambassador Adlai Stevenson was obtuse about the necessity of winning blocs of votes with social pleasantries, Marietta knew how to cultivate the delegations, particularly those from Latin America and Africa. She would open her house night after night for diplomatic receptions, and invite a mix of celebrities and internationals who spoke the languages of her guests of honor. Her English butler, Collins, would pass champagne on an antique silver tray while the delegates admired the Trees' eighteenth-century furniture and the coromandel screen they had imported from Ditchley Park, their former stately home in England. Marietta was adept at finding out how the delegates intended to vote, using the same technique she would later teach her two daughters as dinner party etiquette. "Ask them about their childhoods," she said, and that simple trick enabled her to hear, as she put it, the delegates' hidden agendas "almost like a dog hears supersonic sounds."

Some years later, she was able to use that same talent as a member of the CBS board. She once returned from a month at her house in Tuscany to discover Bill Paley feuding with the head of the network, Thomas Wyman. Her first day home, she set about visiting every board member in order to assess the situation. Board member Roswell Gilpatric recalled that she was close to Wyman, but angry that he was attempting to sell CBS to Coca-Cola, thus depriving it of its independence. At the climactic board meeting, she spoke first and movingly, calling Wyman "a fine man" who did not have the "taste and ability" to run CBS.

Despite years of psychoanalysis in the 1950s, Marietta could never transcend a dislike of being alone. Her brother Sam Peabody was always surprised when she confided in him about her lack of self-confidence. "Analysis gave me such energy!" she told her brother George. "I much prefer going to a boring dinner than being alone with a good book, because the book is always there, but the dinner will never come again."

She rarely told her own daughters much about her life. She had learned to keep her own counsel in her childhood, and that lesson served her well in her love affairs. "I knew there were many questions I could never ask my mother," Frances FitzGerald told me. It was "inconceivable" that she would have relaxed on her mother's bed and asked her about her long romance with Adlai Stevenson. "My mother called that kind of thing 'toe curlers'—questions that were so embarrassing they curled your toes! But that was the kind of family she came from. They never talked about anything! And certainly not sex."

Marietta Tree was the firstborn child and the first grandchild of her generation of the Peabody clan, whose original fortune came from merchant sailing ships. Her father, Malcolm Peabody, was an Episcopal bishop; her mother, a Parkman from Boston, was so unpretentious that once, when she was taken sailing on a yacht, she called out to everyone she passed, "It's not ours! It's not ours!" Another time, she slammed on the brakes of her car when she realized that her son Endicott was holding hands with his girlfriend in the backseat. "I had such an awful relationship with my own mother, I was determined not to repeat it with my daughters," Marietta Tree once told a friend.

Marietta's childhood winters were spent in Philadelphia at the rectory in Chestnut Hill, her summers in Northeast Harbor, a lovely town of New England lobstermen and aristocrats off the coast of Maine. Northeast Harbor was only thirteen miles, but a psychological world, away from Bar Harbor, the elegant summer colony favored by Pulitzers and Morgans. "To the Bishop and Mrs. Peabody, Bar Harbor was a dangerous place! The bishop thought of it as entirely populated by very decadent rich people who spent their mornings lying by a large heated swimming pool at the Bar Harbor Club waiting to drink their first martini before lunch," recalled Susan Mary Alsop, who as Susan Mary Jay became Marietta's first and closest friend.

Marietta's grandfather Endicott Peabody was a rector, who founded the Groton School with financial support from J.P. Morgan. He ran it for fifty-six years, educating Roosevelts, Dillons, and Harrimans in the classics and the benefits of cold showers, using up much of the Peabody fortune in the process. He was "a monster," one of his grandsons told me, a frightening figure who treated his own son, Marietta's father, and his grandchildren as if they were "Groton first-formers. Sex was verboten, smoking, drinking—all those things! Divorce was out of the question."

It was difficult for anyone in the Peabody family to earn parental approval. "Good God, Marietta, I have never seen such a rejecting family as yours," Ronald Tree used to tell his wife. Marietta and her four younger brothers had the same taut bones, a similar laugh, a passion for the irreverent, a need to contribute to society, and a subtle resentment of one another. They grew up in a crowd with more than thirty first cousins, but their parents were not affectionate. As the only daughter, Marietta appeared to have suffered more than her brothers: Endicott, known as "Chub," Sam, George, and Malcolm junior, known as Mike. Perhaps as a result, she became deeply competitive with them, except for Sam, to whom she felt close. "We all competed with each other for what little affection there was," Sam Peabody told me. "My brothers and my cousins on both sides of the family were absolutely amazed by Marietta, and also very jealous of her. They tried to catch up with her, but she was impatient and had other things to do." She was the powerful sibling who had a difficult time sharing center stage. She often made her brothers feel insignificant.

Frances was a powerful role model. A stern matriarch and a passionate advocate of civil rights, she was once arrested at a demonstration in St. Augustine, Florida. At the time, Tree was at her grand house, Heron Bay, in Barbados with her husband, Ronnie. "Don't you dare leave Florida unless you get arrested! Otherwise there is no point," Marietta shouted at her seventy-four-year-old mother on the telephone. Several days later, a telegram arrived during lunch. "Oh, good news, everyone! Mrs. Peabody has been released from prison!" Ronnie Tree announced at the table. As it happened, the British Queen Mother was a guest that day. "Mrs. Peabody released from jail? Oh dear, she will be so disappointed," the Queen Mother said.

Marietta had to assert herself from an early age if she wanted attention. "Go ahead and hit me with a stick!" she shouted at one brother. "I dare you! You won't do it!" When her brother took her up on the dare, she began to sing so that no one would see her cry. "She had an expression we all picked up—'sib riv,'" George Peabody told me. "She was the most generous person in the world, but only on her turf. If there was any suggestion that *I* was getting any power, then the needle came."

When her brother Mike was deputy assistant secretary of HUD, he learned that his sister was meeting privately with his assistants, "trying to get her projects through." "They would come in all starry-eyed and say, 'Your sister is just wonderful!' I had to blast her for going behind my back!" When Endicott was running for governor of Massachusetts, Marietta did "very little" to help his campaign, according to several members of the family. "She didn't like it that Chub was getting in the national arena—that was her turf," George told me. She also was opposed to his conservative views on the Vietnam War. "Endicott was fighting the Kennedys in Massachusetts, and they stuck together as a family. He was upset that he didn't feel the same support," Sam said. When George became a management consultant, Marietta said to him, "None of us quite understand what you do." Even Sam was not immune from "the needle." "I learned not to ask her for favors," he told me. "Let's make a list of the four or five real stars in our family," she said, as an adult, to George.

On her mother's side, her grandmother Parkman, a rich Bostonian, was a considerable scholar who knew classical Greek. A trustee of Radcliffe College and a glamorous rebel, she waited until she was thirty-five to get married, after having had "scores of famous affairs," according to Mike Peabody. After having five children, she decided child rearing was not for her. She turned the responsibilities for her children over to her firstborn child, Marietta's mother, and resumed a love affair. Not surprisingly, Marietta's mother resented her ever after.

A family expression was "a Peabody or a nobody." At home there were prayers every morning, grace at every meal, and Sunday school. "The Peabodys stood for something!" Sam Peabody said. During the Depression, Marietta and her brothers were often taken to call on the poor. Politics were discussed constantly. Jane Addams, the founder of Hull House, was a close friend of Marietta's mother and a frequent visitor to Northeast Harbor. Mrs. Peabody was active in the Girls' Friendly Society, but when her granddaughter Penelope Tree, Marietta's second child, married a South African musician, she was very upset. "Oh come on, Mother, you went to jail over civil rights," Sam told her. "I believe in justice, not intermarriage," Mrs. Peabody snapped.

Almost from birth, Marietta confounded her mother. "They couldn't believe it! Mrs. Peabody once read to Marietta and me a bit of a diary she kept," Susan Mary Alsop told me. "It was written in 1921, and I remember it vividly: 'Malcolm and I find it increasingly difficult to comprehend Marietta. She is enchanting and everybody is crazy about her . . . but she is also very independent-minded! Happily, we are going up to Groton next week and Malcolm has already written to his father to ask if he would see Marietta and talk to her and help us understand.'"

Marietta bucked her parents constantly. When she was a teenager, her father lectured her about smoking. "During the argument, Marietta lit up a cigarette! I remember my father hit the ceiling!" George Peabody said. But Marietta had forged a strong ally in her grandmother Parkman, a kindred spirit. "'Mapa,' as we called her, worshipped Marietta," Mike Peabody said. "They were so much alike, and they understood each other. Mapa would do anything for Marietta." She even counseled her on her techniques with men. "Always remember what fragile creatures men are," she said. "They are even more scared than you." Marietta and her grandmother had "a common enemy," Frances FitzGerald said. "That had to be very difficult for *my* grandmother—their enemy." Marietta's alliance with her grandmother appeared to infuriate her mother.

By the time Marietta was a teenager, "every boy in Bar Harbor was in love with her," according to William McCormick Blair, Jr., the former U.S. ambassador to Denmark and the Philippines, who was a close childhood friend. "When Marietta used to come to Groton to visit her grandfather, the dining room would stop." Her parents did everything to try to tamp down her spirit, even insisting that she leave the dances at the Bar Harbor Club long before the band stopped. "When she would drive in with a date, her father would be on the porch with a watch, and Marietta was never allowed to linger in the car. That infuriated her!" Susan Mary Alsop recalled.

Marietta attended St. Timothy's school in Maryland, then finishing school in Florence, where she studied French and Italian. On her return she expressed a desire to get a degree in political science. Her father insisted she attend the University of Pennsylvania, because she could remain at home, although her younger brothers were allowed, she recalled bitterly, "to go to Harvard, to do anything they wanted."

It was 1939 and Marietta was in the middle of her junior year at Penn. Perhaps to escape her parents, Marietta determined to marry before she finished school. Susan Mary Jay was engaged to Bill Patten, who introduced Marietta to his friend Desmond FitzGerald—"Desie," as he was called. He was a Republican lawyer, "devastatingly handsome" and "intolerant of fools," Sam Peabody said. The Peabodys were suspicious of his family, who were from Long Island and spoke with clenched teeth, as if they were "social people." Marietta's parents were furious when she fell in love. "They called him second-rate," Frances FitzGerald said. Later, he would become deputy director of the C.I.A. "My mother used to say to me that her whole childhood could be summed up with a song from *Porgy and Bess:* 'There's a Boat Dat's Leavin' Soon for New York,'" Frances FitzGerald said.

They married on September 2, 1939, while Hitler was invading Poland. The guests listened to the radio all during the reception, and it was obvious to everyone at Marietta Peabody's wedding that their lives would soon be turned upside down. It was less obvious that the war would begin to free Marietta FitzGerald, as it freed scores of other women.

A few years ago, Marietta Tree started to draft her memoirs. "Write down what you really think about everyone," Arthur Schlesinger told her. "Tell the truth." It was an impossible assignment, for Marietta always camouflaged her opinions in the gentlest of casings, even phrasing most negative thoughts as questions. She was able to write only a few pages of detached and girlish prose. Some of the observations she made about her life were quite telling, however. For Marietta FitzGerald, the war was "heady liberation."

> *I don't think anyone realized we were pioneers of the feminist revolution. My new friends were trade union officials, politicians, reporters, movie directors, and I was particularly fortunate in my new women friends. Mary Warburg, Minnie Astor (later Fosburgh) and Dorothy Paley (later Hirshon). . . . They led me into a world a long way from the rectory in Chestnut Hill, Philadelphia, and introduced me to Valentina clothes, Ed Murrow, the Rockefeller Institute, Orson Welles, house parties, mahjongg, a good skin doctor, the Urban League, smoked salmon at "21," interior decoration, psycho-*

analysis, Thomas Mann (the man), "The Game," Bill Hearst, mascara, the American Veterans Committee, Edith Sitwell, impressionist and fauve paintings.

She was twenty-three when she arrived in New York with Desie. She couldn't cook, knew almost no one, and immediately became pregnant with Frances. "Oh, she was so dowdy then!" her friend June Birge said, but she was determined to learn. She registered for classes at Barnard and pushed her pram in the park with her new friends Mary Warburg and Ethel Roosevelt, the President's daughter-in-law, whom she knew because Franklin junior was a Groton boy. When the war began, she and Mary Warburg went to work for Nelson Rockefeller, taking visitors from Latin America all over New York. Touring a prison infirmary, she tugged at Warburg's sleeve. "Look at that marvelous gangrened toe!" Another time, at Riker's Island, Marietta was served "the most disgusting scrambled eggs with the inmates," Warburg said. "How can you eat this?" Warburg asked her. "Someone has to," Marietta replied.

She was hired by *Life* magazine as a researcher. She wrote in her memoirs, "After the Personnel Officer of *Life* Magazine telephoned me to say that I had been chosen . . . I sang, hugged myself, danced around the room, and must have frightened the people with my entrechats. . . . It was my first real job." Her first day at work, she looked up her friend Mary Warburg's name in the *Life* research stacks. "Marietta called me and said, 'You know what they have you down as? A socialite! How could they?' To be called a socialite was the most disgusting, nauseating thing in the world!"

Discovered to be a major beauty, she was photographed by Horst for *Vogue.* With Desie posted in the Far East, Marietta was quickly the toast of the town. When her brother Mike came down to visit from Groton, he answered the telephone. "This is Tony," a man said. "Who is Tony?" Mike asked Marietta. "Anthony Eden," she said. "We're going to dinner tonight." Eden, the British foreign secretary, was in New York to drum up support for the war. Marietta wrote her parents of parties she was giving: "Great fun—had the Astors, the Bennett Cerfs (he's a publisher), the Warburgs, Covarrubias (a Mexican painter), Barbara Mortimer [later

Babe Paley] . . . and the Larry Lowmans (he is in charge of CBS television)—everyone on their toes and they didn't leave until 3. Feel a little drawn today."

What did her parents make of such behavior? Attempting to rein her in, they wrote to her, counseling her to get pregnant again when Desie came home on leave. Marietta was furious.

> *Thank you in a way for your two letters . . . counselling me to be affectionate to Desie and to enlarge my family. I am 28 years old. . . . What I would like every once-in-a-while is a little approval from you both—as a matter of fact that is what I have always wanted all my life from you, and never felt—or certainly rarely felt that I had it—as compared to what you give Endicott and Mike, for instance. You have done so much more for me than most parents that I have no cause for complaint and overflow with gratitude—but I do get approval from others (even in the family) and can't be entirely wrong—and naturally I would rather have it from you two than anybody else—except Desie.*

She was beyond her parents' bromides now, beginning to live life on the pinnacle. One night Bill Paley invited her to dinner with Ed Murrow and the English publisher Lord Beaverbrook. Beaverbrook was then the czar of British arms and airplane production, with a reputation for "force and a wicked charm used to manipulate people," she wrote. That night, the German army had advanced to the suburbs of Moscow. "If Hitler defeats the Russians, which he probably will," Beaverbrook told them, "we are in for a thirty-year war." After V-E Day, Marietta encountered Beaverbrook again. Fearlessly, she reminded him of his prediction. "He turned purple," she wrote, "and said, 'I never said any such thing.'" The *Life* researcher, always trying to be accurate, [said], 'Oh, yes, Lord Beaverbrook, you did say that, and Bill Paley and Ed Murrow are witnesses!'"

She shared an office with Earl Brown, the Time Inc. expert on city politics, baseball, and unions. "He was the first black that I had ever met and I was sweatily polite to him to show how unprejudiced I was," she wrote. One day Marietta lost a phone message for him from the union leader Walter Reuther. Brown yelled at her, and she yelled back. "But in my anger," she wrote, "I suddenly saw a person . . . not a black man. . . . I never saw his color again nor did I see anybody's color after that." A woman of her class and her era, she had been reared to believe that unions were "corrupt or Communist." At *Life,* she was made aware that the Newspaper Guild had fought for the benefits she enjoyed. She joined and became the shop steward, collecting dues and attending meetings, where she "learned to outmaneuver the few Communists in the union. Afterward, I generally went dancing at El Morocco, and enjoyed the contrast of white plastic palms, champagne and dancing with men in black tie and uniforms."

Early in the war, Madge Kingsley, the wife of the playwright Sidney Kingsley, called her. "Come meet us at '21,' because we have two extra men for dinner." Mary Warburg went along. "We got to '21' and there was John Huston! There was an immediate electricity between John and Marietta. . . . I wasn't so lucky. The other extra man was an embalmer." Huston was the son of the actor and singer Walter Huston, and had just made *The Maltese Falcon.* Marietta FitzGerald was oblivious; in fact, she had never heard of him. She told a biographer: "I couldn't think of anything to say, so I said, 'Are you any relation to Sam Houston?' He thought for a bit. 'Who's Sam Houston?'" Huston had a rogue's charm. At the time he met Marietta, he was carrying on a love affair with Olivia de Havilland, whom he had directed in *In This Our Life.*

He was taken with Marietta, and later said, "She was the most beautiful and desirable woman I had ever known." He would become, according to Dorothy Paley Hirshon, "the passion of her life. She was radiant when they were together." Huston exuded danger and masculinity, although he was quite circumspect with Marietta when they were with friends.

Marietta Tree was consistently drawn to men who could expand her dimensions, yet not enslave her with their demands. No one could have been a better teacher than Huston. He swept her along into his New York; they stayed out all night drinking at P.J. Clarke's while he told her amazing stories, including the entire plot of *The Treasure of the Sierra*

Madre. He took her to meet Lillian Hellman, whom she adored, and each weekend he was in town he would follow her out to Long Island, where she often went to stay with Minnie Astor.

On Long Island, Bill and Dorothy Paley were right down the road at their estate, Kiluna Farm. At that time, Dorothy Paley set the tone in New York; she was a dark, brainy beauty on the international best-dressed list and, much to Bill's discomfort, as passionate about interventionist politics as Marietta. Marietta and Dorothy became fast friends; they worked together to open a nursery in Harlem. "We painted like crazy," Dorothy Paley Hirshon told me. "And that was not the sort of thing she liked." But she showed up when she promised, as she would all her life.

Marietta FitzGerald fit in perfectly in her new world with John Huston, but she was, from time to time, overcome with guilt when she thought about Desie in the Burma theater, for she "had a very high idea of duty," according to Dorothy Hirshon. Her friends knew that Huston was eager to marry her. He had begun to pressure her to tell Desie about their relationship. Marietta resisted; she said she was not "head over heels in love" with him, and she was well aware that he was impossible as "marriage material," in Mary Warburg's phrase, for he had a string of women.

Her marriage to Desie, however, had been destroyed by the war. "I had been waiting for him to come back—I mean literally every day—and when he finally did it was wonderful just as I imagined it would be, and then, boom, the divorce," Frances FitzGerald told me. Having learned what it meant to be free, Marietta was not about to return to the staid life she envisioned as the wife of a Park Avenue lawyer. "Now I was expected to give up my job, give up my new friends, as Desie naturally wanted to see *his* old friends," she wrote, adding self-mockingly, "and the last straw, give up half of my closet space."

As she had once escaped the rectory through her marriage to FitzGerald, she appeared determined to get away from her husband. When Desie came home on a leave, she told him about John Huston. "I didn't hear from her for three days," Huston remarked. "I could see that she'd been through an ordeal; her face was drawn and her eyes were swollen. Desmond had agreed to give her a divorce, but only on condition that she see an analyst and undergo therapy before starting proceedings."

FitzGerald was cleverly attempting to buy time, but his ploy did not work, for one weekend at Kiluna, Marietta met the man she would ultimately marry, Ronald Tree. Tree was twenty years older than Marietta, polished and discreet.

He had the same chiseled features and slicked-back hair as Desie, but he was international and very rich. He had been reared as a generalist, and believed that he would live out his life in the style of an English lord, occasionally writing a book of architectural history. Tree's immense estate in Oxfordshire was the retreat of Winston Churchill, Brendan Bracken, the British Cabinet, and the London smart set—the David Nivens, Noël Coward, Diana and Duff Cooper. Tree's wife, Nancy, of the Virginia Langhorne family, was a niece of Lady Astor; she was, like Ronald, an Anglo-American who had taken on the ways of her adopted country. She had filled the seven reception rooms and twenty-four bedrooms of their eighteenth-century home, Ditchley Park, with important furniture and "had a way of making a room look so old and so perfect," William Paley once told me. Later, she was a principal of the design firm of Colefax and Fowler.

Perhaps Tree's greatest appeal was that he, more than John Huston, shared Marietta's passion for politics. The Office of War Information sent Tree on a speaking tour to help shape public opinion in favor of the British; Archibald MacLeish dispatched him to Harvard to speak to the Nieman fellows. For Marietta, Tree must have seemed romantic, sweeping into New York from harrowing journeys on the Pan Am Clipper from Lisbon; once, he was trapped with an alleged Vichy traitor for three days by bad weather. Inevitably, he would call Marietta when he arrived in the city, for his marriage to the witty but high-strung Nancy had fallen apart.

One day at the end of the war, a package was delivered to Mary Warburg's apartment. "It was a box from Ronald Tree. I thought, How strange. I opened the box, and inside was the most beautiful blue-lacquered Fabergé box. On the lid was an 'M' made from diamonds. I thought, Ronnie has gone out of his mind! Later, I learned that the box was for Marietta. . . . But until then I had no idea that anything was going on."

Her divorce, according to her brothers, would become a central fact of her life, for it pitted her finally and definitively against her family; there was no turning back. The divorce would as well color her relationship with FitzGerald's daughter, for she knew that Frankie adored her father, yet she moved her an ocean away. "I felt my life was over when she married Ronnie," Frances FitzGerald said later.

Marietta's father was now in Syracuse, the bishop of central New York. One day Marietta announced dramatically that she was arriving to discuss "the situation." "A plane flew over," Sam Peabody recalled, "and I can remember my father saying, 'That's Marietta's plane.' He was dreading it! My father was closeted with Marietta in his study for what seemed like days. Not only did she announce that she was going to Reno to be divorced but that she was going to marry Ronald Tree! This was outrageous!" Marietta's parents enlisted her brothers to move against her. "I remember writing a letter to her saying how terrible this was," recalled Sam Peabody. "Endicott did the same thing. Marietta wrote me back, saying how hurt she was by my letter. And that, of all people, she depended on me for support. I wrote her back and said, 'I'm with you,' but I don't think she ever forgave Endicott, and that was the beginning of the split."

A picture of Marietta Tree as a bride shows her posing in front of one of the great doors of Ditchley. She is smiling and looks joyous, very Hollywood, as if she were playing a role. Her petticoats are causing her skirts to billow out. The caption in her scrapbook reads, "Owner!" but the new mistress of Ditchley arrived to find a gloomy and hostile environment. She wrote in her memoirs of their arrival:

> *The huge front door was open revealing part of a hall of height, depth and grandeur beyond my experience and imagination. [There were] busts of gods and ancient heroes, bosomy beauties, huge statues of classical heroes, a painted ceiling of gods and goddesses, [with] acanthus leaves and eagles and flags strewn all over them. . . .*

*Lined up from the door and reaching back into this huge, pale
and gilded space were the indoor staff who served in this palace num-
bering over thirty people. . . . Never did I think I would walk into
my next house with my beloved and my sweet little daughter, a pale
and bewildered six-year-old, into what looked like the first scene of
"Marie Antoinette Comes to Versailles."*

Marietta Tree was then twenty-nine years old, chatelaine of a vast
estate of more than three thousand acres, run in pre–World War I–style
grandeur in the grim winter of 1947. Marietta received little support
from her parents, who had forged a new closeness with Desmond
FitzGerald, even encouraging him to purchase land in Maine. Frankie
"had to eat her dinner alone on a tray in one of those great gloomy halls,"
Dorothy Hirshon remembered. "She was a very unhappy child." Her
school in Oxford had little heat. "We used to warm our pencils in a fire
so our hands wouldn't freeze," Frances said. Rationing was in effect; there
was little fuel or food. The Trees relied on the farm for supplies. Marietta
was without domestic skills; she was a magazine girl who liked to talk
politics, and her first assignment as the mistress of Ditchley was to hire
"a cook for the servants," according to Sam Peabody.

Additionally, the acerbic and popular Nancy Tree remarried and
mounted a campaign against her former husband's bride. Lady Astor, her
aunt, called Marietta "Mrs. Reno Tree," according to Sam Peabody. "It
was Nancy Tree's house! Everything in it was Nancy Tree. She had done
the whole house . . . the servants . . . everything! It was not easy. She was
the intruder!" said Dorothy Hirshon. The chief housekeeper was loyal to
Nancy Tree. Each time Marietta made a suggestion, she would say, "Well,
the first Mrs. Tree always like to have it done this way." Marietta later
wrote that the woman "was so like the sinister housekeeper in the movie
Rebecca that I was determined to get rid of her as soon as I learned her
job myself."

It was said that Marietta opened up a drawer in her dressing table on
her first night at Ditchley to discover a note from Nancy Tree: "Who's
the puss in my boots?" Sometimes during weekend house parties, Nancy

Tree would appear and make a terrible row, wanting one or another of her pictures or urns back. Overwhelmed, Marietta's puritan character caused her to be overly solemn with the sardonic British upper class, and she was a social flop. Taken to visit Henry Moore by the art critic Kenneth Clark, Marietta stared at Moore's monumental statues in his garden. "Could you tell me what you *mean* by these images, Mr. Moore?"

Her first encounter with Winston Churchill was "frightful," she wrote. She had no idea that Churchill did not address women at the table. She drank "three glasses of champagne and [it made me] feel warmer and more relaxed." Churchill decried "the rationing system after the war, which he condemned as a drag on the free market." Marietta challenged him, saying it was unfair that the rich could luxuriate in "self-indulgence." "I was John Calvin addressing the sinners," she later wrote. "Go on, give it to him," Sarah Churchill, his daughter, whispered in the silence. "The argument was dropped like a lead balloon," Marietta wrote, and for the rest of the meal she stared "remorsefully . . . at my plate."

She learned to do her homework. If Ronnie's interest was furniture, she would bone up on it. If the British upper class wanted to be frivolous at dinner, she would not insist on talking about the machinations of the Labour Party and the new prime minister, Clement Attlee. She began to assemble her own set of friends.

Swept out of Parliament by the triumph of the Labour Party, Tree was now crippled by the new British tax laws; as an American in England, he was forced to pay double tax. Nor had Anthony Eden done anything to help him create a position for himself after the war. Tree felt betrayed, according to friends, for he had backed Eden during the Munich crisis. "It was quite lazy and selfish of Anthony," a friend said. Tree felt he was losing altitude; he made the decision to sell Ditchley and regroup in America. But before they left, Marietta and Ronnie gave one last great ball.

It was July 1949. Marietta was just pregnant with her second daughter, Penelope. She wore billowing peach chiffon. In her two years in England she had turned her former antagonists around. The night of the ball was unusually warm. The great trees of Ditchley were illuminated with hidden lights, a French technique, new at the time. The terrace was filled with titles, including the young Princess Elizabeth and Prince Philip, who "stood by themselves" for much of the evening, according to Sam Peabody.

Marietta had invited every American friend she had in London, including a man from Northeast Harbor she hadn't seen in years. "This man drank a bit too much of Ronnie's excellent champagne and . . . he lurched onto the dance floor and cut in on the future Queen! It was to die!" Susan Mary Alsop said. "Immediately, one of the members of the royal household rushed to Marietta and said, 'Mrs. Tree, this guest must be removed.' Supremely loyal, Marietta answered, 'What do you mean, remove him? He is an old friend of mine. He is a beautiful dancer, and I am sure that Her Majesty is enjoying herself very much. I only hope that he will dance with me!'" After midnight, the guests dined on cold salmon, savory cheeses, and salads, and Susan Mary remembered Marietta feeling wistful. "I'm going to be so homesick for England back in New York. What am I going to do without this wonderful place and our lovely life?" she asked her old friend.

She was entering the fourth phase of her life, the New York years in which she would become a public figure. Marietta had to start over again in New York; she was a rich woman who had once worked as a fact checker, married to a man who had no defined work. Returning to the city in 1949, she complained of "low energy" and developed illnesses from stress. "Ronnie loathed New York," Sam Peabody said. "He had many friends, but no position or focus." At first, Marietta felt compelled to take on a superficial role as her husband's hostess, "trying hard to amuse Ronnie with constant entertainment," Peabody said. She loved the pace of New York and the intelligent conversation, but Ronnie first wanted to escape for much of the year to Barbados, where he had built a Palladian retreat on the water.

Marietta believed, she later told friends, that psychoanalysis saved her. For five years, she went every day. She developed the cool, disaffected style of the professionally analyzed; later in life she appeared to behave as if her years of therapy had freed her from feeling any restrictions from her family. Marietta and Ronald began to lead separate lives. They spent much of their time apart, although they remained loyal and close companions. "I know that at times I've not been easy—leaving my beloved Ditchley & starting life again here caused me much pain which in turn I must have communicated on to you," he wrote her, adding, "You have given me Penelope & words cannot express the wonder of that."

Ronald Tree became a colonial power in Barbados, where he developed a large resort called Sandy Lane. Marietta threw herself into reform politics in New York and worked as a drone at the Lexington Democratic Club, often taking Frankie with her. It was then considered a noble calling to fight the clubhouse politics of New York, where machine bosses such as Carmine DeSapio, in his silk suit and dark glasses, delivered the votes to the county leaders.

In the Trees' fabulous house on East 79th Street, Marietta began to entertain her old friends from the war as well as everyone she met in New York politics. In the dining room at "Little Ditchley," as the house quickly came to be called, Lillian Hellman might go at it with Bill Paley over Stalin, or Arthur Schlesinger, down from Harvard with his then wife, Marian, would decry McCarthyism and Cold War Republican politics. Ronnie, spending more and more of the year in Barbados, was absent from many of these dinners. In retrospect, the smart, brittle conversation that he had spurned seems naïve and provincial. Marietta's friends argued over reforms, but they were unable to see the larger picture, to imagine that the ramifications of the Kennedys' machinations to obtain power were possibly dangerous for the country, that Manhattan could unravel without the domination of the party bosses, or that an incomprehensible wild card like Barry Goldwater might just reflect the new populist mood in the country. Theirs was a tight group that confirmed one another's opinions, and for them it was a golden era.

Once, Marietta had fought the Establishment; now she was at the center of it. By the Kennedy years, she was written about frequently in the rotogravures. She posed for the *Times* swathed in fur on her way to the United Nations. The U.N. job catapulted her into fame—"Our Top Girl at the UN," *Look* magazine called her. Her recipe for loin of pork appeared in the columns, as did her views on international life. "She still blushes when the Russians anger her," one writer wrote in *Look*.

For years, those closest to her have speculated about Marietta's relationship with Adlai Stevenson. He called her Zuleika Dobson, after Max Beerbohm's fabulous English heartbreaker and became her mentor. When he lobbied for her U.N. appointment, Marietta wrote him, "My gratitude to you flows like Victoria's cataract for appointing me to the U.S. Del[egation]—for I realize now that all my life had been in preparation and in hope for the last two weeks. I only hope that the results [are] as constructive as the soaring fulfillment." The intellectuals of the "silent generation" revered the divorced and single Stevenson and jockeyed for his attention. A circle of rich, accomplished women fought over him, including newspaper heiress Alicia Patterson, Ruth Field, and Jane Dick of Chicago, but his sons have always believed that the woman he intended to marry was Marietta Tree.

Marietta first met Stevenson in 1946, through Ronnie Tree. In those days he was a rather whimsical idealist whose desire to be Illinois governor seemed a fantasy. Marietta contributed to his first campaign and wrote him from Ditchley when he swept into the statehouse in 1949, "No one can believe the vote! All congratulations!"

Back in New York, she was determined to be at the 1952 Democratic Convention and got a menial job on the state committee so that she could be part of the crowd. In Chicago, she was sharply observant. Adlai, she later told one historian, looked "like a pyramid" addressing the crowd. "I was irritated by his views on civil rights and Arab-Israel affairs—they were not my views," she said. "Marietta was always trying to move Adlai to the left—those conversations I can remember," Frances FitzGerald said. Stevenson respected her nerve and listened to her as much as he did to the cynical Alicia Patterson. "[Alicia] scorned my liberal views," Marietta said. Marietta was not afraid to get her point across. She told Stevenson's biographer John Bartlow Martin that she sensed Adlai was "anti-Semitic," and that that infuriated her. "Why do you always have to say a 'Jewish banker'?" she would scold him.

Within Marietta's circle, the relationship was commonly discussed. She worked doggedly in the 1956 campaign as the New York head of the Volunteers for Stevenson, and traveled with him and Alicia Patterson around the world. At campaign headquarters in New York, Marietta often walked around in her stocking feet. Stevenson drew closer and closer to her. Once, in the late 1950s, he was staying at a villa near Lake Como. Alicia was his guest. Hearing that Marietta was set to arrive when she departed, she refused to leave. "It was a nightmare," said a man who was Stevenson's aide at the time. "Alicia was in a rage that Marietta was coming. I had to walk her around the lake until she finally agreed to get on the train."

One night in 1960 at her house in Barbados, Marietta was with Arthur Schlesinger and Adlai Stevenson as Stevenson labored mightily, writing and rewriting the speech he planned to give at the 1960 Democratic Convention. Marietta supported Kennedy; she was desperate for Stevenson to throw his delegates to Kennedy, Schlesinger remembered, but she was careful not to hit too hard. She knew Stevenson and Kennedy did not get along. She never forced the issue as Stevenson endlessly rewrote into the night.

What was their relationship? At a Princeton archive there are dozens of letters and notes from several unpublished interviews with Marietta Tree that suggest a true intimacy. Marietta told John Bartlow Martin that Stevenson spoke constantly to her of his mother. "He told me she was massaged on her bed and he used to watch her, and he was very interested [in this], especially her bosoms. . . . She turned him into an aural man. Through all that reading aloud. You know he couldn't learn anything by reading—he had to listen." He talked to Marietta about his first encounter with a prostitute: "It horrified him."

Her later letters to Stevenson were quite intimate. By then they had developed pet names for themselves: he sometimes playfully referred to her as "that lump," and they called each other Mr. and Mrs. Johnson. Once, in her U.N. days, she wrote him from London, where she was on a trip with Ronnie:

> *A., Have been here a week, and it seems eight. We have been fêted, entertained, wined, dined, balled, tead, theatered, etc. by the warmest friends. . . . Why can't I enjoy all this? Real answer. Because am far away from Johnsonville. . . . I pray [your trip to Los Angeles]*

not too exhausting and overladen with pâté de foie gras. Heedst the five pound promise.

I know a bank where the wild thyme grows and keep enclosing myself in the dream of it. M.

"I always assumed that Adlai Stevenson was in love with my mother," Frances FitzGerald said. "The fact that she wasn't going to do anything about it made it all the more interesting." She had long ago made the decision never to leave Ronnie. They appeared quite content leading separate lives. Once, at a dance at Brooke Astor's, Adlai and Marietta danced the whole night, and "his hand was way below her waist," a friend said. "It was clear that he was crazy about her." "She hated the whole subject of sex," FitzGerald told me, although she had a clear memory of traveling in Spain with her mother and Adlai. "Our rooms were quite close together, and I had the feeling that Adlai was roaming around." Stevenson stayed at the Waldorf Towers in New York, and Marietta confessed to Susan Mary Alsop that when he was in town she came home at "four in the morning." Friends learned never to ask Marietta certain questions, for she was not beyond telling lies to protect her private life.

Walking with Marietta in London near the American Embassy one day in the summer of 1965, Adlai suddenly said, "Keep your head high. I am going to faint." She tried to revive him with mouth-to-mouth resuscitation. When he fell, his briefcase came open; pink classified cables flew all over Grosvenor Square.

"When they got Adlai to the hospital, Marietta was standing up at the top of the stairs absolutely sobbing as if her heart would break," Mary Warburg said. Susan Mary Alsop flew back to Europe with her from the funeral. "She just reminisced about him. . . . It was quite apparent how much she loved him. When we got to Paris, I was desperately worried that she might jump into the Seine, and I called her at the crack of dawn every day." Grieving terribly, Marietta left to join Ronnie in Florence at a villa they had rented. She remained in bed for much of that month, but Ronnie didn't comment. "His courtesy and good manners never deserted him," Alsop said.

When Ronald Tree died in 1976, he left her only her two houses, which, despite a real estate slump, she immediately sold. The mansion on 79th Street, now a consulate, brought her only about half a million dollars. In the last years of her marriage, they had pulled closer together. Once, staying at Mary Warburg's, she opened a top drawer in the guest room to find some of Ronnie's shirts that he had left there. She began sobbing "uncontrollably," Warburg remembered. She set about reorganizing her life. "I made a list of what to do," she told a friend, "and I realized I had every qualification to go on corporate boards." She went back to college and studied accounting to prepare herself.

Marietta Tree lived to see Manhattan fill with crack addicts and the homeless, but she remained without cynicism, so optimistic that she became active in the Citizens Committee for New York City to try to alleviate the new misery. She "spent thousands of hours and she raised millions of dollars for us," Michael Clark, the Committee's director, said. Each year she would write "four to five hundred personal letters" to raise money for youth programs, drug-counseling services, and block associations, but ironically she gave very little money herself. "A cousin of Marietta's told me that the *P* in Peabody stands for parsimonious," Clark said.

She had an enthusiasm, a certain zest. Frankie and Marietta were once out walking during a garbage strike. "As we were stepping through tons of trash on 57th Street, my mother kept saying, 'Isn't New York wonderful? I can't think of anywhere else in the world I would rather live!'"

"What would you have liked to ask your mother that you never got to?" I asked Frances FitzGerald.

"I wish I truly could understand how my mother moved away from her family and became what she became," she said.

We were sitting in Northeast Harbor in the small cottage on the water that FitzGerald shares with her husband, the writer James Sterba. FitzGerald has her mother's posture and perfect elocution, but she measures her words carefully. She writes examinations of American culture and politics and lectures on foreign policy. She won a Pulitzer Prize for her study of the Vietnam War, *Fire in the Lake*. She waited until she was fifty to marry.

Frances and Penelope have always called their mother Marietta, as if they understood from an early age that she was not maternal. If they wanted her attention, they had to enter her world. Marietta did include Frankie in many of her activities, taking her in the summers to Venice or with Adlai Stevenson to Africa, where she met Albert Schweitzer. "I got the sense from my mother that I could do something from the earliest age!" she said. In later life, when she saw in herself certain traits of her mother's, Marietta would "go bananas," FitzGerald said, but she could never transcend her emotional legacy with her children. Like her mother, Marietta didn't "analyze personal relationships. She pushed away a lot of things," FitzGerald said.

As a mother and a wife, Marietta was unfailingly correct, but as her own mother had been with her, she was, as Dorothy Hirshon said, "fairly detached." Frankie saw her mother as "a glamorous and incredible figure," but she never felt intimate enough with her to work her way through her closets or borrow any of her clothes. As a young woman, she was often wary of bringing boyfriends to Barbados, because her mother would dazzle them. "I was often in a rage," she told me, but later she began to understand that her mother couldn't help pulling focus in a crowd. "My mother had to have all the guys in the room," she said. Once FitzGerald and her new husband were visiting her mother on Sutton Place. Suddenly, Marietta dropped to the marble floor of the foyer and did "fifteen perfect push-ups," as if to demonstrate her physical superiority.

Her mother encouraged her need to achieve. When FitzGerald was in her twenties, she left for Vietnam to write about the war. "My mother arrived on a tour for the State Department. I went to meet her in my jungle khakis, and she was all in white with this fabulous hat! Here was this vision! I remember being furious, but also very proud because she was so beautiful. . . . I went to join her somewhere in the jungle, and my plane had to make an emergency landing. I looked down from the plane, and I saw her doing laps in the South China Sea next to a destroyer. I was having anemic hallucinations, and she was being fêted with tea dances. But when she saw the horrible condition I was in, she said, 'We are leaving.' She took me to Singapore and stayed with me in the hospital for weeks. She saved me then. I was able to get back to Vietnam, and then months later I returned to New York. When I arrived, there was Robert McNamara in the library! I had expected to be the conquering hero in my house, and there was the enemy being entertained." (Marietta's brother Sam had also observed her need to accommodate men in power. "It irritated the bejesus out of me that she would sit down with Henry Kissinger and see nothing wrong," Sam Peabody remarked.)

Penelope was a toddler when her mother attempted to regroup in New York. Penelope became a shy, fragile child who would often cling to the curtains when visitors came. She was, however, doted on by her father, who would spend hours with his daughter, appearing to find in Penelope the companion he longed for in his wife. "Your mother says it is time to come out of the water," Tree used to tell Penelope, as if trying to drive a wedge between them. "Ronnie is so permissive with Penelope," Marietta would complain to her friends. "He lets her do anything!" On the night of Truman Capote's legendary Black and White Ball in 1966, Marietta and Ronnie encountered sixteen-year-old Penelope in the library, dressed in "ravishing but very scanty black leotards," Susan Mary Alsop recalled. Capote himself had invited Penelope to the ball; Betsey Johnson designed her outfit. The next morning, Penelope recalled later, Diana Vreeland called to tell her she should become a model. Within two years, Penelope left home and moved in with the English photographer David Bailey. Later she moved to Australia, where she now lives with a psychotherapist with whom she has a son.

For years Penelope appeared to believe, according to friends, that she had never really gotten a chance to know her mother. "My feelings are so complicated about her that I don't understand them," she told me. I asked her what she knew about her parents' early relationship. "I know they met at a party. That's really about all. My mother never talked to me about anything like that." When Penelope's daughter, Paloma, was born, Marietta, according to a friend, "began to realize what she had missed not being close to her daughters." She attempted to make up for lost time, flying to Sydney frequently to see her grandchildren and calling weekly on the telephone.

Penelope and Frankie learned to come to terms with a basic fact: "Marietta was the least introspective person we had ever known," Frances FitzGerald told me. "Anything that might have hurt her, she just wiped out."

The day of her last party in June of 1991, Marietta had remained in bed until dinner in order to have the strength to get through the evening. She was determined that no one except her older daughter should know that she had inoperable cancer. She had been reared to be "a Christian gentleman," one brother said, and could not admit to herself or anyone else that her body had let her down. "She was trying desperately not to sink, which was the running theme of her life," Frances FitzGerald said. In the last year, a friend had taken her home from a party. "How are you?" he asked. "Very, very lonely," she said.

She greeted her guests as if nothing were the matter, giving her customary little gasp of pleasure: "Hello, beauty!" and "How wonderful you look!" The small details were as flawless as ever—her brown leather seating chart with its tiny paper flags was by the door; her waitress, dressed in a starched black bombazine skirt, offered champagne.

It was a warm night, and she had thrown open the bay windows of her Sutton Place apartment to the great lawn and beyond, to the shimmering necklaces of lights on the Queensboro Bridge, which spans the East River. "Wouldn't it be wonderful if our city's bridges were lit?" Marietta had remarked years earlier to the then mayor, John Lindsay. "New York could seem so much like Paris!" Lindsay took her suggestion and did it.

After dinner the guests moved into the peach drawing room, where Marietta settled into a green velvet window seat. She began to talk about the past. This too was out of character, but she began to describe the first night she had ever been kissed. Roosevelt was president then and she had marched with a boy out onto the lawn at her grandmother's house. "I closed my eyes tight and I waited. When the boy finally kissed me, it was so disappointing! I wanted something more. I don't know what I wanted, but I did want more."

She had long kept her cancer a secret. Eight years earlier, she asked her brother Sam to take her to the hospital, where she had a lump removed from her breast. "She never mentioned it again," he said. Tree appeared to believe that she could will her recovery through the sheer force of her exuberance. She never slowed down until this year, when the cancer recurred. By the time the lump was visible on the mammogram, the cancer had spread. Marietta concocted an elaborate hoax for her brothers and friends. "I have antibiotic poisoning," she said. Only Frankie knew the truth, and she was uneasy about being the keeper of the secrets. Marietta increased her activities, attending every lunch and dinner she could. Winston Churchill had told her when she was a young woman, "Age is a somber period." She determined for her it would not be so. In June she ran into the historian Robert Caro. "I have decided to write my memoirs, and I want your help," she told him. "Call me in the fall!" She was wearing bright red stockings, Caro remembered, and looked "stunning."

In Maine in late June, Sam Peabody walked into his sister's bedroom. She was in bed, staring into her hand as if, he said, "she were facing the end of her life for the very first time." For much of the month, she was too weak to get out of bed. "I don't know what is the matter with me," she kept saying. "I haven't been in bed since I had Penelope."

One night in July, she went to dinner with Punch and Carol Sulzberger, the owners of *The New York Times,* and former *Times* executive Sydney Gruson and his wife, Marit. The Grusons and the Sulzbergers had been close to Marietta for more than thirty years. They were overcome with worry, for Marietta was wearing a black patch over her eye and complained of double vision. She had lost twenty pounds. The evening was fraught, but the next day Marietta left a message on Sydney Gruson's answering machine: "That was simply the best and finest time I ever had in New York."

She wouldn't admit that she was dying, not to anyone, not to herself. Sitting in her doctor's office with Frankie, she suddenly turned to her and said, "You know, I am not sure that I would have done this for *my* mother." "Don't be silly," Frankie said, then thought, My God, she is probably telling the truth. "I said to her, 'Well, you are a much better mother than your mother was to you.' And she said, 'I am afraid that isn't so. I would love to do it all over again.'"

In late July, Penelope arrived in New York for her annual visit. She was told then that her mother was gravely ill. To friends who would call, Marietta said, "It is so marvelous having Penelope and Frankie here with me. They are taking care of me so beautifully!"

Several days before she died, Marietta instructed her secretary to accept all invitations for the fall. She wrote to a friend in Australia, "I am thrilled you are going to be here before Thanksgiving and look forward to it greatly. . . . At the moment I am laid up, but expect to be on my feet by Labor Day." She never gave in, even at the moment she died. "Get me out of here," she told Frankie. "She went down swiftly like a beautiful sloop hitting an iceberg," FitzGerald later wrote to Marietta's childhood friend Bill Blair.

Marietta's funeral was in Northeast Harbor at the tiny stone church where fifty years earlier she had married Desmond FitzGerald. Brooke Astor brought flowers from her own garden and arranged them "as if for a party." Frankie and Penelope taped Marietta's tiny scarlet leather 1991 appointment book from Smythson's to the top of the box containing her ashes as it went into the ground. The book was filled with appointments through Christmas. The last thing George Peabody remembered seeing of his sister was a bright flash of red.

DECEMBER 1991

Diana Trilling

The first time I went to see Diana Trilling, she announced briskly: "I hated your aunt." My tape recorder was running. I was there to interview her about my father's older sister, Anita Brenner, a 1930s intellectual. She quickly elaborated. "Maybe 'hate' is too strong a word to express how I really felt. Envy is a better word. In fact, I envied your aunt. In the 1930s she was taken very seriously for her writing and for her opinions at a time when I was not. She was a celebrity! Something occurs to me. Was she in fact a lesbian? I see her walking into a room. She clumped. Something else: she never did the humane thing, much less the right one."

I knew that Trilling, then a vibrant octogenarian and notorious intellectual matriarch, liked to test the mettle of first-time visitors. I had been told that it was a sport for her, a form of mental hazing. If I wanted a relationship with Diana I would have to adhere to her order of social business: she would not surround you with approval, shower you with hyperbole, or for that matter, endorse your projections. Diana and her husband, Lionel Trilling, had reigned for years as arbiters of a rarefied circle that explained culture and literature. The first tenured Jewish professor in Columbia's English department, Trilling had the sheen of an Anglophile. In the Eisenhower and Kennedy years, "Li and Di" were at the center of a tiny world of New York liberal intellectuals at a time when in their eyes ideas—"the life of significant contention," she famously called it—colored the discourse of the era.

Trilling had positions on everything and everybody—Zabar's declining standards, arcane feuds that predated Eisenhower, the decline of cultural references of current Columbia University students, the cupidity of the younger generation of publishing baby sharks, the wardrobe mistakes of movie stars.

Diana never forgot a dagger. She nursed and reiterated her grudges. The poet Randall Jarrell once insulted her house gift of a coconut cream pie: "What's that, pus?" he asked her. The critic Alfred Kazin once famously asked her husband, Lionel: "When are you going to dissociate from that wife of yours?" She recorded that Lionel himself accused her of "being the worst person he had ever met and of having ruined his life." With close friends, her conversation was laced with imperious commands: "It is necessary to be precise" or, "I think you don't have your facts right" or, "You need to rephrase your question." The most innocuous remark could provoke an acid bath. "It's a nice day," editor Wayne Lawson once told her as we were leaving lunch. "It is not," she snapped right back. Seeing an audience of Beats, she wrote of the shock of "so many young girls, so few of them pretty, and so many blackest black stockings; so many young men, so few of them—despite the many black beards—with any promise of masculinity." Only later would she write without a hint of irony, "I was never taught to please . . . I was in middle age before it broke upon me that people made life more pleasant and profitable for themselves by undertaking to please others, often at some cost in honesty." This insight did not seem to make her a diplomat. Diana gave no quarter in her writing or with her friends—a trait she described as a reverence for brutal honesty.

Trim and handsome with protuberant dark eyes from an early childhood thyroid disorder, she could dazzle you with fine-tuned calibrations and a surefooted ability to upgrade personal observations into a cultural context. Attempting to clarify my aunt's place in the literary pantheon of the Roosevelt years, she said, "If you were a woman—and an intellectual—in the 1930s, it was very difficult. There was a diminution of respect. You would be admired at one moment and made of no consequence the next. I watched it in relation to myself. I did not become a writer until 1941. It was your fate as woman—you had to keep yourself at the level of celebrity or you just ceased to exist."

A few years earlier, Trilling had confronted the writer Patricia Bosworth. "Your father must have been a Communist," she told her and Bosworth later wrote: "When I didn't answer, she ordered: 'Admit it. If you don't I'll have to conclude that you've been brainwashed,'" Bosworth noted in the *New York Times.*

Bosworth, the daughter of a cold war liberal lawyer, Bartley Crum, and I had originally met Trilling at a time when each of us was working on a family memoir. Diana had known our relatives and felt no need to gloss their images. My aunt Anita, she insisted, had been "reliable" even though she was a Trotskyite. Yes, she had been an "exceptionally gifted" writer and an intimate of Diego Rivera and Frida Kahlo. But what Diana recalled was that she gave good parties and was stingy with the maid that she and Diana shared at the beginning of the Depression. Despite her protestations, Bosworth could never disabuse Diana of her misguided notions about her father's politics.

I began to visit Diana as often as I could. I admired her sense of order, of adhering to form even for our casual tea dates. When I would telephone, Diana would first insist that she was very busy, maintaining a strict work schedule—dictating to one of many of a series of assistants and secretaries. She presented herself as a model of a disciplined life—she projected a desire to remain in control at all times. By then Trilling had a severe case of macular degeneration and could no longer read except with the help of a magnifying lamp. She was frequently in search of new secretarial help—they were all hopeless, she would say with desperation, and might I know anyone with whom it would be possible for her to work harmoniously? She would choose a time and a day—always teatime. She lived near the Columbia University campus in a ground-floor apartment that seemed unnaturally dark. She had a passion for order; the Claremont Avenue apartment was always fastidious, her paper napkins had a monogram. Her living room had prominent bookshelves and Walker Evans photographs, sturdy sofas that did not contradict the 1930s intellectuals' aesthetic disdain of luxury and comfort. When I would arrive, Diana would be seated on a sofa. She was perfectly groomed, with her dark hair pulled back into a neat chignon; she often wore shirtwaists. A tray would be arranged neatly with tuna sandwiches and butter cookies. She would have prepared the tuna salad herself. She knew every inch of her kitchen, she claimed, and continued to cook as much as possible for herself. The tuna flowed out of the sides of the crusts—The cooking was important to her; she bragged about her pot roast, as if it connected her to a roseate version of a difficult childhood. When I would ask about those years, she would answer imperiously that she was writing about this period in her memoir and I would just have to wait.

In our visits, Diana complained she felt she was in the shadow of her husband Lionel Trilling, star professor and interpreter of literature. He was the patriarch of two generations of Columbia intellectuals. Best known for his collected essays, *The Liberal Imagination,* Trilling was "perhaps the most intelligent man I ever met," his former pupil Norman Podhoretz once said of him. His gift was illuminating the very bones of books, how they worked rather than what they meant. Trilling also analyzed Matthew Arnold, Henry James, E.M. Forster. Discussing *Pride and Prejudice,* he noted that Elizabeth and Darcy first spoke with very different syntax and by the conclusion, sounded much the same.

Their son, James, was born when Diana was forty-two. Diana often asked me about my own daughter, who was ten years old when we met. "No matter how responsibly we do our work, that is not our primary concern," Diana would say softly. "We are somehow deficient as mothers. Your self-consciousness increases, your energy diminishes. Having babies! How are you going to have the energy to do it all? I had my household going by nine A.M., but the children are so mentally demanding, your thought process is taken up." She did not resent the time. "There is a point when your children become so interesting to you that you don't want to spend a day away from them. My preoccupations were domestic. My time was taken up by my husband and children," she said.

It would take years for her to write professionally. She would remind friends that she did not even begin at *The Nation* until she was thirty-nine, and did not publish her first full-length work, *Mrs. Harris, The Death of the Scarsdale Diet Doctor* until she was in her seventies. She established herself as a reviewer at a time when reputations were made by trenchant analysis—James Agee, Clement Greenberg, Mary McCarthy, and Randall Jarrell frequently weighed in with their opinions on the arts. If Diana did not take on the big, sprawling themes of the literary sisters, the Trillings' place in "the Family" as Podhoretz called the group, was as its moral arbiters. They were a small circle, trading quips and insults at nightly parties. They quarreled over public matters from Trotsky to Joe McCarthy and accused each other of "breaking ranks," delighting in their feuds and fissures. Podhoretz's memoir *Ex-Friends* is as dense as a legal brief, detailing years of squabbles of this period.

Diana described friendships with the terse language of the Paris peace talks. Lillian Hellman "made an approach" and sent "a strong overture" to her and Lionel seeking "an alliance." Her friends received letters and notes typed on blue or gray stationery with perfectly chiseled sentences, as if written for posterity. She remarked that "Lionel taught me to think and I taught Lionel to write." Her collections of essays show an acute gift of observation, a sense of middle-class cultural history, a contrarian's view. She read a novel a day and reviewed fiction weekly, published essays and articles in *Partisan Review* and *Commentary*. Her opinions were feisty and muscular, praising Saul Bellow as "talented and clever" but attacking *Dangling Man* as "not the kind of novel I like." Nabokov's *Bend Sinister* had "four successful moments." She championed Norman Mailer's literary acuity in *Partisan Review* soon after he was bannered across the front pages of the *New York Post* for stabbing his then wife, Adele, perhaps saving his reputation when he was a pariah among the smart set. She tenderly defended Allen Ginsberg and the Beats, although the essay struck many who read it in 1959 as patronizing. When she turned a gimlet eye on the murderous intent of Jean Harris, she angered feminists who felt that the death of Herman Tarnower could be somehow justified as sexual rage. She loved the bright lights that narrative brought her, and kept a photo of herself with William Buckley on *Firing Line* in her dining room.

The list of women with whom she had complex relations was stellar, beginning with my own aunt Anita. By the time Diana and Anita Brenner met each other in 1929, Anita was established as a young literary star. Her thesis *Idols Behind Altars* had been published to rave reviews two weeks before the stock market crash. The book established the twenty-four-year-old as a *wunderkind* anthropologist and introduced the notion of the pagan influence in Mexican culture to a wide popular audience. Anita was taken up by the circle around Lionel Trilling and was a frequent contributor on Latin American affairs to *The Nation* and the *Times*. She had posed nude for Edward Weston's camera and had made a reputation for boldness—it is Anita's round derriere that is the stunning Weston pear-shaped nude on display at the Museum of Modern Art.

By 1935, Anita was known for her support of and friendships with Diego Rivera, Frida Kahlo, and the Italian socialist Carlos Tresca, and entertained often at her brownstone in Brooklyn Heights. On Halloween night 1935, Anita decorated her house with pumpkins and sugar skulls, as if for *dia de los muertos*, the day of the dead. Whittaker Chambers, then a Stalinist agent in hiding, arrived at the party, coming above ground for the first time. Almost sixty years later, Diana had perfect recall of the evening. "I recoiled when I saw him," she said. "He put out his hand to shake mine and I would not touch it. No one would speak to him." Chambers's subsequent notoriety for using a pumpkin to hide the microfilm which would implicate Alger Hiss as a communist agent was linked to the trauma he experienced at Anita's party, Diana firmly believed. "I am convinced he chose a pumpkin for a hiding place as an unconsious act because of the dreadful night at Anita's," she told me, a perception that she passed along to Chambers's lawyer during the Alger Hiss espionage trial.

Diana's circle included Mary McCarthy and Lillian Hellman and later Gertrude Himmelfarb, author and wife of Irving Kristol, and even Daphne Merkin, who dedicated a novel to Diana. Merkin later noted in the *Times* that Diana was criticized by no less than Mary McCarthy and Hannah Arendt for her efforts to obtain cultural cachet beyond her established place as muse to Lionel Trilling and "peerless hausfrau." At the end of her life she wrote her seductive memoir, *The Beginning of the Journey*, filled with testy judgments on former foes and a nuanced portrait of her husband. The title was an ironic comment on Lionel's novel *The Middle of the Journey*, and in her book she revealed his foibles—he was, for all his eloquence and intelligence, an alcoholic, abusive to her and cowed in childhood by his doting eccentric aunts and mother. If fear had marked her childhood, it did not mark Diana's final years. She never lost her passion or her curiousity and was as interested in gossip about movie stars and famous people as she was frantic about time, determined to break loose from all who had diminished her and held her back.

The portraits of the young Diana Rubin and Lionel Trilling on the cover of *The Beginning of the Journey* suggest what Diana often said about their relationship. "We believed in achievement, not happiness," she told Patricia Bosworth. Lionel Trilling appears epicene and effeminate, his hands clasped over each other, staring moodily into the distance like Lord Byron. As a young woman, Diana radiates the dignity and loneliness that would mark her life. Isolated from a social life until she got to Radcliffe, Diana often remarked wistfully that Lionel was catnip to women—he reputedly had a mistress for years whom Diana knew—and she remarked from time to time on her own feelings of being thwarted, both emotionally and sexually. She edited the letters of D.H. Lawrence and was jealous of Lillian Hellman's remarkable ability to seduce men. When Lionel complained he felt blocked as a fiction writer because of his inability to indulge in unbridled sexual passion, Diana encouraged him to have many affairs to free his creativity. Over the years, friends have wondered if Trilling was confused about his sexual identity; he was an unlikely Lothario.

It was a strange love between them. "We were never in love the way that people are in love in popular songs," she wrote, adding that "over a lifetime we loved each other very much, increasingly with the years, although in middle life we quarreled a great deal and often threatened each other with divorce." A man with Lionel's childhood would have daunted a lesser woman. He was a pampered toddler of such rarefied prettiness that his mother felt the need to hang a sign on his baby carriage: Please Don't Kiss the Baby. The baby was cosseted with a squirrel coat and fur blankets. Later, young Trilling had a nanny who brought lamb chops on a silver salver to the playground while his other friends ate from a lunch pail. He told Diana that his lifetime dream was to be able to have such a pail. His mother and his aunts followed him to summer camp and then forbade him to go away to college, but his mother read to him voraciously from the Brontës, Jane Austen, Henry James. Lionel's family had grand ambitions; his aunts collected art and his uncle Hyman Cohen owned a racing sloop, the *Zinita*. Lionel's mother schemed for her son to be the heir apparent. Cohen, cold and feckless, occupied Lionel's imagination. Trilling tortured himself with the richness of the drama that his uncle's story might yield for fiction: How could he not write about Hyman Cohen making the Bermuda Race in 1920?

The upwardly aspiring Cohens did not approve of his marriage to the daughter of Polish Jewish immigrants. It was an act of rebellion for Trilling to marry her. Lionel's father was a hyponchodriac, "a Mr. Woodhouse without an Emma," Diana wrote. A gifted tailor, he was a bad businessman who thought a prosperous living could be made by manufacturing fur-lined coats for open roadsters at a time when the roadsters were going the way of the horse and buggy. He was as well given to sudden rages. Diana tells of his ripping up his wife's lace blouses. His grandson James Trilling would speculate convincingly in the *American Scholar* that these destructive attacks were an undiagnosed form of ADD, attention deficit disorder, which was passed down through the Trilling men.

Diana Rubin was born in 1905 and reared at a time when women wore steel-reinforced corsets and were banned from clubs and restaurants and arrested for smoking cigarettes in public. As a girl, she slid down haystacks in rural Larchmont before the family moved to the city. The youngest of three children, Diana was musical and a talented singer. Even in old age, her voice remained melodic and evoked Radcliffe in the days of speakeasies and boys in raccoon coats. Unlike Lionel's father, Diana's had a gift for money. He began as a braid manufacturer and then moved on to own a silk stocking business. A successful businessman with progressive ideas, he built a modern steel and glass factory on Long Island that was studied by architecture students, and recognized the unions. He was an early vegetarian, eating only cereal and olives, an exercise fanatic who experimented with Christian Science. Diana's father talked to her about becoming a political journalist in the style of Walter Lippmann; he evoked the victimization of Jean Valjean. Although he was not a reader, *Les Miserables* was the singular book of his life. When she was a young woman, her father took her around the world. She saw, she wrote, the Paris of Proust and the Parc Vendome, the Rue de Rivoli. She went to the west coast of South America, steaming to port with her father on a launch reserved for VIPs.

Yet for all its luxury, her childhood was a paradigm of the Eastern European "culture of cruelty." Children were not treated as precious, and Diana, the youngest of three, was a special target for her mother's envy and rages. "Pleasure was not the principle of our home," she wrote. "I learned early in life that to laugh before breakfast was to cry before dinner." She became a fearful child, afraid of the dark, of burglars, of germs. Later, she would suffer panic attacks. Her mother, a beauty, often told Diana how unattractive she was: "You'll never catch yourself a man to hold onto," she told her. Her father, when he wasn't doting, could also be harsh, suggesting when she sang for guests that he would build her a stage in the toilet. He would praise her, then belittle her. She wrote that his defiling her talent with a reference to excrement forced her to take seriously his ban and her mother's mockery. "Without psychoanalysis, I would not have been enough free of it even to make a start as a published writer," she wrote.

"I never had firm emotional ground under my feet," she calmly noted. Diana's mother was volatile and envious, as well as ill through much of her own daughter's adolescence. She was a beauty as a young woman, and had been a showroom model, but became a *balaboosty* in the house. In Larchmont and later on West End Avenue, she made the clothes and did the cooking. She lifted the heavy furniture, beat the rugs, turned out the closets. Her mother had the superstitions of rural Poland, slaughtering kittens in front of Diana, and wiping cinders out of her eye with her tongue. From portraits as an infant posed with one nanny or another, Diana herself became convinced that her mother had a nervous breakdown after her birth. Writing about her childhood in her eighties, she began to see the contradictions: "The father who would build a stage in the toilet was the same father who took care of his employees. The mother who murdered cats also took wounded chickens to bed to nurse them back to health."

As a child, Diana was distressed to move from the rural setting of Westchester County to the ostentatious upper-middle-class Jewish ghetto of West End Avenue of the 1920s. The setting was an arena for the cruelest displays of new wealth, she wrote. The men were flashy, the wives loud and demanding, dressed in showy clothes and diamonds— "their rude voices filled the Schrafft's Restaurant at Broadway and 83rd Street." She returned from Radcliffe to find a mother who was gravely ill in a world that was a strict contrast to the haven of self-conscious plainness of Cambridge. Diana felt "implicated by the coarseness" of the neighborhood. At Radcliffe, Diana studied art history and was convinced that the Polish imprint of her childhood prevented her from being invited into the elite social circle of her favorite professor, although he later invited her to be his assistant at the Fogg Museum. Trained as a dutiful daughter, she felt compelled to return to live at home in New York to search for a job. "My Jewish name stopped me at the door of the Metropolitan Museum and the Frick Art Reference Library," she wrote. By any interpretation, it was a dreadful period in her life. Her mother was dying; Diana could not come to terms with her complicated feelings. "I was jealous of her and angry at her," she wrote, and she never truly understood the history of failed communications between them, the lack of intimacy. Diana wondered if she truly remembered her as she was or if she romanticized their only shared link—a love of singing.

On her deathbed, her mother requested that Diana sing her a Russian lullaby. In later years, she rarely spoke of her mother, but she said in a conversation with Patricia Bosworth, "I have suffered very much from women, very little from men. I'm outraged by one woman lawyer after another coming on those television shows . . . you see their eyes steely and their mouths, they're scary people."

She was introduced to Lionel in a speakeasy by Clifton and Polly Fadiman, who thought that two people with such euphonious names should meet. They slept together early on in their relationship, an act which Diana described as the boldest of her life. Lionel, then without funds or any visible means of supporting his future wife, announced to his mother that he intended to marry—her response was to faint. At a subsequent Trilling seder, Lionel's spinster aunts refused to shake Diana's hand. Diana's father had a similar reaction. "Two damn fools can't get married," he said, although he agreed to pay for the wedding and to give them a $5,000 wedding gift, a substantial sum in 1929. Although Lionel's aunts and rich uncle Hymie attended the wedding, none of them sent gifts. Diana had married into a family as destructive as her own. Soon after, Lionel broke with his relatives for good. Marrying Diana had been an act of rebellion. Although he lived until the age of seventy, his uncles and aunts outlived him and remained in their large Park Avenue apartment. However aware they were of his accomplishments, they never spoke to him again.

Diana later wrote that she, like the women of her era, had not been trained to be "custodians of their fates." She insisted that Lionel attend her singing lessons with her to confirm that she had talent. Her teacher, an early feminist, reacted angrily: "Why do you have to have his approval? It's your voice, isn't it?" She was being spoken to in the language of women's liberation, but her response was to burst into tears.

Soon after, in 1931, she experienced her first panic attacks, clinging to Lionel through the night in the throes of a nameless and overwhelming terror. Unfamiliar with the language of psychiatry, she consulted a neurologist who asked her a question that would remain with her a lifetime: Why did she want Lionel always to be with her? She answered unhesitatingly: "I wanted Lionel to be with me because I wanted to be more dependent on him than he was on me." Her response, she later wrote, was the first hint of what would become a crippling neurosis. Lionel's refusal to exert parental authority over her "exposed her to all the illicitness and temptation I had been taught to fear."

In 1999 in the *American Scholar,* James Trilling noted his mother's failure to link her own mother's nervous breakdowns to her history with phobia. Although she lived long enough to learn of a possible genetic tie, Diana preferred psychoanalytic explanations for all maladies. In *The Beginning of the Journey,* she portrays herself frequently as the family scapegoat. She was convinced, she wrote, that her brother was allowed power over her because he was a boy and her sister because she had a physical handicap, a curvature of the spine. Both Lionel and Diana had the strictest allegiance to Freud; James argued that his parents could not recognize the physiological conditions which afflicted them both. His father's ADD, he wrote, was surely mislabeled as neurosis as was his mother's panic disorder and agoraphobia. As evidence, he cites Diana's older sister Celia who "used to grimace and smack her lips while making convulsive yet deliberate grasping motions with her hands." Today we would see this as Tourette's syndrome, but Diana viewed it solipsistically as a mockery of her own identity. "She was the dark side of the body: abandon unredeemed by pleasure, debility unredeemed by pain," James Trilling wrote. Diana spent much of her life trying to leave her sister behind. In this she was abetted by Lionel: "Her older sister is an ugly caricature of D. and I was frightened," he wrote in his notebook when he first met her.

Celia finally did marry, in a nursing home, shortly before her death. James Trilling reports that the marriage sent Diana into a rage, as if Celia's decision had but one purpose—to defile her own relationship with Lionel. Yet again envy—a sense of being tormented—seized Diana. "Celia in all her decrepitude could find a husband, while Diana, a widow still in her early seventies, was condemned—even self-condemned—to spend the rest of her life celibate."

We were having tea in Morningside Heights. "What did you think of Mary McCarthy?" I asked her, trying to make idle conversation in one of our encounters. I hadn't yet learned to avoid talking about successful women with Diana, and predictably, Diana exploded as if she were under attack. "Why are you asking me that? I had no use for Mary McCarthy. We had nothing in common. In fact, I have spent a lot more time with you than I ever did with her." She was churlish, she said, because McCarthy had called her a "Trotskyite" in her last memoir. "There were constant factional disputes—the dictates came from Moscow. Mary should have understood my feelings about Moscow Gold, as we called it. It was a culture in which friendships were smashed easily. There was no end to the attack!"

While she spoke, the telephone rang repeatedly. "No, darling! I am all right! Dinner? There is a place here called Caballere. . . . Is that good? Rupert's? Too noisy. The Caballere is perfectly all right . . ."

Diana turned back to me and without being asked changed the subject to a favorite conversational topic, her relationship with Lillian Hellman. "If what you mean is to ask me about Lillian, well, that is another story. She approached us. She made an open overture. She said to Lionel at a party, 'Why don't you and Diana want to be friends with me?' Lionel and I became her friends very reluctantly."

In Diana's later years she was often asked about her feuds with Hellman and with Norman Mailer. The rage and sense of betrayal she felt from both of her former friends echoed her childhood. The facts of the matter appeared to be the following: At the height of her success as a playwright in 1958, she met Norman Mailer at a party at Lillian Hellman's. Mailer's first words to her won her over: "Now, what about you, smart cunt?" She was titillated by this and flattered by his bad-boy flirty approach. The friendship continued with antic eyeball who-could-outstare-the-other competitions, according to Peter Manso's biography of Mailer. Diana was clearly attracted to him, but she waxed superior, suggesting that she and Lionel "gave Norman some kind of legitimacy in the midst of all his *meshugas*" and added, "We did for a lot of other people as well." The undercurrent of the Trilling-Mailer friendship was soon to be Lillian Hellman's feeling that Mailer was her own discovery.

By 1977, Trilling and Hellman were both cranky septuagenarians with no intention of retreating into quietude. They shared a publisher and their competitive enmity for each other exploded on the front page of the *Times:* Diana accused Lillian of having kamikaze-like ordered the cancellation of *We Must March My Darlings,* a book of Diana's collected essays, because Diana attacked Lillian's politics in several critical sentences in the book. Diana believed that Lillian had told Mailer to rewrite a positive quote he had given, rendering it useless. She never forgave him. Nor would he apologize to her. Later, Hellman would turn on Mary McCarthy with a similar fury, and sue her for remarks made on a talk show. Diana told Patricia Bosworth, "Someday I think my obituary is going to read: 'Diana Trilling dies at 150. Widow of distinguished professor and literary critic Lionel Trilling. Engaged in controversy with Lillian Hellman.'" Shortly before Hellman died, Diana learned that "in those last days, when her vitality ebbed, all one had to do was say, 'Diana Trilling' or 'Mary McCarthy' for her strength to be restored. So you see, I was of some use to her in the end."

In 1981, during a lull during jury selection of the Jean Harris trial, the out-of-town reporters asked Diana, Why in the world was she interested in Mrs. Harris's case? It seemed a strange assignment. She was then in her seventies and every day would make the long trip to a Westchester courthouse to share the press seats with the other reporters. It was an act of boldness by any stretch; she had no experience with the grit of reporting, no history as an interviewer. Harris refused to see her, preferring to tell her version of events to Diana's competitor Shana Alexander. At first Diana tried to finesse the questions to raise her interest into a larger cultural context. She had always been interested in cases, political cases like Hiss and Oppenheimer, with direct bearing on society, and also situations and persons—LSD, the civil rights movement, the death of Marilyn Monroe—which illustrate "private and public dilemmas."

In fact, what might have motivated her was simple: She wanted back in the game. One rainy April night, Diana drove to look at Herman Tarnower's house. She recorded that she felt uneasy when she visited Tarnower's house, "as if I was appropriating other people's lives for my own purposes." Water dripped off her plastic hood and onto the top of her nose. Contempt overwhelmed her. "What I was looking at was a low two-storied house, not large but large enough to make a sizable bad impression. I saw a Japanese—Japenoid—manifestation, a sort of domestic pagoda. The facade was incoherent with terraces; every terrace seemed to be backed by glass. It was a small busy statement of deference to the East." Drenched, she presented herself to Tarnower's Belgian servants, Henri and Suzanne van der Vreken, wondering if she should fumble in her bag for a letter of credentials.

I tried to imagine Diana at this moment in this scene. She was coldly rebuffed by Tarnower's staff. I wondered what could have driven her to remain, as she did, wishing fervently she had a spyglass to see Dr. Tarnower's pond and private Buddha. "Imagine one's private pond in Westchester with a private Buddha to row to—it was absurd! A Westchester pagoda was absurd, this expensive trumped-up serenity was absurd. This was what came of our winning the war in the Pacific: America now had rights on the peace of the Orient!" Suddenly, as she started away, the scene at Dr. Tarnower's lake dissolved and was replaced for Diana by the vision of a swimming pool with a dead body, not of Tarnower, but of no less than Jay Gatsby.

Diana fled Armonk to go home to reread Fitzgerald and feast upon the moral implications of Tarnower's sordid tale. She charged Tarnower with vulgarity, as if being nouveau riche had brought about his death. "But surely the way in which taste is exercised—every kind of taste: in art, and architecture, and decoration, dress, food, manners, and speech—is the firmest clue we have to how someone pursues his life in culture and therefore to the style of moral being he would legislate for us, if he had the power."

Embarrassed by Jean Harris's intellectual boasts, Diana criticized her high-flown sentences: Tarnower "read Herodotus for fun" and argued over syntax. Diana rose up haughtily and dismissed him as a fool: "As a famous diet doctor, Tarnower was one of the hidden tyrants of culture" who had clearly sinister ambitions to dictate "the way in which we were to conform our bodies to an arbitrary consumer ideal." Her greatest ire was reserved for Tarnower's spartan Scarsdale regime: the grapefruit, boiled cabbage, and eggs of the Thursday allotment, the absurd inflation of the "epicurean" allowance with its melon and strawberries and espresso coffee. She interpreted all manner of darkness and pretensions into the Scarsdale Diet, but wasn't it just as possible that Tarnower or, more to the point, his ghostwriter, was trying to pad a two-sheet diet plan into a full-length book?

She was no more sympathetic to Jean Harris. She lost all sympathy for her and revised her entire manuscript after the trial because she was unable to get a fix on Mrs. Harris's personality. "I'd swing from an extreme of sympathy to an extreme of disenchantment. When she was charming, I was charmed. When malice took over, as it so often did without her being at all aware of it, I'd scarcely remember that I'd ever felt anything but dislike of her—I would think, how can anyone fail to see that this woman is dangerous?" she wrote. Diana ascribed her feelings to Mrs. Harris's "lack of an emotional core." As it happened, I reread *Mrs. Harris* and Diana's childhood memoir within days of each other. I was startled to find that much of what she saw in Jean Harris seemed connected to what she later wrote about her mother. It seemed to me that the parallel meant that even an observer of such acuity could continuously see and repeat the patterns of childhood.

The last time we spoke Diana turned the conversation to what her life had been like in the 1930s. She was as well starting to write recollections for *The New Yorker* on her days at summer camp. Peter Manso had offered to help her with the second volume of her memoirs, but she turned him down emphatically. She wanted, she said, to stay on her childhood. Later, she would write stunningly about a state dinner she attended at the White House in the Kennedy years. Her description of shopping for a dress—long versus short?—and arriving at the White House in a friend's station wagon from the train was as rich a portrait of literary mores in the 1960s as any account published.

What was apparent was that Diana was moving without sentimentality or compromise toward a new understanding of the society she had influenced. There was an atmosphere of Arnoldian formality about these equivocations; it was not a frivolous pursuit. The *Times* even remarked on her grudging tone: "The strange difficult ungenerous unreliable unkind and not always honest people who created the world in which Lionel and I shared, and to which we tried to contribute, are now most of them dead. I inscribe their names here on this poor monument: Elliot Cohen, Herbert Solow, Henry Rosenthal, Philip Rahv, Dwight Macdonald, Fred Dupee, Margaret Marshall, Delmore Schwartz, William Barrett, James Agee, Bernard Haggin, Irving Howe."

In our visits, Diana would reminisce with equal intensity about her early married life. Her father lost everything, then died at a time when Lionel was trying to establish himself in the difficult, unwelcoming atmosphere of Columbia in the 1930s. Diana had figured out a way to serve a crowd for Sunday tea parties. She would buy fish spread from Weisbecker's, a local deli, then mash it with cream cheese and liverwurst. "I could feed fifteen people for a dollar," she said proudly, remembering her skill as "the housekeeping goddess of reason," as Robert Lowell called her. As we talked, she kept the television on to monitor the O.J. Simpson trial on *Court TV.* Although her vision was mostly gone, the high contrast of the screen made the drama available to her. She announced that she was writing about the case for the *New Republic.* She had by then completely rethought her feelings about the "smarty-pants" she had known. "I don't know that intellectuals have made any great contribution to political wisdom," she said. She was particularly horrified by the lack of intelligence in the intellectual argument coming from Los Angeles. She used the term "nondimensional," and then did a flawless imitation of TV-speak. " 'It is racism' or 'it is economic' or 'it is class-engendered' and if you are a conservative, it is because of the 'welfare programs.' " "The fact is," she said, "it is something that goes beyond and combines all those things." Diana had always defined herself by nuance and oppositions. She remained a woman with a beautiful mind convinced of the honor of rejecting easy answers and received wisdom. Her voice was haunted by melancholy, but had a spirited urgency. The last time I spoke to her, she hung up quickly and unapologetically. "Darling, I must go work," she said.

JUNE 1999

Jacqueline Kennedy Onassis

People were told to move along briskly the morning after Jacqueline Kennedy Onassis died. By ten o'clock that Friday in late May, hundreds of mourners from all over the city and the suburbs had gathered outside her grand apartment building on Fifth Avenue. It was known in New York that Mrs. Kennedy, as she would remain forever in the national memory, lived a few blocks north of the Metropolitan Museum, across from Central Park; the traffic was backed up in every direction. Sound trucks from the networks were forced to park a block away. "My God, there are reporters here from China and Japan," the UPI man said as he scanned the crowd. A woman with teary eyes worked the line with her toy Pomeranian on a pink leash: "I was with her just two days ago with the dog!" A reporter bellowed into her cellular phone, to Reuters. "Anyone on the desk want an interview with a woman who said she walked with her with the dog?" Nearby, a Haitian nurse openly wept and crossed herself repeatedly in the bright sunshine.

The death of a public figure in New York is always choreographed like a splendid pageant, but the police had never experienced anything that remotely resembled the tributes that came that morning. I watched from behind the blue-and-white police sawhorses as clusters of men in suits, women in running shorts, mothers with babies in strollers, and young women in crisp spring linen dresses on their way to offices dropped bouquet after bouquet into the purple impatiens planted outside the entrance to her building. Such care had gone into the selection of these flowers—single buds of the palest tulips the pink of a baby's palm, cascading lilacs, and tiny unfurled roses. One woman had gone to Mrs. Kennedy's own florist and asked what she would have liked. "Anything small," he said and then repeated the obvious. "She was very discreet." All morning they came and carefully laid their tributes.

Much of Jacqueline Kennedy Onassis's fame came from her looks and whom she married and from murder. But it was heightened by a curious detachment she had, a certainty held in reserve. (The breathiness of her voice, some felt, could be explained by the fact that she was shy.) She had good manners as well, and a keen sense of her place in history, and something else: the allure of her secrets. She was often playful, sometimes sly; yet sadness, even melancholia, seemed to lurk just beneath her surface. Soon after President Kennedy was assassinated in 1963, Mrs. Kennedy went to visit Minnie and James Fosburgh in Katonah, a charming town outside of New York City. Kitty Carlisle Hart was visiting as well. Kitty Hart's husband, director and playwright Moss Hart, had also recently died, and the two widows spent hours together in private. To lighten the atmosphere, Mrs. Hart suggested that they all play Walter Mitty. "What would you be if you could be anything at all?" she asked Jackie Kennedy. "A bird," she replied, as if her desire to escape her destiny could not be imagined in human form. All that weekend Mrs. Kennedy agonized. She went over and over the President's final moments, as if she blamed herself for his death. If I had turned to the left, if I had turned to the right, what if I had moved six inches in the car? What if we hadn't gone to Dallas? Would Jack still be alive?

It has become a commonplace for writers and reporters to say that the one person they wanted to interview was Jacqueline Kennedy. Now she was gone, with all of the questions unasked, unanswered. So many opinions and facts we will never know: What did she really think of Rose Kennedy, Lyndon Johnson, Judith Campbell Exner, and Christina Onassis? Did she know that the White House logbooks were sometimes fictions, notable for their omissions? In later years, she often mentioned "Jack" in conversations, as if to flatter her companion that she was sharing something, but those small remarks never added up to very much. It was a charming trick she had learned, an implied confidence. A pretty British reporter who later wrote about the episode in *The Spectator,* claimed that Jackie had once rescued her from Ted Kennedy's drunken sexual advances on a train. Mrs. Kennedy gave the reporter, Noreen Taylor, the impression that she was not repulsed by the exuberance of the Kennedys but almost wished that she could have their boisterous resilience. She was quoted as having admitted she had "learned not to fight her emotional makeup." She once wrote of the family, "How can I explain these people? They were like carbonated water, and other families might be flat." But, much as she might have admired the Kennedys, Jacqueline Kennedy also understood her fame and its odd paradox: her only enduring stardom would come from silence.

It was the morning of May 20 when most people heard the news of her death, although Jackie Kennedy had died the night before. New York had had a particularly glorious spring; the forsythia and the tulips on Park Avenue lasted longer than anyone could remember. The Knicks and the Rangers were battling for championships, and there was a feeling that the city was coming back, basking in the energy from the new mayor. Early that morning, my eleven-year-old daughter awakened me with a certain jauntiness of tone, as if she were privy to inside news. "Jackie Kennedy is dead!"

Television kept running the footage that had defined my generation's childhood: Jackie as a young woman on a horse at Merrywood; Caroline and John as toddlers, scrambling on the beach in Newport, their hair riffling in the wind; Jackie in her "Schiaparelli pink" suit diving out of the Lincoln convertible. The world she created for herself became part of the cultural language of the era: George Plimpton's elaborate toasts to eight-year-old Caroline with a champagne flute full of cocoa, poetry recitations, pirate treasure hunts with longboats borrowed from the Coast Guard, French conversations just for the heck of it, and *cadeaux* of ancient Roman heads to her longtime companion Maurice Tempelsman. We were reminded of how beautiful she was when she was young. Those creamy shoulders in strapless gowns, the startling dark eyes on the sides of her head, the cap of dark hair.

On TV her life seemed fully documented, but the truth was always quite deliberately hidden. Did she ever let her hair down with her close friend and school chum Nancy Tuckerman? Somehow I doubt it. Mrs. Kennedy appeared to be a woman whose intimate friendships came from a shared history. All that week in May there had been conversations among a certain group in the city about the gravity of her condition. It was said that she was near death, but even her closest friends did not believe it. And then Mrs. Kennedy was dying so quickly. Her friends rushed back from Europe, from their houses in the country, and felt almost betrayed that she had never let on how serious her lymphoma was. Why were they surprised? They knew that Jackie Kennedy was of a world that believed that discretion was the highest ideal.

There were, of course, many tears that morning. And in numerous houses in America, mine included, the questions of children: "Mother, why are you crying?" In my daughter's voice, I could suddenly hear my own, thirty years ago, demanding of my own mother crying in front of our black-and-white Motorola that November of 1963: "Mother, why are you crying?" I could see my then thirty-nine-year-old mother sitting cross-legged in her pedal pushers, weeping, oblivious to my pre-teen presence. And now here on another television set again, were all the phrases we associate with any description of Camelot. For *The New York Times,* she was "the young woman in widow's weeds," but the editorial writer, like everyone else, was struggling to describe the intangible, the subtext of this woman who chose not to let herself be known except by her children.

"Why don't you act more like Jackie Kennedy?" my mother used to ask when I was a teenager. "Talk less. Project mystery." My mother and Mrs. Kennedy were of a generation reared not to express their thoughts publicly; they knew etiquette and bromides and a sense of the appropriate. When confronted with an enemy, Mrs. Kennedy refused to make eye contact, impeccable to the last.

It was the autumn of 1960 when she first began to ascend. As Jacqueline Kennedy drifted along the campaign trail, her husband's advisors, miscalculating the mood of the country, wanted her to be invisible. It was the first time fashion had come close to political power. When Mrs. Kennedy was campaigning in New York City Castro was in town and the Yankees were in a World Series. Here was the wife of the Democratic candidate—a Catholic!—and a woman out of a Cole Porter lyric, very Côte Basque, fey. She had quite cunningly invented her own style. For years, she had very deliberately copied Audrey Hepburn's look. She took Hepburn's image—the naïf, the gamine—and made it her own. She was dressed, as Hepburn was, by Givenchy and Balenciaga. She wore the ballerina skirts of *Sabrina* and the *Funny Face* leotards. In private, she often sought the guidance of the great fashion diva Diana Vreeland, who was involved with every aspect of Mrs. Kennedy's glamorous wardrobe as First Lady.

America was ready for her; young marrieds had put their Depression-era upbringings behind them and were suddenly prosperous, impatient with the dowdiness of Mamie Eisenhower and her pink-and-green decorating schemes. We bought Vaughn Meader's *First Family* album to imitate Jackie's accent and hundreds of thousands of copies of a Hallmark Christmas card of an angel she had painted. For the middle class who had grown up with the idea of Yankee virtue, Jackie Kennedy made luxury, frivolity, and European glamour de rigueur.

Our mothers suddenly sported double-breasted knockoff suits and skimmer dresses and threw away their Claire McCardells. My mother worried that she was not flat-chested enough to "get away with," as she phrased it, those skinny tops. "There goes Jackie in her Pucci and her Gucci," our mothers used to tease. They were obsessed with her style and suddenly wore low heels and, later, khaki pants and navy T-shirts. Mrs.

Kennedy taught our mothers to read *Vogue* and *Women's Wear Daily*, to wear black and more black and tie their hair back with a velvet bow.

On the morning after Mrs. Kennedy died, many women I spoke with mentioned their mothers; and mine, too, was on my mind. I could hear my mother's voice a few days before she died. She was lying on a paisley chintz sofa in my house in Manhattan, ravaged by cancer, trying desperately to project the idea that nothing in the world was the matter. She entertained herself by reading a copy of *W.* magazine. "My God, look at those Bouvier sisters! Here is a picture of Jackie and Lee Radziwill out shopping in Paris on the morning after their mother died!" I expected my mother to make a remark about unseemly appearances, but she surprised me: "Isn't that marvelous? Such élan vital! I admire those girls. This is what I want you to do after my funeral. Imitate Jackie Kennedy. Never waste a moment in your life."

That Friday afternoon, John Kennedy, Jr., walked out of his mother's apartment in his running clothes. He would later glide down Park Avenue on his Rollerblades and wind up on the front page of the *Daily News*. There was a murmur of disapproval from some of the reporters, but I thought, His mother would approve. Earlier that day, John had come out in front to address the crowd, and the photographers had descended on him in a single wall. He wore a dark pin-striped suit; his eyes were red and puffy. When he appeared, many people in the crowd began to yell: *"El hermano! El hijo!"* And over and over, "John-John!" In the imagination of the mourners, John Kennedy, Jr., was perpetually three years old, paying tribute to his father with a heartbreaking salute. A family friend later said that he and Caroline had been "stunned" by the reaction to their mother's death and the hordes who came and camped in front of 1040 Fifth Avenue, a measure of how successful Mrs. Kennedy had been in making her children believe that they had a semblance of a private life. John said that he was grateful for the wishes of the crowd and he hoped that the family would be able to observe the next few days "in relative peace."

He was so like his mother then, addressing the nation after the assassination, thanking the country for the eight hundred thousand letters she had received. Nearby, several reporters scurried about doing their person-in-the-street interviews for their afternoon deadlines: What did Mrs. Kennedy mean to you? I observed one young woman hold herself a bit away. She wore a felt-and-leather bomber jacket and looked a bit out of place in this elegant neighborhood. Jenny Garcia, thirty years old and a guard in a men's shelter, told me she was "compelled" to come. "I identified with Mrs. Kennedy," she said. "I'm a single mother, after all."

As the tulips and sweetheart roses piled up in the flower beds, every thirty minutes or so the doorman filled his arms with bouquets and took them to the basement, where two close friends of Mrs. Kennedy's attempted to work them into funeral wreaths. I watched Ted Kennedy, newly married, arriving with his wife. Then William Kennedy Smith strolled toward the apartment building. He smiled and appeared quite nervous; perhaps he had heard the reporter next to me cry out, "There's the rapist," despite his acquittal. As Ted Kennedy and William Kennedy Smith shambled in, their lips tight, I wondered how Jackie had explained the death of Mary Jo Kopechne at Chappaquiddick to Caroline and John. Soon, Eunice Shriver appeared, her face lined and drawn.

When she was a young woman, Jackie had called the Kennedy sisters "the rah-rah girls" and compared them to a pack of gorillas. They referred to her as "the Deb" and imitated her baby voice. As Mrs. Kennedy was dying, the sisters asserted themselves once again: I was told that one Kennedy sister had been by the bedside as Jackie lay in a semi-coma. As her friends visited her, whispering their last goodbyes, pressing religious medals into her hand, the sister narrated in a loud voice: "—— — says she loves you, Jackie!!" And then there were the discussions— how to bury her, where to bury her—and the questions: Should the funeral be public, semiprivate, or perhaps even held at the apartment? Incredibly, Caroline and John were left with no clear instructions from their mother. The Kennedys lobbied for a state funeral but Caroline held firm, insisting that the ceremony be private and by invitation only. Although Mrs. Kennedy tried to avoid public life, she did have a passion for history and her family's place in it. When she got off the plane to Washington from Dallas in 1963, the first thing she did was ask someone on the White House staff to research Lincoln's funeral.

Mrs. Kennedy was ambivalent about publicity. When she dined at a popular restaurant in New York, the owner would tell her when photographers waited to ambush her outside. "I can't face the press," she would reportedly say. "Why don't you go out the side door if you want," he would suggest, and Mrs. Kennedy always answered, "Oh, I guess it's all right," and then sighed and cast her eyes down. At one point, that May Friday, Hillary Clinton called to announce that she would like to attend the services. The family at first was unsure what to do; they believed that the arrival of the First Lady would make Jackie's funeral a total public event. "I want to come as a friend," she said. And so the decision was made to hold the funeral mass at St. Ignatius Loyola, where Jackie had gone to church as a child, and then fly her body to Arlington Cemetery. Mrs. Kennedy had determined that she wanted to be near the President. A woman who had a complex view of her privacy was to be buried in a public place as a national figure in the company of military heroes and legendary American men.

There is no question that her background was unusual. She was the daughter of a bossy and imperious mother who, in her second marriage, to Hugh Auchincloss, was so determined to prove to the world that she was now rich that, according to one biography, she hired more servants than she had rooms at her Newport estate, Hammersmith Farm. Jackie's father, Black Jack Bouvier, was an appealing drunk who often dated women his daughter's age. The year young Jacqueline Bouvier spent away from her family in Paris as a college girl was, not surprisingly, the happiest of her life. At twenty-one, she wrote an autobiographical remarkable essay in polished and flashy prose, which helped her to triumph over a field of more than a thousand college seniors to win the 1951 *Vogue* Prix de Paris, a contest the magazine had devised, as it quaintly phrased it, to "dissolve the 'no experience' barrier that exists between the young and the professional world." Scanning later photographs of the Prix de Paris applicants, they appear to be girls from the Seven Sisters who wore cashmere sweaters, circle pins, and white gloves. The self-portrait Jackie Bouvier turned in to *Vogue* reveals her unusual detachment and wit. Here it is, uncut, just as she typed it that spring, forty-three years ago:

A self portrait written from the author's viewpoint is liable to be a little biased. Written from the viewpoint of others it would probably be so derogatory that I would not care to send it in. I have no idea how to go about describing myself but perhaps with much sifting of wheat from chaff I can produce something fairly accurate.

As to physical appearance, I am tall, 5'7", with brown hair, a square face and eyes so unfortunately far apart that it takes three weeks to have a pair of glasses made with a bridge wide enough to fit over my nose. I do not have a sensational figure but can look slim if I pick the right clothes. I flatter myself of being able at times to walk out of the house looking like the poor man's Paris copy, but often my mother will run up to inform me that my left stocking seam is crooked or the right-hand topcoat button is about to fall off. This, I realize, is the Unforgiveable Sin.

I lived in New York City until I was thirteen and spent the summers in the country. I hated dolls, loved horses and dogs and had skinned knees and braces on my teeth for what must have seemed an interminable length of time to my family.

I read a lot when I was little, much of which was too old for me. There were Chekov and Shaw in the room where I had to take naps and I never slept but sat on the window sill reading, then scrubbed the soles of my feet so the nurse would not see I had been out of bed. My heroes were Byron, Mowgli, Robin Hood, Little Lord Fauntleroy's grandfather, and Scarlett O'Hara.

Growing up was not too painful a process. It happened gradually over the three years I spent at boarding school trying to imitate the girls who had callers every Saturday. I passed the finish line when I learned to smoke, in the balcony of the Normandie theatre in New York from a girl who pressed a Longfellow upon me then led me from the theatre when the usher told her that other people could not hear the film with so much coughing going on.

I spent two years at Vassar and still cannot quite decide whether I liked it or not. I wish I had worked harder and gone away less on weekends. Last winter I took my Junior Year in Paris and spent the vacations in Austria and Spain. I loved it more than any year of my life. Being away from home gave me a chance to look at myself with a jaundiced eye. I learned not to be ashamed of a real hunger for knowledge, something I had always tried to hide, and I came home glad to start in here again but with a love for Europe that I am afraid will never leave me.

I suppose one should mention one's hobbies in a profile. I really don't have any that I work at constantly. I have studied art, here and in Paris, and I love to go to Art Exhibits and paint things that my mother doesn't put in the closet until a month after I have given them to her at Christmas. I have written a children's book for my younger brother and sister, as it amuses me to make up fairy tales and illustrate them. I love to ride and fox hunt. I will drop everything any time to read a book on ballet. This winter I am trying to catch up on things I should have learned before. I am taking typing and Interior Decorating outside of college and learning to play bridge and trying to cook things from recipes I found in France. I am afraid I will never be very successful over a hot stove.

One of my most annoying faults is getting very enthusiastic over something at the beginning and then tiring of it half way through. I am trying to counteract this by not getting too enthusiastic over too many things at once.

She came of age in an era when young people drank at the Bemelmans Bar at the Carlyle and used expressions like "tipper tapper" when they meant typewriter or, as in her delightful essay, "jaundiced eye" and "Unforgiveable Sin." Like her fashion inspiration, Audrey Hepburn, she was a 1929 baby, admired for her beauty from an early age. As a young woman, she was voraciously curious and described herself as an aesthete. Her interests were rarefied: obscure French poets, nineteenth-century Indian court paintings, mystical religions. There was something of a party girl underneath the Vassar smarts. It was there in the little-girl voice, and it was there in her sophisticated understanding of the way things work. When she applied for the Prix de Paris, she imagined an entire *Vogue* "dream issue" with the theme of nostalgia: "You can swish out to lunch at your new little restaurant in a jacket cut like a Directoire Dandy's; you can wrap yourself in a great Spanish shawl in your own very U.S.A. living room; you can dance as you used to in the twenties in a wisp of a flapper's sheath. It is always fun to pretend, and we think that these harking-back clothes will make you feel quite secretly mysterious. Call them nostalgic; they are really just variations on the theme of coquetry."

She envisioned celebrities in designer frocks: "Madame Pandit Nehru in a Mainbocher sari standing on an Indian prayer rug," "Princess Alexandra of Greece in a dress like Grès's calla lily tunic, standing beside a Greek statue." Her ideas for costume couture were equally high-flown: a voluminous deep red taffeta to evoke "The Doges of Venice"; a dress with a trumpet skirt to suggest "the Spanish look"; and a cloth greatcoat for "Sherlock Holmes and the Scottish Highlands."

The details of her *Vogue* proposal suggest the woman of fashion that Jackie Bouvier was to become. She was interested in the "romanticism of the far-off and the bygone" and imagined how glamorous a reader would feel wearing a spangled jacket that "reminds them of Blood and Sand." She designed a basic sheath dress and a three-page layout to show women how to use it with big hats, schoolgirl blouses, red chiffon scarves, or an apron ("Wear it under a great striped taffeta apron to your parties at home and feel as if you have stepped out of *Tales of the Arabian Nights*"). For a college girl, her tastes were flossy: she suggested articles on Proust and the literary history of the madeleine; an obscure Scott Fitzgerald story, "Please Show Mr. and Mrs. F to Room No. . . ." She even suggested nostalgia gossip, such as a few sentences on the *Titanic*'s sinking, a picture of Lindbergh, Man O' War, goldfish swallowers, and Shirley Temple.

When Jackie Kennedy died, it was revealed unexpectedly that she had been a magpie; her houses were filled with her clothes and papers, and reportedly some of Jack Kennedy's suits were preserved in a trunk. Her *Vogue* essay hints at this tendency. In it, she created "Moments for Memories," special dresses that years later "laid away in folds of tissue paper will be your own very special piece of Nostalgia."

Her letters evoked the Edwardian era; friends treasured her thank-you notes on the famous Wedgwood blue stationery with "1040 Fifth Avenue" engraved in white, or, if she was in residence on the Vineyard, the distinct white scallop shell. Her handwriting was girlish, with its sweeping loops and fat letters; there was no sense of hurry in her prose. Once, when she was still living in the White House, she wrote to Lady Dorothy Macmillan before the president was due to arrive at Birch Grove, the British prime minister's country home: "Please think of Jack as someone David Gore is bringing down for lunch—and just do whatever you would do in your own house—his tastes are distressingly normal—plain food—children's food. . . ." On another occasion, as Jack Kennedy lay in the hospital recuperating from a spinal problem, Marietta Tree sent him "a heavy British biography," according to the historian Richard Reeves. Mrs. Kennedy penned a fast thank-you note. "It was really so sweet of you to send Jack the biography, but at the moment Jack is only reading his favorite author, Cholly Knickerbocker."

Her physical manners were equally polished. She always jumped to her feet when she was introduced to someone. Once she was visiting the Children's Storefront school in Harlem. As she sat in the office of Ned O'Gorman, the founder, a drunken homeless man wandered in. The visitors in the room froze, but Mrs. Kennedy rose. "How lovely to meet you," she said as one friend held her back.

There are friends of Mrs. Kennedy's who believe that had she not met Jack Kennedy in Washington in the summer of 1952, she would surely have been a writer. A short story she wrote for the *Vogue* prize showed, at the very least, Jackie Bouvier's early perception of the hypocrisy in her family relationships and an interest in the macabre. Her grandfather Bouvier had died three years earlier, in 1948. The gambling debts Black Jack owed to his father canceled his share of the estate. He was, however, named trustee for his sister, Edith Beale. There was great conflict in the family when Black Jack lost a portion of her estate to bad investments. Another thorn in his side was that his father's mistress had received $35,000, a great deal of money at the time.

"Christmas Story—The Violets" is set two days after the death of the grandfather of a young woman named Sophie. The entire story, a scant five hundred words, takes place in the drawing room of the grandfather's house. "I was sitting beside my grandfather's coffin looking at him as he lay in his dark blue suit with his hands folded. I had never seen death before and was ashamed that it made no more of an impression on me." Sophie hears the family arguing over who will get the yellow damask Louis XVI sofa. "I was glad he couldn't see how his children behaved once he was dead." Suddenly, a doorbell rings. A man enters with a bunch of violets, flowers that implied Eliza Doolittle and Covent Garden, a lower class. An aunt is peremptory with him, snatches his violets, and places them near "a sheaf of gladioli," and then asks Sophie to leave the room so the coffin can be closed. Sophie picks up the violets and holds them near her face. "I knelt on the bench beside the coffin and put the violets down inside, beneath my grandfather's elbow, where the people who came close to the coffin would not see them."

Once I had a long conversation with Mrs. Kennedy at a party she held to promote one of the books she was publishing. It was 1983, not long after she had burrowed into her life as an editor at Doubleday. Living in New York again, she retreated into seriousness and went out only with close friends. She often stayed at home and read. By then she knew all the freight entrances all over the town that would allow her a quick escape from the paparazzi, but from time to time she would promote a project or a cause, such as the preservation of Grand Central Station. On this night, Mrs. Kennedy celebrated the publication of *Maverick in Mauve,* a diary kept by a nineteenth-century grande dame, Adele Sloane, the grandmother of the wife of her stepcousin, Louis Auchincloss, a woman whose wedding in 1895 cost $1 million and featured private railroad cars for the guests and a bridal gown with an eleven-foot train from Worth. At the party, held appropriately at the Museum of the City of New York, Mrs. Kennedy in the corner talked quietly to friends. She wore a pale jacket and a slim black skirt. Again, there was that intangible sadness, the sense that she was holding herself apart. I was attending as a reporter, and I expected Mrs. Kennedy to shy away from me, but she did not. There was no trace of the baby-doll voice as we talked. What had interested her in the diary was not the detailed descriptions of the Mauve Decade, she told me, but the character of Adele Sloane herself. She used the words "survival" and "survivor" several times, and it was impossible not to believe that her fascination for this diary had something to do with feelings of identification. "What was so moving to me was the spirit of this woman, and the dignity with which she lived her life, and her basic character," she said. "That her life would seem to be ideal, and then tragedy would strike her—losing her child, for example. And that her life was not going to be so perfect after all, that she would have enormous difficulties, but somehow her spirit and her character would carry her through. You realize, especially when she writes so movingly about the death of her child, how difficult her life could be."

Although she was one of the most famous women in the world, Mrs. Kennedy appeared to believe that other people were much more interesting than she was. Once, swimming off Martha's Vineyard with the singer Carly Simon, she looked overhead and noticed helicopters in the sky. "Oh, look, Carly! They know that you're here," she said with no irony in her voice. Her letters were filled with lavish regard for others, as was her conversation. Like all shy people, she rarely felt comfortable talking about herself. In the last years of her life, she confided to one friend, she had taken up meditation. But she had always seemed to have an ability to obliterate anything unpleasant in her life. In the midst of her acrimonious divorce negotiations with Aristotle Onassis, Mrs. Kennedy held a small dinner party at her apartment. It was a summer night and extremely warm in the apartment, and one of her friends grew faint. Mrs. Kennedy and her escort for the evening, a television producer, took the guest into the library and stayed with her. As the guest recuperated, she overheard a long and affectionate conversation about Onassis. "Do you remember how he used to love to roam around the city at all hours of the night because of his insomnia?" Mrs. Kennedy asked the producer. "Remember that night he ran into you on Park Avenue at two A.M. and brought you home for a drink and came into my bedroom, so happy that he found someone he knew I liked? He was just like a dog with a bone!" Mrs. Kennedy's musical laugh filled the room.

The same friend later wondered whether this quality of transcendence explained Mrs. Kennedy's ability to detach herself from the infidelities of the men in her life. There is a theory among Kennedy historians that, in fact, Mrs. Kennedy clocked very little actual time in the White House. She appeared only when she had to, preferring to remain at her rented country house, Glen Ora, in Virginia, with Caroline and John. Jackie Kennedy is not known to have spoken of the President's infidelities. When at a lunch last year a friend was talking about bisexuals and made a comment, a joke really, about how she would hate to be involved with a bisexual because then "everyone would be your enemy," Mrs. Kennedy replied, "Well, all men are unfaithful anyway." Then they spoke of reaching a certain age and their expectations that a man should be faithful. A woman of a certain age should not have to put up with bad behavior. Oh yes, Mrs. Kennedy agreed. There was no bitterness in her tone.

A few days before she died, Jacqueline Kennedy made it clear to her friends that she did not want them talking about her even after she died. Mrs. Kennedy was an admirer of the poet William Butler Yeats, who theorized that the mask one wears in life is the mask one becomes. Some days before she died she told one friend: "I don't get it. I did everything right to take care of myself and look what happened. Why in the world did I do all those push-ups?" Her letters continued to be cheery. To Kitty Hart she wrote, "What a surprise, but I feel fine and we will still have a lot of laughs!"

On Sunday, May 22, the day before Mrs. Kennedy was buried, I walked back over to her apartment building. By this time, the crowd was somewhat unruly; the police department had closed Fifth Avenue to traffic. One reporter called the Empire Wok, a local Chinese restaurant, on his portable phone. "Prawns and peanuts!" he shouted. "Bring it to 1040 Fifth Avenue, and tell the doorman it is for a reporter in the mob."

I arrived early at St. Ignatius Loyola the next day for the funeral. The reporters were already gathered behind the grassy island in the middle of Park Avenue. This late in May, the tulips had lost their blooms. The UPI photographer had saved a place for me directly behind the tree in front of the church. We watched the crowd being held behind barriers on 84th Street. One man in the crowd held a sign: CAMELOT WILL BE REUNITED IN HEAVEN.

In front of the church, the New York police and the Secret Service were out in force supported by the private Kennedy family security detail. The true female friends began arriving wearing discreet little black suits, Upper East Side women from Zip Code 10021, with their big blond hair, mourning weeds; their arms and legs were bare because it was so hot a day.

And then there was the odd business of the arrival of the First Lady. It is well-known that Mrs. Clinton has uncertain taste in clothes, but her suit with the large carnation pink collar was a mistake. Everywhere she went that day, the bright swatch of Dallas pink caught the camera eye. A few moments after she had gotten inside, another car pulled close to the reporters, but behind them, on the east side of Park Avenue so that the passengers would have to walk through the crowd. Out bounced a smiling Robert Kennedy, Jr., with his mother, Ethel, waving and beaming, acting as if his aunt's funeral was a campaign stop. Not long after, Caroline and John arrived with their mother's mahogany coffin. The bright sun put the entire scene in high relief, and from where I stood you could just see the blowing lilies of the valley in the shape of a cross on top of Mrs. Kennedy's coffin. Caroline walking with her brother beside her mother's body moved slowly, her head bowed. It was impossible not to remember the moment in William Manchester's *Death of a President* when the six-year-old Caroline sees her mother break down at her father's funeral at St. Matthew's Cathedral. "Don't worry, Mummy, I'll take care of you," she said, taking her mother's hand.

At St. Ignatius Loyola, a group of close friends had been asked to read—Jane Hitchcock chose the Twenty-third Psalm but insisted that Jackie would prefer the traditional King James Version. A short while later, I heard the final prayer from a nearby radio: *Our sister Jacqueline has gone to Christ. May Jacqueline be at peace, may she be with the immortal God.* A few moments passed, then the pallbearers emerged with the coffin. Caroline and John followed, and John put his arm around his sister. One by one, the entire Kennedy family gathered—Ethel, Teddy, the cousins—and then Hillary Clinton took her place on the left. The steps to the church filled with Kennedys. One by one, they came and stood facing the crowd, as if they had rehearsed this final scene. Then they waited for the coffin, looking straight ahead. The photographers were

still, startled by the tableau. The family gazed directly at us, into the cameras, appearing to understand the historic importance of the moment. The only sound I could hear was the clicking of hundreds of cameras. "I've waited my entire life for a shot like this," a photographer near me said, "and now I don't want to take it."

AUGUST 1994

And then, once again, there was another crowd of mourners standing in front of a New York City apartment building on a humid summer night. Five years had gone by since Jacqueline Onassis's death and now, incredibly, the crowd had moved downtown to the loft district known as Tribeca—the triangle below Canal Street. On a July Friday, John

Kennedy, Jr., with three hours of instrument training, had taken off in a single-engine private plane with his wife Carolyn Bessette and her sister Lauren to the haze of the Martha's Vineyard evening fog.

In the days that followed, enduring the collective ritual of observing and mourning another Kennedy tragedy, it was sometimes difficult to remember the paradox of John Kennedy, Jr.'s life. He was the son of a martyr who was a practical joker; he wore celebrity lightly and, like his father, had a deft, whimsical side. He was one of the most famous people in the world, but he had always inhabited his city with a silky smoothness, riding its subways, Rollerblading through the park, interviewing witnesses at the District Attorney's office, as if he were any other law school grad. He wasn't. Kennedy had to have his own secretary as a young D.A. to cope with his mail. From time to time, he would meet terminal cancer patients from Ireland whose last wish was to have a photograph taken with the young Kennedy prince. He tried to live a life without all that, making his way through New York offices, like Carolyn and Lauren, as harried professionals taking pride in how crammed their calendars were. Busy up to the last minute with city preoccupations, Kennedy worked hard at his job as the publisher of *George.* All that Friday, he was in meetings attempting to plot the next stage of his magazine's life. Carolyn Bessette, it was later reported, was preparing her clothes for that weekend's Kennedy wedding at Hyannis. She told her shopper at Saks that she was apprehensive about getting on a plane. Her husband, she said, had only recently learned to fly and had just had a cast removed from his leg. Lauren Bessette was busy as well at Morgan Stanley, unable to break away from investment banker meeting after meeting. Then, it was early Saturday morning and all over America friends and family called each other: "Are you watching TV?" It took ABC an hour after CNN was reporting Kennedy's disappearance to round up their correspondents and stop the morning cartoon format.

Two days after he and Carolyn were buried at sea, I stood in the crowd at Varrick and North Moore. I thought about the day after his mother died when John had come out on his Rollerblades and taken off down Fifth Avenue, determined to keep the game going, no matter what. The hundreds of people outside his building lined up quietly behind the police barricades. They moved ghostlike and hushed past thousands of flower arrangements, burning candles, and signs, folded letters, crumpled photos, newspaper headlines festooned with ribbons. The sidewalk in lower Manhattan had become a holy shrine that resembled the villages of *curanderos,* mystical faith healers, in central Mexico at festival time. But there was nothing celebratory in the atmosphere. The voices were muted, some people were crying. The smell of scented candles and incense hung in the air; every few seconds a strobe flash of a camera lit the dark night. GOD WANTED AN EDITOR/PUBLISHER, JOHN-JOHN. A DESIGNER: CAROLYN. AN INVESTOR: LAUREN, one sign said, a metaphor for the career identity that is the symbol of a certain New York life. I moved along with the crowd reading the signs out loud like a prayer. YOU'RE ALL TOGETHER, NOW. It took almost an hour to move through the line. On the glass door of Kennedy's building was another poster: ANOTHER SON MET GOD'S SON ON JULY 23, 1999. GOODNIGHT, SWEET PRINCE.

Kay Thompson

No one who knew Kay Thompson could explain what motivated her to run away from her New York life. Thompson seemed weary of her public persona, an identity so firmly established that one friend called it "the *Eloise* and *Funny Face* thing." In 1962, at the very height of her celebrity, she suddenly and mysteriously moved to Rome and took a splendid maisonette at the top of the Palazzo Torlonia, near the Spanish Steps. From her terrace she could see the baroque domes of the city. Thompson had just brought out a new edition of the third of the Eloise books, *Eloise at Christmastime,* and the quirky and poetic voice was unmistakable:

> *And when we awakened*
> *he'd come and gone*
> *and in all of this midnight and dark*
> *we could see these reindeers zimbering*
> *through the trees in Central Park*
> *We could even see this tail-light*
> *on Santa Claus' sleigh*

and Emily had a baby pigeon
on absolutely Christmas day

Eloise was more than a best-selling book; the dolls, toys, and wardrobe it produced were one of the first publishing saturation-marketing gambits. The author of *Eloise,* however, appeared to believe that her creations had overwhelmed her; she was in retreat. When she complained to her editor Richard Grossman that "the world is coming apart," he said casually, "Why don't you move to Rome? There is nothing you can do here in New York that you can't do there." So she picked up and left "with only a toothbrush," she later told a friend.

Thompson was a woman of certitude and imagination, known for her exacting standards about every aspect of her appearance and career. In Rome, there was the matter of a particular shade of beige she envisioned for a chiffon scarf. "It must be not quite bone, not quite pink, definitely not greige, perhaps the exact color of the sky one hour before sunset or just after twilight. It could even be red! You know what I mean?" she said to fashion illustrator Joe Eula. The walls of her new apartment had to be "the exact hue of the water at Ostia." A jacket she required for an appearance on *The Garry Moore Show* had to be "burgundy and no other shade! A silk velvet—thin, thin, thin! Balenciaga and definitely not Chanel," she told the costume designer Robert Mackintosh.

Kay Thompson's Eloise was published in 1955—Thompson insisted that her name be above the title, as on a marquee. By then Thompson had sung on the radio with Fred Waring and André Kostelanetz and had coached Judy Garland, Lena Horne, and Joan McCracken at MGM. Later, with Andy Williams and his three brothers, she had a daring nightclub act. William Randolph Hearst and Maurice Chevalier had attended her opening at New York's elegant Le Directoire in 1948. But even after Thompson became a star, she was as restless as a six-year-old.

Eloise was a curious doppelgänger for Kay Thompson, a kindred spirit. Like her creator, Eloise was contradictory, both brazen and yearning. She was an imp of the perverse, a refreshing antidote to the coy and correct heroines of most children's literature. She "skibbled" through the

Plaza hotel, ordering up room service and crayoning walls. She "sklonked" kneecaps and said "rawther" and "absolutely," but a genuine pathos neutralized her grandiose ways.

Thompson always insisted that *Eloise* was not for children but for "precocious grownups," a phrase she approved for the book's jacket. She had a singular fondness for words. "Boring" was a favorite Kay Thompson adjective; she pronounced it as if it were a musical phrase, extending the first syllable. So too with her other cherished descriptions—"too boring," "divine," "heaven." The Thompson superlative was "pure heaven," conferred rarely.

The 1950s were Eloise's period, and she helped to define them; there was even a special room at the Plaza where one could pick up a telephone and hear the voice of Eloise herself. The voice was, of course, that of Kay Thompson, theatrical and breathy: *Hello, it's me, Eloise.* Her pronouncements were droll: "Getting bored is not allowed." "Sometimes I comb my hair with a fork." By 1963, more than a million copies of *Eloise* and its sequels had been sold.

Kay Thompson was tall and skinny, with blond hair, strong sharp features, and extraordinary agate eyes. She was handsome and offbeat, and possessed a kind of mannish look that was not in vogue at the time. Later she would grow to resemble the writer Isak Dinesen, but as a young woman there was an ebullience in her face, lightness around the edges. She was notorious for her style—the trailing scarves, the toreador pants. "She could take ten yards of black jersey and wrap it around and make it look like a Schiaparelli," her friend the critic Rex Reed recalled. It was difficult to separate her from Maggie Prescott, the brittle and hilarious fashion editor she played in *Funny Face,* the 1957 Stanley Donen film starring Fred Astaire and Audrey Hepburn. Thompson might stride into a room gaily singing, "Hello, hello!" as if she were eager to be noticed, but she was generally thought to be isolated from people. Over the years her friends have speculated about the zigzags of her life, the conflicts in her personality. She was prudish, even priggish about language and behavior, yet drawn to the uninhibited world of theater. She lived in dazzling settings, but would often spend days alone. When she went out in public she pulled focus completely, but she was seldom intimate, and so wary of relationships that very few people had her telephone number. "I really don't know what made her tick," said Lena Horne. "Kay is a recluse hiding behind a pageant," another friend remarked.

In Rome she lived in a series of smallish rooms that she made into a "palace of crystal and tinkle," Joe Eula recalled. Thompson installed floor-to-ceiling mirrors, which had to be laboriously hauled through the garden of the palazzo and up an exterior elevator to the maisonette, which she called the *superattico*. Her drawing room had almost no furniture, except for zebra-skin rugs—"the zebes," she called them. Thompson shared the apartment with her pug, Fenice, who, like his mistress, often wore a scarf tied jauntily around his middle. Fenice went everywhere with her in Rome, seeming to exist on a diet of green Chuckles, which Thompson insisted he preferred. Her devotion to the pug was such that she reportedly sawed the legs off her grand piano in order to move it into her bedroom at the top of a spiral staircase, where she would play songs for him. But Thompson was restive in Rome, searching for a new project to utilize her prodigious energy. She turned down a featured role in *The Pink Panther,* as she had earlier turned down one in *Auntie Mame,* with a crisp wave of her arm and a single word: *No.*

The playwright Mart Crowley met her during these years. He had studied art, and Thompson discussed with him the idea of doing some sketches for a book she was working on called *The Fox and the Fig.* Crowley recalled that Thompson often resented it when people she met "expected her to be the Diana Vreeland parody she played in *Funny Face.*" She seemed to believe that the caricature had come to define her, and her eccentricities were not too far from Maggie Prescott's in the movie. There was a reason for the confusion. One day she announced to Crowley that she wanted to have tiny Oriental lacquered tables for her bare living room. She was determined to paint them a shade of red she had seen in a Revlon ad. "We went out and we bought ten unpainted raw tables that were twelve inches high. 'No higher, no smaller,' she said. They needed priming, but did we do that? No. So we went out and bought nail varnish—cases and cases of it—and we sat around on the marble floor with the zebes and painted those tables for days, and we never got through." *The Fox and the Fig* was also left uncompleted.

Crowley believed they were friends, but after Thompson became displeased with his work, he said, for some time he could no longer get her on the phone. However odd their relationship, it would have been inconceivable to Crowley at that time that the creator of Eloise would retreat from life completely and attempt to take America's most popular six-year-old with her. "Eloise is me. All me!" Thompson once told her friend Eleanor Lambert, the fashion publicist. "No, Kay. Eloise belongs to the world," Lambert recalled answering. She says she was surprised when Thompson did not reply.

"I think the story of our lives comes through these wonderful people we run into. You run into a stranger and: 'My God, the electricity!' And then you come into something terrible, and our lives are ruined by this," Kay Thompson once told the writer Stephen Silverman in a telephone conversation. Since 1973, when Thompson and Eleanor Lambert staged an elaborate fashion show of American designers at Versailles, Thompson has slowly withdrawn from public and social life. She now lives quite purposefully as a recluse in a large apartment owned by her goddaughter, Liza Minnelli, on East 69th Street in New York. She is confined to a wheelchair, but often wears a favorite red Halston sweater and dancing shoes; her feet tap frequently to a beat that only she can hear. She routinely turns down interview requests. "Make them go away," she tells Allen Eichhorn, Liza Minnelli's publicist.

A theme of Kay Thompson's life has been a relentless search for privacy. She returns calls, even from friends, haphazardly, if at all. When she does call back, however, she will often stay on the telephone for an hour, then hang up and call right back to add a thought to the soliloquy that has gone before. She is part of a generation of women who speak in great, colorful dramatic arcs. "You have led me down the garden path, and I have followed!" she recently told a friend. News radio is often on in the background when she calls. She reads constantly and has strong opinions. She told me she was convinced that O.J. Simpson was innocent. "You don't expect me to agree with Dominick, do you?" she asked testily, referring to the writer Dominick Dunne and his coverage of the Simpson trial in *Vanity Fair.* Often she will end conversations with a vibrant "Think pink!" "Think Pink" was the remarkable opening number in *Funny Face,* in which Thompson instructed her staff at *Quality Magazine* to "banish the black, bury the blue, burn the beige. Think pink! And that includes the kitchen sink!" At times she will close with another favorite phrase: "Be brilliant!"

Thompson's age is a subject of bemused speculation among her friends. Several believe she is close to ninety-five, although she shrieks when that figure is mentioned: "Heavens, no!" An official biographical entry gives her birth date as November 9, 1912, although some references add "disputed." One music encyclopedia placed her date of birth in 1902. Very little is known about Thompson's early life. She was close to her sister Marion, but she rarely talked with friends about her childhood. Like Eloise, she seemed to exist center stage with her family off in the wings. She was born in St. Louis, where she was called Kitty Fink. She attended the same high school as Tennessee Williams and later went to Washington University. Thompson's father, a jeweler, encouraged his daughter's musical ability. According to a 1936 *Radio Guide,* Thompson had informed her family at the age of four that she would be an actress even though she was not as pretty as her two sisters. "Ugly Ducklings Can Have Beaux," *Radio Guide* cruelly titled an early Thompson profile. The words below were equally mean: "When she looked into the mirror and a homely girl stared back, Kay Thompson went to work with a will—and made that homely girl a star!" By the time she was sixteen, she was a prodigy on the piano, performing Lizst with the St. Louis Symphony.

At age seventeen she moved to Los Angeles and took a job teaching diving at a summer camp. As a singer, she was talented but not appealing enough to be recognized as a natural radio star. She sang with the Mills Brothers before they were well-known, and worked in San Francisco clubs. She had her nose straightened and lost her original name for the more euphonious "Thompson." She was strong-willed, ferociously ambitious, and would not compromise her standards. According to a 1948 column in the New York *Daily News,* in 1934 she was fired from a radio show where she had been singing top forty hits. Soon after, she was hired to sing with Fred Waring, but he fired her too. She made two records for Victor, but the *News* columnist reported that the head of the company had hated them and refused to release them. She worked for André Kostelanetz, but he replaced her with Alice Faye.

The composer Hugh Martin met Thompson about 1935, when he became her rehearsal pianist. Later he was part of her group, Kay Thompson's Rhythm Singers, on CBS. "She was the cutting edge. The sophistication was in her singing and in her conversation," Martin recently recalled. "She was to vocal arrangements what Louis Armstrong was to jazz."

During the Depression the Shubert brothers controlled Broadway. As a young choreographer Agnes de Mille worked for them and later described in a memoir the aura of "evil magic" about Lee Shubert. Without the protection of Equity, dancers had no security and earned a pitiful "thirty-five dollars a week, twenty dollars for rehearsal, and a little loving on the side," she reported. De Mille encountered Kay Thompson in 1937 in a Shubert production called *Hooray for What!*, a debacle that would prove traumatic for both of them. That show could have made Thompson's name in the theater. Harold Arlen wrote the music, the book was by the venerable writing team of Howard Lindsay and Russel Crouse, and the lyrics were by E.Y. "Yip" Harburg.

In rehearsal, Arlen quickly realized that Thompson not only could act and sing but was also a gifted vocal arranger—an entirely new field at the time. Hugh Martin of Thompson's Rhythm Singers and his later collaborator Ralph Blane followed Thompson from CBS to *Hooray for What!* At CBS, Martin had observed her technique: "She did not come to the studio having made the arrangement. She would use us as her tools, the way a painter uses pigment. I would sit there and watch her fingers and try to soak up all the changes of key. At a certain point, when she felt the arrangement had reached its zenith, she would stand up and say, 'O.K., over to you!'" During *Hooray for What!*, Martin recalled, "Kay would be sitting in front of the footlights during rehearsal with a bandanna around her head, sweat pouring out, looking like the chic-est thing in the world while all of us were clapping and singing 'Down with Love' and 'Buds Won't Bud.'"

The Shuberts wanted to turn *Hooray for What!* into a bosomy–chorus-girl revue, and Lee Shubert felt that Thompson was not sexy enough. He and Vincente Minnelli, the director, battled over this and every other artistic decision. "Rehearsals were a horror," de Mille recalled. "The bosses . . . were prowling the aisles whispering. I developed a tic from snapping my head to see who was spying behind me." Thompson was "grim-lipped and sardonic," de Mille wrote, and Minnelli and Arlen took to their beds. The Shuberts fired dancers and singers capriciously. De Mille was dismissed in the lobby, only hours before the leading man. One night, as Thompson was leaving the stage, she felt a tap on her back and heard the words "That will be your last performance."

Martin was in the basement of the theater when Thompson was fired. "I will never forget the cries, the sounds, and the sobs that came from her dressing room," he said. She was so devastated, Martin recalled, that in the end "she could not face thinking about it. It was banished from her life." *Hooray for What!* became one among many taboo subjects for Thompson, who resisted any unpleasant talk. Martin remains convinced that the humiliation kept Thompson from ever doing another Broadway show.

By then Thompson had married the trombone player Jack Jenney, who recorded "Stardust" and later played with Artie Shaw. Jenney directed Thompson's recording sessions and appeared with her in a 1937 Republic movie, *Manhattan Merry-Go-Round.* In 1939 they wrote a song called "What More Can I Give You?," but shortly after, Thompson left Jenney for CBS radio producer Bill Spier, who was among the first to broadcast a symphony hour of music from Europe. Thompson worked on Spier's show and reportedly traveled with the CBS crew abroad. Spier was married with three children, but he divorced his wife and married Thompson. Spier was "a boy genius," his third wife, the actress June Havoc, told me. Spier was tall and dark, a concert-level pianist with a lethal sense of humor. He would later produce *Suspense* and introduce the Dashiell Hammett character Sam Spade to radio.

As Thompson became increasingly well-known, Spier felt he was on the periphery of her life. She was exuberant, but kept her distance. Her friends remarked that Spier seemed to understand the contradiction in her personality: bravado was her disguise.

There is a portrait of Lena Horne in the MGM days with Kay Thompson, who is leaning against a wardrobe rack. She is all legs, in a sleek straight skirt with a wide belt and high sling-back pumps. Her face is radiant. Her friendship with Hugh Martin was responsible for having propelled her in 1944 into a relatively new position as a vocal arranger at the elite unit of MGM run by Arthur Freed, the producer of *Singin' in the Rain, An American in Paris, Gigi,* and other major MGM musicals. Freed brought Cole Porter to Metro for *The Pirate* and promoted the careers of Judy Garland and Lena Horne. The Freed unit, recalled Hugh Martin, was "the most intense concentration of talent I had ever seen."

Freed worked with Roger Edens, a gentle Texan who would later produce *Funny Face.* Like Thompson, Edens was a person with diverse abilities. He was Judy Garland's mentor as well as a composer. As a producer, Edens had signed Hugh Martin and his collaborator after the success of their show *Best Foot Forward.* Martin and Blane's first score for MGM, *Meet Me in St. Louis,* was a triumph for Edens and for Judy Garland, and "The Trolley Song" was nominated for an Oscar. One day Martin announced to Edens that he was leaving Metro to go off to the war. "Hugh, how are we going to replace you?" Edens asked. "There is someone much better than me: Kay Thompson," Martin told him.

In the history of popular American music, Kay Thompson's role has been largely unreported. Her vocal arrangements helped bring jazz rhythms to MGM musicals; she taught Lena Horne to sing loud and gave Judy Garland a new sound. Horne says Thompson was "a major part of my time out there at MGM. Professionally she developed me as a singer completely. I had the groundwork there, but I did not know how to get it out. She is the best vocal coach in the world."

In Los Angeles, Kay Thompson and Bill Spier took a bungalow at the Garden of Allah, the hotel which had once been a haven for Sheilah Graham and F. Scott Fitzgerald. Later, she papered her apartment on Beverly Glen with tiny clusters of flowers from candy boxes; the walls and ceiling were completely covered. Thompson and Spier gave lavish parties for their musician friends. Through her friendship with Thompson, Lena Horne met her husband, the arranger Lennie Hayton. During Thompson's Hollywood years her urge to perform was subsumed into improvs she would do at parties, often with Judy Garland or Roger Edens. Much of this material was later recycled for her nightclub act. For Cyd Charisse, who starred in *The Band Wagon* and *Silk Stockings,* Kay was "a bundle of energy. I remember her flying by in the rehearsal hall with all this vivaciousness and energy—there was nobody more enthusiastic about everything than Kay." She wore pants that laced up the front like those by Jack Cole, whose sophisticated modern-dance company included Gwen Verdon and Carol Haney, Charisse said. Often Thompson would break into a jitterbug just for the sheer fun of it.

Roger Edens became a pivotal figure in Thompson's life. They were creative allies who shared the same birthday. Edens was married and by all accounts romantically unavailable to Thompson, but deeply connected to her emotionally. Each year on their birthday they threw an elaborate party. They would write songs for each other and rehearse their numbers for months. "Kay would have no clue what Roger was doing, and Roger would have no clue what Kay was doing," said a friend, Leonard Gershe. "People would die to get invited!"

When Edens and Thompson sat together on a song, such as one originally written as a vehicle for Greer Garson in the 1946 film *Ziegfeld Follies,* it was deadly satire. Garson had starred in *Madame Curie,* and "Madame Crematon" was a Thompson-Edens send-up of her great-lady character. It was high camp and witty, a set piece in which an imperious actress announces to reporters her plans for her next weighty part— Madame Crematon, the inventor of the safety pin. The night came when Vincente Minnelli and Arthur Freed were to hear it for the first time. "They all assembled at Arthur Freed's house," says Hugh Fordin. "Kay was playing the role, and Roger was playing the piano. The song ends with a big hurrah-hurrah, and there is silence from Garson. Finally Garson's husband says, 'Your house is beautifully appointed, Arthur.' There was no way Greer was going to do this. Kay and Roger went out and sat in the backseat of Edens's car, speechless. Finally Roger said, 'Goddamn it. Judy is going to do it! She is the perfect mimic, and she will just mimic you.'" In the film, Garland, in a sleek satin dress, with a long chiffon scarf in her hand, did Kay Thompson.

Judy Garland eventually came to rely heavily on Thompson's coaching. She was a belter then; when she sang a ballad it was with no subtlety in her interpretations. "Judy just had a big voice," said Rex Reed. "Kay softened the tones and made her hold certain notes longer. She is the one who put the sob in her voice. Judy was always running out of steam on notes and she would have to catch her breath. She'd say, 'Oh, God, I ruined it.' And Kay would say, 'You didn't ruin it—use it!'" Thompson coached her through *Ziegfeld Follies, The Harvey Girls,* and *The Pirate,* in which she sang Thompson's arrangement of the song "Mack the Black."

Much has been written about the relationship between Judy Garland and Kay Thompson. You could see Thompson's style like a shadow print in a Garland performance. There was the hand on the hip—a gesture Liza Minnelli later inherited. And Thompson had a distinct bow—one arm perpendicular, the other behind her back—which Garland used. In later years, when Garland's anxiety was so crippling that she would cancel concerts, Thompson could pull her out of her emotional funks. But Thompson was often contemptuous of Garland's lack of discipline and her reliance on pills. "I got so tired of taking care of her," she told a friend and Garland became family for Thompson, who often traveled with her and her young children, Liza and Lorna.

By the end of Thompson's time at Metro, her style was fully recognizable: you could tell which singers had been trained by her. Lena Horne recalled: "She said to me, 'All right, it's there. We just have to bring it out.' I began to sing with some kind of assertiveness through my training with her." Thompson instructed Horne specifically to use more breath. "Kay would play jazz, and I would sing. She took what little I had, and it just got bigger and bigger. We both liked jazz and jazz musicians, and musicians have a tendency to develop sounds you hear coming from an instrument."

Arguably Thompson's best work was her complex arrangement of the Harry Warren and Johnny Mercer standard "On the Atchison, Topeka, and the Santa Fe" in *The Harvey Girls.* She and Edens wrote a complicated series of lyrics introducing each Harvey girl ("We were schoolmarms from Grand Rapids, Mich / But reading, writing, 'rithmetic were not our dish!"). Ralph Blane assisted Thompson on the vocal arrangements. He later told Hugh Fordin, "Kay would write twenty ideas while I threw out nineteen! They would just come to her like that, she was so fast! Kay could have been a great composer had she settled on one theme or idea. She could never discipline herself to do the same thing twice."

In Thompson's last days at MGM, her marriage to Bill Spier was unraveling, and she was looking to escape. "I had a headache for two years, and I said, 'I have to get out of this place! It is just too much!'" Thompson attempted to blame MGM for her unhappiness: "I learned that in a big studio you are so categorized that you have to become what people think you are or get out. So I got out," she once said. "Everything was saying, 'You are going someplace else, and you are going to do something else.' So my contract was up on May 17. The choreographer Bob Alton said to me, 'You can always have an act.'"

In 1947 the standard nightclub act was Hildegarde or Jean Sablon, just standing and singing in front of a band. Andy Williams and his three brothers were also restless at the Freed unit, and Thompson had a daring idea, completely new for its time: a club act where she would be center stage with four men behind her, choreographed as a theater piece. Thompson called her new career "the saloon beat." For a time, the novelty of her idea commanded her imagination. Thompson enlisted the best talent at MGM for advice, and Bob Alton agreed to help her with the staging and movement.

Eloise began then too, as a vocal riff, shtick to pass the time between friends. One day Thompson was late for a photo session at Alton's. "I drove the car across a golf course—Bob's house was right there. I got out of the car and I opened the door and went a few steps and he said, 'Who do you think you are, coming here five minutes late?' I said, 'I am Eloise. I am six.'"

Eloise became an alternative persona for Kay Thompson, much as the dummy Charlie McCarthy was for the ventriloquist Edgar Bergen. The little girl's noxious voice allowed Thompson to express contrarian thoughts and ideas. Eloise took form as a lonely and whimsical child who created her own world. She immediately became part of Thompson's daily conversation. "The boys loved Eloise! Andy gave himself two names, Junior and Melvin. They gave her names, too," Thompson recalled.

Thompson and the Williams Brothers opened their act at El Rancho in Las Vegas when Thompson was in residence in Nevada getting her divorce. A charged romantic atmosphere existed between Williams and Thompson, friends say. "She was madly in love with Andy," according to Leonard Gershe, but Williams denies this. However close they were, Thompson was determined that the act would be hers alone. Thompson, Williams remembers, exerted complete control. "At one time my brother Dick wanted to compose or arrange one of the songs. Very soon it was decided that that wasn't the way it was going to go."

There was no question but that the act was unique: "Now we are used to seeing a girl with four or eight guys, but at that time vocal groups had never done anything but stand around the microphone at the end of a number and put their arms up. It was that static!" Williams said. "We acted out scenes like a miniature Broadway show. When we got on the stage at El Rancho Vegas, we realized that no one could hear us. We hung microphones from a beam across the stage—this had never been done before. Kay got up there and hung the mikes herself!"

They received $2,500 a week at a time when Sophie Tucker, according to Williams, commanded $5,000. Eight weeks later, Thompson and the Williams Brothers moved to Ciro's in Los Angeles. "Walter Winchell began writing about us. Within a year we were making $15,000 a week," Williams said. When they opened in New York in April 1948 at Le Directoire, *Variety* headlined: KAY THOMPSON'S N.Y. CAFE WOW CUES ANSWER TO WAIL FOR 'SOMETHING NEW.' The review continued, "Miss Thompson is an atomic bomb of rhythm songapation with her equally supercharged vocal vitamins, the four Williams Brothers."

Thompson was taken up immediately. Her signature numbers— "Jubilee Time," "Pauvre Suzette," "Louisiana Purchase"—sounded fresh in postwar New York. "She was really a throwback to Cole Porter and Noël Coward," recalled Nina Bourne, who later worked on her books at Simon & Schuster.

Through Leonard Gershe, Thompson came to know D.D. Dixon, a young and stylish editor at *Harper's Bazaar.* Dixon would later marry

Johnny Ryan, a stage manager, and become a well-known social figure in New York, but as a young woman she often traveled with the photographer Richard Avedon and helped him organize shoots for the magazine. Ryan had a gift for understanding what was new, and she was fascinated by Thompson. "Kay would call me and do Eloise on the phone. She would say 'This is Eloise' in that funny little voice. *I knew nothing about technology,* but I finally said, 'Kay, you really ought to get a tape recorder and write this down!' This was the 1950s, and I did not even know what a tape recorder was. Ryan said, 'There is a fellow across the hall, a great friend of mine, Hilary Knight.' He used to make little drawings and shove them under my door. One morning he made a drawing of a fat little prissy, pretty girl with frizzy blond corkscrews. She had a satin ribbon in her hair and a bulging belly, and she was facing a little girl who looked just like Eloise. I called Kay and said, 'I have a drawing of Eloise.' And Kay got enormously interested."

A black leather scrapbook rests on a shelf in Hilary Knight's apartment on East 51st Street in New York. In it is the entire publishing history of *Eloise* and the phenomenon it became. Knight, a student of the painter Reginald Marsh, was twenty-eight when he was introduced to Kay Thompson in 1954. He was starting his career as a magazine illustrator and was influenced by the work of the British artist Ronald Searle. The son of two New York artists, Knight is modest and thoughtful. His small apartment is crammed with vintage theater recordings and his own sketches and paintings.

"I just *knew* this little girl," he said of Eloise. "D.D. took me to meet Kay—I believe it was her last performance at the Persian Room. We went to the lobby, and I remember sitting with her, and she told me about the book. We pretty much started working on it right away."

For Thompson, Knight was "Princetonian—shy, gentle, and soft-spoken." She had written, she recalled in a 1957 interview, "12 lines on a piece of paper and handed it to him. 'If you're interested, get in touch with me.' Then I spoke a few words of Eloisiana and left." That

Christmas, Thompson received a card from Knight, a highly stylized picture of an angel and Santa Claus streaking through the sky. On the top of Santa's pack was Eloise. "It was immediate recognition on my part. There she was, in person. I knew at once Hilary Knight had to illustrate the book," Kay Thompson said.

"I holed in at the Plaza and we went to work. I just knew I had to get this done. Eloise was trying to get out. I've never known such stimulation. This girl had complete control of me. Ideas came from everywhere. Hilary and I had immediate understanding. . . . We wrote, edited, laughed, outlined, cut, pasted, laughed again, read out loud, laughed and suddenly we had a book."

"I did a sketch of the little girl, and we worked together. It was a total collaboration," Knight corroborated. "Kay talked about the way she looked, the little costume. The attitude was a combination of several different people. One was a woman, Eloise Davison, a food writer at the *New York Herald Tribune* and a friend of my family. All of these people—Nanny, Eloise—are really Kay," Knight said.

On the opening page, Eloise announces, "I am Eloise. I am six." Eloise's facial expression and pose invoked classical portraiture of great men—Ingres's wealthy noblemen, Jacques-Louis David's Napoleon. Illustrator Joelle Shefts thinks Knight's perfect pitch for the body in motion "put him in a league with [Sir John] Tenniel, [Arthur] Rackham, and [Edmund] Dulac." Knight was able to temper the darkness of Thompson's text by spoofing Eloise's pomposity and splattering her across every page. There is an ingenious quality to his elegantly crafted drawings, an economy of line—almost as if they were preliminary sketches.

Soon after the text and drawings were completed, Thompson recalled, "we took Eloise to Jack Goodman at Simon & Schuster, and he recognized and understood Eloise immediately. We all became close friends, and the book went into print—only a thousand copies the first time, just to see how it went."

How it went was immediately: Jack Goodman, the editor of S.J. Perelman and Irwin Shaw, issued a memo dated November 18, 1955: "Thursday evening first copies came off press. Friday morning at 9:30

people in the office who had taken home copies came in making considerable noise. Friday morning at 11:30 we ordered a second printing. Friday afternoon, *Life* magazine told us they are running a story on *Eloise* (pictures and text in two colors) in their December 5th issue." Goodman then rounded up blurbs from a roster of distinguished authors. "To me, *Eloise* is the most glorious book ever written about an endearingly frightful little girl. Completely enchanting, and you can quote me fulsomely," Cornelia Otis Skinner said. Noël Coward's appraisal was printed in the ads: "Frankly, I adore Eloise." Soon the book was selling four thousand copies a week; it shared the best-seller lists that spring with John O'Hara's *Ten North Frederick* and *The Quiet American* by Graham Greene.

Richard Grossman, who worked on the original Simon & Schuster promotion campaign with Jack Goodman, later would edit Kay Thompson and become a close friend. "Kay had a clear idea of what she wanted—to get out of the 'saloon business,' as she referred to it, and be respected by classy people." With success, a whiff of myopia crept into her relationships. Barron Polan, Thompson's agent, who had helped make her singing career, took her to court over commissions on the *Eloise* books. He lost. Thompson, who was often cranky and left a trail of ruptured relationships with longtime friends, frequently used the expression, "I'll cut them off at the knees."

Eloise, although only six, had a temperament that resembled her creator's. She was isolated and self-involved. In an introduction to a special edition of Ludwig Bemelmans's classic, *Madeline,* Anna Quindlen called Eloise pathetic. "When I think of Eloise grown up," she wrote, "I think of her with a drinking problem, knocking about from avocation to avocation, unhappily married or unhappily divorced, childless."

Thompson became caught in the downdrafts of celebrity. She lived at the Plaza, purportedly rent-free, for many years, but she could not escape her idea. She staged tea parties at which she presided as Eloise, and helped to create the special Plaza menu for children, which offered "Teeny Weenies" and "Eggs Eloise." In Dallas, Thompson helped launch Eloise clothing at Neiman Marcus; Eloise dolls were sold at Lord & Taylor. At Simon & Schuster, Richard Grossman suggested to the publisher Robert Bernstein that he might enjoy working with Thompson manufacturing Eloise novelty items. Bernstein set up Eloise Ltd. and took Thompson with him when he left for Random House, where Bernstein later became president. "Kay was such a perfectionist that getting something she was happy with was not easy," Bernstein recalled. Their only book project together was Bernstein's idea, the poignant and sentimental *Eloise at Christmastime* in 1958:

> *So if no one remembers me*
> *and no presents can I find*
> *I'll know I don't deserve them*
> *It doesn't matter*
> *I don't mind*

Thompson turned down a chance for Eloise to endorse caramels, but agreed to a disastrous adaptation of *Eloise* for CBS television. The cast was stellar—Ethel Barrymore, Louis Jourdan, Charles Ruggles, Monty Woolley—but the script departed wildly from the book. In it, Eloise was caught in the middle of her parents' threatened divorce in a hotel filled with intrigue. John Frankenheimer directed, and called the experience "a nightmare." The reviews were savage. TURKEY WAS THE SPECIAL, one headline said of the Thanksgiving production. Just as she had done after *Hooray for What!*, Thompson, acutely sensitive to criticism, burrowed in and closed and locked another door. She resolved, she told friends, that she would never allow Eloise to be dramatized again.

Shortly after *Eloise* and all that followed came Thompson's role as the redoubtable Maggie Prescott in *Funny Face,* who storms her way to Europe and lands in France singing the enduring "Bonjour, Paris!" "I never considered anyone else for the part," Stanley Donen said. If *Eloise* placed the nightclub performer in the public mind as a hypersophisticated and world-weary woman, Thompson's image was solidified with her staccato interpretation of a fashion editor inspired by Diana Vreeland. Like Vreeland, Thompson was brassy and shrewd: "She's got to have bizzazz!" she declaimed about one model, and "bizzazz"—a Vreeland word used in *Funny Face* by Gershe—entered glossy fashion copy.

Funny Face had originally been inspired by Leonard Gershe's friendship with Richard Avedon and his wife, Doe, a model. Gershe was impressed by Doe's beauty and her ambivalence about her profession, and he talked about the Avedons with the English writer Clemence Dane. By way of background, Gershe told some of the stories D.D. Dixon Ryan had regaled him about her fabulous boss, Diana Vreeland, and her famous aphorisms such as "Pink is the navy blue of India." "What a glorious idea for a musical—the fashion world, a fashion photographer, and a model who doesn't want to be a model," Dane told him. "Why don't you write it?" He did, and for years, Gershe's play, *Wedding Day,* as it was first called, languished. Robert Alton wanted to direct it, but only if Kay Thompson would play the fashion editor. Thompson, Gershe recalled, "had never got over *Hooray for What!* She turned it down flat. She was afraid to go on the stage."

Two years later, Gershe met Roger Edens, who was looking for a movie to produce on his own. Edens had several suggestions for Gershe's script: move the wedding to the end of the story and borrow several songs from George and Ira Gershwin's 1927 stage musical, *Funny Face.* And so the musical was turned into a film script. *Funny Face* went into production in the summer of 1956. Throughout production, there was an undercurrent of tension on the set. Fred Astaire, who played the photographer, seemed to take an instant dislike to Kay Thompson. "He liked willowy women," Gershe said. "There was no reason for it. She never did anything to him. She found him a prima donna and mean to Audrey." Thompson told Stephen Silverman, "Stanley never yelled at anyone, except Fred, sort of, at the end." During the filming of Thompson and Astaire's duet, "Clap Yo' Hands," Thompson was playing the piano. "Fred said, 'Stanley? Come over here.' Stanley said, 'O.K., stop the camera.' And Fred said to him, 'What is she doing on the piano?'" Moments after Thompson and Astaire finished dancing up the stairs, Thompson told Silverman, "Fred grabbed me out of the blue and said, 'Where did you learn balance?'"

In Paris, Thompson and Hilary Knight went to work on a sequel to their best-seller. Thompson was determined to put Eloise in a small Left Bank hotel, the Relais Bisson. As Knight dutifully sketched Paris scenery—the Pont Neuf, pigeons at Fouquet's—Thompson's eccentricities became more evident. "When we were in Paris," Knight said, "Kay was going to come back to New York to do a song called 'Bizzazz' on *The Ed Sullivan Show*. We went to Balmain, and they gave her a fabulous beige chiffon dress and jewelry for her appearance. I forget what the reason was, but she decided that she did not like it. She threw it in the tub and washed it! She just ruined it."

Like the original, *Eloise in Paris* was fresh and inventive. Thompson's text was enchantingly fey:

> *When you are in your chambre which*
> *   is your room*
> *you are allowed to fall on the bed and*
> *   sort of sklathe*
> *yourself into these large pillows for*
> *   a while*
> *because here's what you are*
> *absolutely fatiguée*
> *which is tired tired tired*
>
> *The absolutely first thing you have to do*
> *is put on your bedroom slippers*
> *which is pantoufles*

Simon & Schuster planned a record ad campaign for *Eloise in Paris*. Thompson was photographed at book-and-author lunches with Dean Acheson; Eloise endorsed Renaults and Kalistron luggage; and Thompson recorded the song "Eloise" with Archie Bleyer.

Soon after, Richard Grossman had the idea of sending Thompson and Hilary Knight to Moscow. The pair set up at the National Hotel. They often went to the Bolshoi, Knight later recalled. Thompson wore three cashmere sweaters, special wool fezzes, and a red coat made of guanaco, a thick camel-like fur. In Moscow, she deliberately wore a dress "inside out" to a wedding, Knight remembered. When she came back she made an album, *Kay Thompson Party: Let's Talk About Russia,* on which she held forth in a daffy monologue: "The plumbing was divine—I had my own stopper for my own bathtub! . . . I said to Hilary, 'Can you stand it? Here we are in Moscow!' It was heaven." And Thompson and Grossman composed a song called "The Moscow ChaChaCha," which Thompson recorded.

On the day she met the American designer Norman Norell, Thompson painted two red dots on her eyelids. "Norell was intrigued by the subliminal flash-of-red effect," Hilary Knight said. When Robert Bernstein walked into his office on his first day at Random House, he was greeted by a half-dozen pigeons flying around and a sign saying WELCOME TO RANDOM HOUSE, FROM ME, ELOISE. Thompson jumped out of a closet.

By the summer of 1966, Thompson was living in Rome, and Hilary Knight returned to work with her on their fifth Eloise collaboration. Knight had drawn hundreds of sketches for a new idea—Eloise lolling in an overflowing bathtub and deluging movie stars in fox coats and the Plaza hotel's long-suffering manager, Mr. Salomone. However celebrated Thompson had become, she was unable to reconcile her public and private lives. The mania for Eloise seemed to have taken over her life. Thompson continued to play her public role with gusto and little noticeable ambivalence. Knight recalled the atmosphere as odd and frenetic. Thompson hung his drawings all over the studio and snapped, "Think of this as a movie." They worked all day long and into the night. Thompson would compliment Knight's sketches—"That's great, Hil,"—but the next morning, he recalled, "that drawing that was so glorious would have a big clot of rubber cement on it, and there would be a piece of paper over the drawing." She refused to accept any of his suggestions. In the end, the idea was too thin to sustain. Even the working title seemed false and affected: *Eloise Takes a Bawth.*

A few weeks before *Eloise* was published, Hilary Knight had received a call from Thompson's secretary asking for a meeting. When he arrived he was handed a one-page agreement to sign. Thompson had written an unusual addendum to her publishing contract. She would own the copyright to Knight's drawings, and any future Eloise books would be locked in at the same royalty split as the first—70 percent for Thompson and 30 percent for Knight. "I totally trusted her," Knight said. "I signed it without really looking at it. I totally signed my rights away." During the years of their collaborations, Knight would occasionally raise the subject with Thompson. Finally she agreed to discuss the onerous contract with Morris Ernst, a distinguished literary lawyer. Ernst, who agreed with Knight that the contract was unfair, "got nowhere with her. He was overwhelmed by her," Knight explained. Nevertheless, Knight and Thompson had soldiered on.

Many artistic collaborations are not entirely congenial. It is said that Gilbert and Sullivan communicated through letters because they could not stand to be in the same room. The union of Lorenz Hart and Richard Rodgers ultimately collapsed, and Bertolt Brecht and Kurt Weill became fed up with each other. Thompson's alliance with Hilary Knight resembled most closely the partnership of Lewis Carroll and John Tenniel. As with Tenniel's drawings for *Alice in Wonderland,* the charm of *Eloise* was greatly enhanced by Knight's vision, but Thompson insisted on complete control. At times, the writer and artist were so exasperated with each other that their editor had to write to Knight urging him to stay calm. They would become strained, imagining slights and betrayals where once there had been a productive, even joyous exchange of ideas.

As early as 1962, when Thompson moved to Rome, she clearly had lost any detachment about her relationship with her six-year-old alter ago. Thompson later said, "People make Eloise what they want her to be. So why should I come in with a Mexican hat and a dish of spaghetti? The book was out one day when Elsa Maxwell left a note that said, 'Dear Miss Thompson, How did you know I lived at the Plaza?' And that is exactly what has taken place . . . the idea of these people playing child!" She ultimately refused to allow *Eloise in Paris, Eloise in Moscow,* and *Eloise at Christmastime* to remain in print. She called the books "rotten" and said, "Eloise is all of us. She is not the girl with the hat on in Mexico."

Thompson seemed to be ready to escape from her creation. Just as *Eloise Takes a Bawth* was ready to go to press, Thompson pulled it from the publisher.

In 1995, Eloise turned forty, but Thompson continues to freeze out Hilary Knight. "She is totally turned off by me. And I honestly can't tell you why," he says. Thompson is consumed by rage and tells friends that

Knight continues to draw Eloise. "All he is entitled to is a share of the royalties," she told Rex Reed. "Eloise has another life, and I am planning it right now." It was to Rex Reed that Thompson gave her last formal interview. In 1972, she told Reed that she was on the verge of publishing her fifth book, *Eloise's Wit and Observations.* She never did. "My life has been *sic transit,* and now I'm sick of transit. No point in saving memorabilia—someone always steals it. I own an orange tree here, a rattan chair there, and the rest is in storage in Rome."

All over America, *Eloise* continues to sell briskly. In 1998 almost 45,000 copies were sold. First-editions are rare, and cost almost $300. "They leave the store usually the day they come in," says Schuyler Hooke, the manager of Books of Wonder on West 18th Street in New York. Thompson continues to turn down all book and film offers, including one from Knopf for her memoirs and another from Francis Ford Coppola. Coppola talked to her on the telephone for hours about Eloise until he finally realized, a friend said, that Thompson was hopelessly tangled with her creation. "Well, goodbye to both of you," he reportedly signed off.

For the fortieth anniversary, there were special Eloise promotions, including an elaborate display in the windows of Books of Wonder. One night Schuyler Hooke was working late when the telephone rang. "A voice said, 'This is Kay Thompson.' Miss Thompson was crisp: 'What is the title of the book in the window?' And I said, 'Well, it's *Eloise.'* And she shouted, 'That is incorrect! The title of the book is *Kay Thompson's Eloise,'*" Hooke remembered. Recently, my telephone rang as well. The voice on the other end was theatrical and enthusiastic, immediately recognizable as that of Kay Thompson. "I don't want my story to be told. I'm too busy working. I have so many projects. I keep them all here in a trunk. But do call again. . . . Maybe someday I will talk."

DECEMBER 1996

Kay Thompson died peacefully in New York on July 6, 1998, at the East Side apartment of her goddaughter, Liza Minnelli. Her will had a surprise—she would allow the publication of the *Eloise* sequels and permit her heirs, her sister Blanche and her children, to sell movie and licensing rights. I was asked to write a essay on Eloise and her creator for the new book. I wrote of visiting the Plaza once again on an Eloise mission—thirty years after my mother first took me to New York to see the mythical hotel where my favorite heroine lived with her nanny and pug dog. When I arrived again, there was a platoon of eight year olds skiddering through the gold lobby where the azaleas bloom in November in the Plaza's Palm Court. I watched them staring dreamily at Eloise's famous portrait with her hand posed jauntily on her hip, her belly poking through her lacey shirt. A new plaque had appeared on the outside wall.

THE PLAZA HOTEL

THE HOME OF ELOISE

Kay Thompson lived at the Plaza while writing Eloise, first published in 1955. Miss Thompson and illustrator Hilary Knight brought this fictitious charmer to life; an exuberant and precocious six-year-old who lived on the top floor of the hotel.

Designated a literary landmark, September 26, 1998.

Clare Boothe Luce

O n one of the last nights that Clare Boothe Luce went out in her life, she was taken to a Chinese restaurant in her beloved Washington. Mrs. Luce ordered velvet chicken, which she said reminded her of the hundreds of meals she had shared with the "Gimo," as *Time,* one of her late husband's many magazines, had so often styled its pet crusader, Generalissimo Chiang Kai-shek. The "Gimo" was now long dead, and Clare Luce was eighty-four years old, weeks away from death, yet her appearance was remarkable. Her skin remained translucent as a pearl, her eyes, despite her near blindness, the cold blue of an aquamarine. She was dressed exquisitely in pastel silks. She could hardly walk, but that night she was "on," talking constantly, telling stories of SALT and NATO, Burma and London, Joe McCarthy and Ike, the "Gimo" and his wife, the "Missimo," with herself at the very center of each anecdote, dazzling a young man from the Federal Trade Commission who had been invited along to meet the legend before it was too late.

The stories were not new, and part of her image was her ability to perform them, no interruptions permitted. Her friends speculated that

her talking was a form of self-protection. In public, she was actressy, calling everyone "darling"; her voice was pure Bette Davis, husky and tough, with a few Connecticut-lady trills thrown in for effect: "tomahtoes," "my deah gahdener." But somewhere in the middle of dinner, she seemed to tire of talking of "darling Douglas—MacArthur, you know" and "Franklin and that dreadful Eleanor," and her voice lost the toughness which had always marked her social persona. She retreated into the realm of the private Clare, a woman of considerable vulnerability, alone at the end of her life without friends to buoy her spirit, without children, without her husband to give her status in Washington. "You know, I have had a terrible life," she finally said. "I married two men I really didn't like. My only daughter was killed in a car accident. My brother committed suicide. Has my life been a life for anyone to envy?"

Clare Boothe Luce was a beautiful liar and a woman of intellectual grit—she created an image for herself based on glamour, brains, flint, and the ability to make people believe that every word she said was true. "Once I was at the White House with Franklin—Roosevelt, you know— and he said to me, 'Clare, if only I could think of a way to try to explain to our great country what I am doing, if only I could think of some phrase which would sum it all up!' I said to Franklin, 'My dear Mr. President, what about using the term "a new deal"?'" This anecdote had endless variations: "I was in London during the blitz with dear Winston— Churchill, you know—and the bombs started falling, and Winston and I were at the Savoy. Winston said, 'The British people have such guts, Clare—if only I could think of a way to describe their struggle,' and I said, 'How about "blood, sweat, and tears"?'"

She told friends stories about how Jock Whitney, David Rockefeller, Averell Harriman, and George Bernard Shaw had wanted to marry her, and how Strom Thurmond had goosed her—all untrue. When *People* magazine, part of her late husband's Time-Life empire, was doing a profile of her, a researcher called Clare's friend Shirley Clurman in a panic. "Mrs. Clurman," the researcher said, "not one word that Mrs. Luce has told our reporter checks out!"

There was hardly need for her to make anything up. By the time she was thirty-four years old in 1937, she had been an understudy for Mary

Pickford; a suffragette; a glider flyer for her patron, Mrs. O.H.P. Belmont; a socialite married to a rich Newport dipsomaniac named George Brokaw, by whom she had one daughter; a divorcée with a ton of alimony at the beginning of the Depression; and, for three years, the managing editor of *Vanity Fair.* "I don't think my position unusual for a woman. I'm following a perfectly natural urge to do what I like," she calmly told a *World-Telegram* reporter in 1933. There were rumors that she had had affairs with Buckminster Fuller and Bernard Baruch, and she had written a best-selling collection of satirical essays called *Stuffed Shirts.* After she married Henry Luce, the publishing tycoon, in 1935, she wrote plays, including one classic, served as a correspondent during World War II, became a Republican congresswoman, and in 1953 was the first American woman to be made ambassador to a major country. When she died on October 8, 1987, *Time* called her "the pre-eminent Renaissance woman of the century." There were memorial services in New York and Washington, attended by friends and associates that included Richard Nixon, Patrick Buchanan, former secretary of state William Rogers, Vernon Walters, and William Buckley, whom she had cajoled to prevail upon Cardinal O'Connor to allow her funeral mass to be held in St. Patrick's Cathedral.

"Things happened to her that didn't happen to other people," a priest who was close to Clare Boothe Luce late in life said. But when she talked of her earliest years, she could never seem to repeat the facts the same way twice. Her father was like a character in a dream. In her biographies, he is described variously as a fiddler, a Memphis Coca-Cola bottler, and the proprietor of the Boothe Piano Company—sometimes the time frame is so distorted that he appears to have had all these professions simultaneously. There is one unvarying, overwhelming fact: William Booth, a descendant of John Wilkes Booth, abandoned Clare and her brother in their early childhood. (The *e* was added to Booth—again sources differ—either by Clare's grandfather, to distance his family from Lincoln's assassin, or by Clare herself, for effect.) Clare's mother, a woman of such beauty that her daughter was said to pale by comparison, was left to fend for herself, and she and the children wound up in a boardinghouse. "Mother always cooked fried eggs by opening the gas jet over the radiator and keeping the window open so the landlord wouldn't smell her cooking and throw us out," she would tell interviewers. Mrs. Booth's maternal efforts were focused completely on young Clare, perhaps because she realized that a blond, curly-headed daughter could be peddled more successfully than a son. Clare had unreserved mother love or at least focus as a child. Throughout her childhood and teens she searched for her father, and she later told friends that she once met him in a subway long after her mother had assured her he was dead. Although he had abandoned the family for a common showgirl, Clare's mother's story to the children was more dramatic: that he had left them for Mary Garden, a famous opera star of the era. "Keeping up the *bella figura* ran in Clare's family," a friend said.

By age ten, Clare was making the rounds at the Biograph studio, trying to fulfill her mother's ambitions that she should be the new Mary Pickford. Mrs. Booth made every effort to shield her daughter from other children. "When I was a child, I was so lonely I became a compulsive eater," Clare said. "My mother's tendency, because of the boardinghouse, was to cook very little and to buy everything at the bakery." Although Clare would lose her baby fat, she never lost her primal devotion to sweets, and she used to insist that her houseguests conform to her lunch menu: naked lettuce leaves followed by a great wedge of apple pie or chocolate cake.

When Clare was still small, Mrs. Booth had the luck to take up with a married tire merchant named Joseph Jacobs, who advised her to gamble every penny she had from her divorce settlement on a single stock. She did, and made enough to take Clare and her brother out of the boardinghouse. Clare was relocated in small hotels in Paris, where she could get "culture" and a patina of the education she lacked. While Clare was perfecting her French her brother was parked in an American military school.

Several years later, Clare was returning from another sojourn abroad when she struck up an acquaintance with the daffy suffragette-socialite Mrs. O.H.P. Belmont. All that "finishing" paid off. Mrs. Belmont was so impressed with her that she confided to Elsa Maxwell, according to Maxwell's autobiography, "I met a girl on the boat who has all the earmarks of talent and success. She's only seventeen and she's poor, but she had beauty and brains to go as far as her ambition will take her. . . . I'm going to give her a push in the right direction."

Eventually Clare would marry Mrs. Belmont's candidate for her, George Brokaw, the alcoholic Newport millionaire who at age forty-three had never attempted matrimony and whose mother, upon meeting Clare, no doubt begged the nineteen-year-old to marry him. Their daughter, Ann, was born almost immediately, but Clare was hardly maternal. "Rich women are not too put upon by their children," she later said. "You don't have to do all the things for a child that those women who had to stay at home did. My Ann had a French governess who took care of her until she was twelve years old and went off to boarding school." Brokaw's Newport world, which Clare would spike in *Stuffed Shirts,* always regarded Clare as a penniless social climber, but neverthe-less as Mrs. Brokaw she was able to move into a limestone-and-marble mansion on the corner of 79th Street and Fifth Avenue. Years later, she would tell the writer Dominick Dunne, whom she met at a luncheon in Newport, "I know all about violence and physical abuse because my first husband used to beat me severely when he got drunk. Once, I can remember coming home from a party and walking up our vast marble staircase at the Fifth Avenue house while he was striking me. I thought, If I just gave him one shove down the staircase I would be rid of him for-ever." Instead, she paid a call on old Mrs. Brokaw and begged her to per-mit a divorce. Mrs. Brokaw did, and in 1929 Clare found herself with a settlement of $425,000 plus $30,000 a year for living expenses. In an unusually ugly custody battle she had been forced to give up her five-year-old to her former husband for six months each year.

Imagine Clare Boothe Brokaw that autumn of 1929. She was twenty-six years old, released from the confines of a vile Newport mar-riage, a nervy glamour girl who claimed that Cecil Beaton had pro-nounced her "drenchingly lovely." (Beaton had made the remark about someone else, according to Helen Lawrenson, and Clare "just pinched it.") She was breathtaking, however; she had had her nose fixed, and had lightened her hair. And although her clothes were often too fussy and her figure was imperfect, she radiated an aura of fragility which camouflaged her brazen intentions and seemed to reduce every man she ever met to a stuttering fool. "That poor little kid," Bernard Baruch used to call her.

At this stage, Clare Boothe Brokaw clearly placed immense value on being known for her style. Her dining room, which overlooked the city, one observer remembered, "was covered with silver tea paper painted over with a panorama of the New York skyline in Matisse colors." The table, which seated twenty, was smoky mirror glass, reflecting the mural of New York and Clare's own skyscraper ambitions. Her living room was also very much à la mode, a study in Chinese red and black and white. It was the era when publisher Condé Nast and editor Frank Crowninshield, with his cane and abundant charm, presided over New York, defining who was elegant and who was not in the pages of *Vogue* and *Vanity Fair.* Immaculate, impeccable Janet Rhinelander Stewart and Mona Williams were considered the arbiters of style, but Clare probably modeled herself more on the irrepressible Alice Roosevelt Longworth, whose feistiness she would certainly have admired. Clare had the money and nerve to prop up her ambitions; she met Condé Nast at a party and demanded a job. When he said no, she showed up anyway—she just sat down at a desk at *Vogue* and wrote captions until he relented.

She was quickly moved to *Vanity Fair,* a man's world editorially and more her style than *Vogue* in 1930. In those days *Vanity Fair* was quartered in three semipartitioned rooms between the elevators and the airy, scented suites of *Vogue.* Clare started off writing captions for the Hall of Fame. One of her first was about Henry Luce, the founder of *Time,* whom she had loathed on first sight. "He claims that he has no other interest outside of his work, and that his work fills his waking hours," she wrote. Soon she was promoted to writing short, tart pieces, and with a facility that never left her she wrote dozens of essays about the world of privilege and pretense: "Hollywood Is Not So Bad," "Portrait of a Fashionable Painter," "Life Among the Snobs," "The Great Garbo," "Talking Up—and Thinking Down," this last a social climber's guide to the art of making sparkling conversation. "The cardinal rule to be remembered is that all contemporary conversation must be limned or suggested against a sparkling background of sex . . . the multitudinous shades of which can be a polite pink at the lobster course to a passionate purple at the grapes," she advised. Wilfred Sheed, in his authorized biography of Clare Luce, observed that her pieces were remarkable because they depended "entirely on flourishes of wit and style," as if the essayist were winging it "on virtuosity and press clippings: not a report but a performance."

The *Vanity Fair* of that era was ruled over by Crowninshield, whom everyone called "Crowny," and his managing editor, Donald Freeman (whom Clare was rumored to have been involved with). The magazine was required reading for the smart set, the best writers and photographers, as well as the nobs they chronicled, would wander in and out of the office all day. Heywood Broun, John O'Hara (another rumored lover), Robert Sherwood, George Jean Nathan, Edward Steichen, George Arliss (who often arrived carrying a snake), Dorothy Parker, Walter Lippmann, and Elsa Maxwell showed up frequently. It became a part of Clare's myth that each morning before she appeared she would already have been attended to by a hairdresser and manicurist, and, according to a *Vanity Fair* copy editor, Jeanne Ballot Winham, she "would be wearing a perfect little suit with lots of frills at the collar and cuffs." Despite Clare's blond fragility, she was, Winham recalled, "a female who had male ideas." Helen Lawrenson, who as Helen Brown Norden worked at *Vanity Fair* then as well as later, once wrote of Clare's ability to social climb: she would call a star such as Constance Bennett and invite her to a dinner for Maurice Chevalier and then ask Chevalier for Connie Bennett. If Clare invented that well-worn trick, she was rewarded with a constant parade of celebrities, who attended her parties and marveled at her style. On her office desk was a sign that read, "Down to Gehenna or up to the throne, / He travels the fastest who travels alone." When Donald Freeman was killed in a car accident in 1932, it was Clare Boothe Brokaw, not "Brownie," as she called the future Helen Lawrenson, who was made the new managing editor of *Vanity Fair.*

Each morning, Jeanne Winham remembered, "Clare would sit in her office poring over hundreds of news photos from the day before, analyzing what we should cover." One of her most popular features was "Ike and Mike—They Look Alike," a clever pairing of photos in which mismatched people resembled each other, and perhaps the inspiration for *Spy* magazine's "Separated at Birth." As managing editor, Clare Brokaw determined who was renowned and accomplished enough for the magazine's Hall of Fame and who received the opposite sort of distinction, "We Nominate for Oblivion." (After Clare left the magazine, she made the 1934 Hall of Fame herself, along with Shirley Temple and Robert Moses.) Even as she helped introduce the newest French painters to America, she realized the obvious—that with a Depression raging, *Vanity Fair* had better forget the froth and turn to politics if it wanted to stay afloat. Once, Condé Nast proposed a satirical cover on "the Forgotten Man." Clare gave her boss a cold stare, according to one of her biographers, and said, "I don't see anything even remotely funny about people being hungry." (Helen Lawrenson later took credit for this remark.) From her bully pulpit, Clare Brokaw enjoyed taking jabs at world leaders, and she mercilessly attacked the Roosevelts. F.D.R., for his part, loathed her, and much later at the White House said to an aide within her earshot, "Will you get that woman out of here!" "Mr. Baruch, I would like you to teach me all about business policy," she had said coyly to the elder statesman when she first met him through Condé Nast, and he was charmed for life. He took her with him to the Democratic Convention of 1932. The reporter Arthur Krock called her "La Belle Dame Sans Merci," but despite her money and fame Clare had her insecurities. "The Algonquin crowd was too much for me," she once said. "I couldn't compete with them." Instead, Clare presided at the weekly *Vanity Fair* lunches in the Graybar Building, where Eggs Benedict were catered by the Savarin Restaurant downstairs.

A well-known Helen Lawrenson story published in *Esquire* had Clare inviting the women at *Vanity Fair* to one of her parties. "Just wear what you have on at the office," she said, and then greeted them at the door wearing a dazzling gown of gold lamé. What is less well-known is that the piece appeared just months after Clare had given Lawrenson $3,000 because she was down-and-out. Clare did have close friends, such as Colleen Moore, the actress, and the socialite Buffy Cobb, although Buffy and Clare once had a falling-out over a man and were not on good terms for ten years.

Clare, of course, was capable of kindnesses: she invited Wilfred Sheed, at age eighteen, to spend the summer at her home in Connecticut.

"Watch out for envy," she advised him. "I don't see why anyone would envy a guy with polio," he told her. "Yes, I guess that might slow them down some. But they'll find a way," she said. Often impulsively, she would paint pictures for friends or take them on trips. But female friends to go the distance with eluded Clare, perhaps because few women wanted to be subjected for hours to hearing Clare on the necessity of the China lobby or on her perceptions of U.N. Secretary-General U Thant. Yet on first meeting, strangers were always impressed by the quality of her mind, her thoughts articulated in chiseled sentences.

Clare was known for her sense of humor, and her humor was very Broadway, a bit weary and angry. Her style was cynical: "No good turn goes unpunished"; "Home is where you hang your architect"; "I can't avoid writing. It's a sort of nervous tic I have developed since I gave up needlepoint." These remarks, part of her personality style, didn't work as well when she put them into someone else's mouth. In *Kiss the Boys Goodbye,* a radical columnist remarks to a maid, "I'll bet the pool's full of scum." The maid replies, "Nawsuh, comrade, you ain't been in yet."

When Clare was young, she loved playing good-natured and girlish practical jokes. Once, in the early 1930s, when she was traveling through Europe with a friend from *Vanity Fair,* a concierge switched her passport with that of a man who was incredibly handsome and well traveled, as Clare discovered when she studied his passport. Unbelievably, the next day Clare found herself sitting next to this suave stranger on a train. "Let me read your palm," she said, fixing him with her Cerulean gaze. "You have been in Morocco, Russia, and Ceylon. You were born in June of 1905 . . ." The stranger was mesmerized, and Clare never confessed it was a gag. "This led to the most wonderful affair," she confided to a friend years later.

In 1935, Clare captivated Henry Luce, who influenced about forty million readers and viewers—one-third of America—with his Lucepress, consisting of *Time, Fortune,* and the *March of Time* newsreels, which interpreted the week's events for moviegoers all over the globe. Luce was easy for her to snag. He left his lovely wife, Lila, for Clare after only three introductions on public occasions. The last of these was a ball Elsa Maxwell gave for Cole Porter, during which while his wife was dancing,

Luce took Clare from her escort and walked her through the lobby of the Waldorf-Astoria to announce without much sentiment or fanfare, and much to her astonishment, that he would marry her as soon as he could obtain a divorce.

She did not say no. Certainly, an often observed maxim about Clare was how much she wanted power. She loved men with "big heads," she used to say, "the Gary Cooper type." She now finally had her dream man, and somewhere in the relentless and self-made Harry Luce she must also have seen her secret self. "A woman's best protection is—the right man," a character observed in *The Women*, the play Clare wrote the year after she married Harry.

She wrote the first draft in three days, while perched in bed with a blue bow in her hair, waited on by her four maids. *The Women* ran more than six hundred performances, and by 1941 had played in twenty-five countries and ten languages, and made the author $200,000. Her women were "dirty little trollops," "double-crossing little squirts," or "Park Avenue pushovers," and her sour attitude toward her sex permeated this, the most famous of her six plays: "She doesn't want to be a woman . . . Who does?" "Oh, Mother, what *fun* is there to be a lady?" "One more piece of motherly advice: don't confide in your girl friends!" Her bevy of females spoke her snappy dialogue, and in all of them there was a bit of Clare—in Crystal, the trashy opportunist; in Mary, the long-suffering wife who exhorts her daughter, "These days, darling, ladies do all the things men do. They fly aeroplanes across the ocean, they go into politics and business." And her martyred Edith allows this playwright to whistle in the dark: "If a woman's got any instincts, she feels when her husband's off the reservation."

"Harry did not like show business people," Clare Luce once confided to her biographer Wilfred Sheed as a means of explaining why she stopped writing for the theater, which had been her true passion. And so Clare became a war correspondent—the "Body by Fisher of the campaign," columnist Dorothy Thompson sneered. Harry Luce didn't think much of liberal Democrats either. "You couldn't be married to Harry and not be a Republican," Clare told Sheed. So in yet another incarnation she went public as an ardent conservative, a Republican congresswoman from Connecticut, a speaker at Republican conventions, and finally as the ambassador to Italy, a stint distinguished chiefly by her belief that she was being poisoned by paint at the official residence.

As Mrs. Luce, Clare was protected from ever having to worry about money or status again. She presided over an immense aerie in Manhattan; Sugar Hill, her twenty-one-room mansion in Ridgefield, Connecticut; and a vast plantation in South Carolina called Mepkin, with thirty black servants who, when Clare was in residence, would float thousands of freshly cut azaleas on the muddy river that fed the Mepkin rice paddies. "Clare did not like to walk in her garden and see silty water," a friend explained. Cabinet officers and prime ministers found their way to her table. Politicians, military men, and movie stars perpetually courted the Luces, hoping to be rewarded with write-ups in *Time*. Apart from the excesses and the guest list, the Luce houses were surprising in their utter conventionality: lots of glass (even a Steuben collection), pastels, and such coldness, a friend remarked, that it seemed as if the Luces were so consumed with their need for power that there was no time to care about cozy domesticity. Or maybe Clare thought this was how the game was played. "Gentiles don't re-cover," she once remarked to the producer Allan Carr when he noticed the stuffing coming out of one of her chairs. But in her Connecticut house every towel, sheet, and pillowcase was emblazoned with her monogram, CBL, like a proclamation of ownership and pride. The pride, however, did not extend beyond the tangibles. She was a mediocre and often reluctant hostess, sometimes taking to her bed if she didn't feel like entertaining, although in one breach of taste the dignitary she neglected in this way was Greece's Princess Sophia. Even without additional irritation Clare was given to black moods, when she would vanish into her bedroom for days on end, terrifying any houseguests and especially her stepson, Hank Luce.

In the beginning they were a supreme couple. Harry was "star-struck," according to a longtime friend, and he loved "displaying Clare." This was not a society drunk but a man of stature. Harry Luce thought so highly of himself that he would publish a four-hundred-page book called *The Ideas of Henry Luce.* Even better, Harry had the power and the money to protect Clare from her critics. Even if Dorothy Parker and the

Algonquin wits and most theater critics sniped at Clare the actress-playwright, as the wife of Time-Life she could be impervious. With Harry behind her, Clare could return to her childhood mindset of never a moment of self-doubt. Often she and Harry would stay up until dawn, head to head, talking about world events. They were an intellectual match; both revered power but lacked time for anyone who wasn't useful. "Clare would be nice to her inferiors if she could find any," Dorothy Parker once cracked. But Clare had gone beyond "Dottie" to become, a friend said, Harry's "idea person." Perhaps to flatter her husband, Clare often spoke in Timespeak, locutions such as "No nitwit he." The Luces traveled constantly, and they would play complicated word games for hours. (*Q:* I know Mr. and Mrs. Pen and their son, a flower. *A:* John Quill.) Above all, Harry was powerful and serious enough to be a father figure for Clare, and in early photographs of the couple, she is radiant.

It is fashionable to say that Clare Luce was a liar, but really she was more of a fabulist, who happened to be married to a supreme propagandist. Like her husband, the son of a Presbyterian missionary based in China, she believed that she understood the notion of truth from the Creation, and her obligation, like his, was to advance that truth. Clare was not the kind of woman who was going to criticize her husband's penchant for twisting journalism to serve his political views. "The weekly fiction magazine," other reporters would call Luce's *Time*—in private, of course. "*Time* today is the gratuitous sneer and the open mouth of shocked belief . . . the clasped hands of Presbyterian piety," a pre-Murdoch New York *Post* once declared. Harry told Clare, according to one of his biographers, that he could fancy no one who was his superior intellectually. "What about Einstein and John Kieran?" was Clare's arch comeback. (Kieran was a famous sportswriter and the star of the popular radio program *Information, Please.*) Certainly, like Harry, she was convinced that her version of history was definitive. And she was not shy about discussing her role in world affairs. It was in her solipsistic war reportage: "I had a talk with handsome, blue-eyed, crisp-moustached General Alexander"; "Madame Chiang read me a bitter article that she had written"; "I ate dinner with the Gissimo, Hollington Tong, and Madame."

Of course, she was aided immensely in her quest for glory by the hype she received from her husband's magazines, a hype that reached such astonishing proportions that when she left for Europe to cover the war for *Life,* Dorothy Parker referred to her dispatches as "All Clare on the Western Front."

Sex went out of the Luce marriage very quickly, according to Clare's friends. Harry wanted a wife who would stay at home, and he had chosen Clare. Just before they married, according to Henry Luce's biographer, W.A. Swanberg, Daniel Longwell, a *Time* executive, went to see Clare in Salzburg and took it upon himself to say that the best thing she could do would be to settle down and have lots of babies and stay out of the magazines. Clare reportedly burst into tears and said she couldn't have any more children. Despite the editor's warning, Clare for years tried to influence the magazines, but Luce's top men always fought her, and Luce would not override them. For her part, Clare was extraordinarily condescending to the Time-Life staff, whom she called "Harry's little people." She took credit for thinking up *Life.*

Later, Clare was even more competitive with Harry, and he didn't like to be beaten. Everything was a challenge to her; she loved jigsaw puzzles and word games and learned to be a superb shot and horsewoman. She often entertained guests by performing an Olympic-quality swan dive off her high board—she was still diving at seventy—and she prided herself on mastering everything she took up, including needlepoint. She would rarely defer to Harry, and at dinners she would hold court at one end of the table while he held forth at the other, reportedly glaring viciously at her every so often. "Clare and Harry were like circles that intersected but did not overlap," Hank Luce explained. "Clare did not care a hoot about China, she didn't understand Presbyterianism, she was ignorant of all the charities and institutions that my father supported."

Clare Luce was wittier and better company than her husband, which was not exactly guaranteed to do much for his ego or their pleasure in bed. "Harry is serially impotent," Clare once told a friend, by which she meant that he could not conduct affairs with other women and keep up a sexual pretense with her at the same time. Nevertheless, however Presbyterian Harry was, he had his share of worldly desires. At one point he almost left Clare for Lady Jeanne Campbell, Lord Beaverbrook's daughter, and Clare remarked, "If Harry marries Jeannie and I marry Beaverbrook, then I will be my husband's stepmother." Lady Jeanne married Norman Mailer instead. There was at times a feeling among those who knew Clare that she was relieved to have the sexual pressure lifted, but she once confided to Wilfred Sheed that this was absolutely not the case. She was tremendously bothered by the lack of intimacy in her marriage, and, worse than that, her female vanity was hurt. "I could tell you an incident that would prove this," Sheed told me, "but I would not betray the confidence. I believe it should die with her." Harry was delighted when Clare decided to run for Congress in 1942. "I am convinced that Harry just wants me out of the house," she told friends.

In January of 1944, Clare, her daughter Ann, and Harry had spent the month of December, as always, at Mepkin, their South Carolina plantation. Mepkin meant family to Clare; she was now a woman of property. Her friend Bernard Baruch, who owned Hobcaw Barony, the plantation just down the road, had told her about Mepkin's availability, and when Clare saw the immense acreage in the South Carolina low country for the first time, told Harry, "This is the most beautiful property I have ever seen in my life." And so, in 1936, Harry bought the seven-thousand-acre plantation for his bride. It was magnificent: sunlight dappled the live-oak trees with their veils of Spanish moss, and the soft South Carolina air gave the place a haunting beauty, which Clare always spoke of as "melancholy." Harry and Clare stocked their plantation with quail and other game for their frequent shooting parties and hired the architect Edward Durell Stone to design several modern brick-and-glass guest houses, which she named Strawberry, Tartleberry, Washington, and Claremont. She used the acquisition of Mepkin as an opportunity for more press, by writing about her new passion for the South in *Vogue:* "Let me say that I am one of Dixie's latest enthusiastic converts. . . . Ah, shades of the Ravenels and Lees and Carters, I blush. . . . I can only plead this extenuating circumstance: we bought [Mepkin] from a Northerner who got it from another Northerner and none of us got it terribly cheap." Later she wrote, "I wasn't going to build a vast plantation house, because that would have been fraudulent. After all, I was a newcomer." In the 1930s there were no decent roads to get to Mepkin, which was deep in rural South Carolina—Ku Klux Klan country. Every year the Luces would take the long train ride from New York to Charleston, where a boat would take them up the Carolina coast and onto the Cooper River, which flowed past their property. Ann adored Mepkin, so for Clare the month of December, when Ann was home from boarding school and later Stanford University, was a cherished and special family time.

It had been especially so that Christmas of 1943, while the war was raging. Ann was then a senior at Stanford, and Clare had long since published her book *Europe in the Spring,* in which she warned America of the danger of Hitler. As Ann had got older, she had grown closer to her mother and, as Hank Luce, her stepbrother, remembered, "just as opinionated." She was tall and sharp-featured, not as pretty as Clare but attractive and very smart, and Harry Luce adored her. He frequently wrote her letters when she was still at Foxcroft, which she would answer by telling him how she had defended the family honor when her snobby classmates made awful remarks about *Time.*

"Did you manage to see your daughter, Ann, as much as you wanted to?" a friend once asked Clare Luce in a taped interview that has never been released. There was a pause as Clare, then an old woman, readied her answer. "No," she said. "When I started to do war reporting and run for Congress, with Ann's vacations from boarding school and college, things didn't always fit together properly." Mrs. Luce, speaking thirty years after the fact, sounded remarkably dispassionate, but perhaps that too was part of the theatrical persona she had developed to camouflage her emotions about the central tragedy of her life. Clare often felt guilty about her absences from Ann. When she left for Europe as a reporter in 1940, she sent her daughter a long, cheerful, and guilt-ridden letter about leaving her yet again. The letter says much about their relationship, which has been portrayed, perhaps unfairly, as consistently distant.

*Annie my darling—You were a grand little trouper about my going
and I really loved you better at that moment, for the swell way you
took it, more than I ever did perhaps before! . . . Hdya like the new
clothes? Do you look adoreable in that little frilled bathing
suit? . . . Is the green tea gown with the frills flattering or isn't it?
Please send me lots of news in your first letter. . . . You'd think perhaps that I'd be the one with the news, seeing as how I'm traveling
to Europe on a big boat. . . . I send you millions, BUT millions of
kisses my sweetheart. Your Mother.*

Just after New Year's of 1944, Ann Brokaw left Mepkin with her
mother. Ann was on her way west to go back to Stanford; Clare was
heading for Los Angeles to give a speech. The trip was special for both
of them. They would have two weeks together, traveling and seeing
friends before Ann was due back at school. "We had such a beautiful
time together on that trip," Clare recalled in the last years of her life. "We
took a train, and Annie took the upper berth and I took the lower berth,
and I can still see her funny little face sticking out. She said to me,
'Mother, I know the strangest thing. I know all of a sudden that I will
never be married.' And I said to her, 'What a funny idea! You're beautiful—of course you'll be married. Don't you want to be?' And she said,
'Yes, I do. Of course. But I never will be.'

"When we got to San Francisco, it was decided that I would drive
her down to Stanford very early. The night before, she came into my
room at the Mark Hopkins and said, 'Mother, you don't have to drive
me down early, because a friend will take me in her car, and you can
come down later for lunch.'"

And so Clare Boothe Luce slept late. "That morning a terrible
woman who had been traveling with us as a secretary for me came into
my bedroom and began to shake me. 'Wake up! Wake up! Your daughter's been killed. Ann is dead!' She screamed at me that Ann and her
friend had been hit by a man who had gone through a light and side-
swiped the convertible. She was shaking me by the shoulders, saying Ann
had been thrown from the open car and hit a tree and broken her neck.

It was so strange . . . I called up Harry. I remember the first words he said: 'Not that beautiful girl. Not that beautiful girl. I'll be right out to take care of everything.' I had to get away from that terrible secretary who brought me the bad news. . . . I called a friend of mine who was one of the officers I had met in that slit trench in Burma and I said, 'I need you terribly badly. . . .' We just walked and walked through San Francisco. . . . I couldn't cry, for some odd reason. And when Harry got there, we took Ann back to Mepkin, because we had all had such marvelous times together there. . . . I buried her in the churchyard on the next plantation."

She blamed herself completely for neglecting her only child, for missing the small moments, and the large ones, of a girl's life that elude a mother building a stellar career. She began to tell friends that everything she had done as a young woman on the make had been a "complete waste"; her years of brittle cleverness mortified her now.

For months, Harry Luce could not pull her out of her depression. Then, slowly, she emerged from her profound grief and sadness into the predictable next stage of reacting to the loss of Ann: she became filled with rage. "What kind of God would take my child?" she asked a priest. Consumed with anger, Clare at first tried to lose herself in the secular world. Some months after Ann's death, she was running as a Republican for the Connecticut seat in Congress It was the most vicious congressional race of her career. She lashed out at the ailing Franklin Roosevelt, who was running for a fourth term. She announced to the world, as she barnstormed through Connecticut, that Roosevelt was so ill that it was doubtful if he could survive four more years. Harry Luce had just acquired a large percentage of the NBC Blue radio network, and Clare used this new acquisition as a forum for her attacks. It was often difficult to feel sympathetic with her, because her anger seemingly knew no bounds. At the 1944 Republican Convention, she excoriated F.D.R. by practically accusing him of murdering "G.I. Joe and G.I. Jim," her term for the dead American soldiers that she said Roosevelt had promised never to send overseas. Coming just as Hitler's death camps were being liberated—and after she and Harry Luce had lobbied for years for America's intervention in Europe—her speech was considered a shocking aberration from a political sharpie. However grief-stricken Clare Luce was, she was sternly criticized for this smear. *The New Yorker* commented that the speech "made it difficult to keep anything on our stomach for twenty-four hours." Even the Bridgeport *Post,* which had always supported her, said that "at times she is positively cruel."

Like her husband, she could be a shrill ideologue. During her 1944 campaign for Congress, Dorothy Parker, Clifton Fadiman, and Tallulah Bankhead showed up to speak out against her—a display which may have inadvertently ensured her victory.

It is difficult to know exactly when Clare began to turn away from the secular world and toward the comforts of the Church. At the end of the war she was in Europe, and soon after Buchenwald was liberated, she asked an American general to take her there. No human being who saw the bodies stacked up there like firewood ever got over it. To survive a world gone crazy, Clare, like many others after the war, reached out to a religion that was pure and uncut by modernity. Harry's Presbyterianism was not sufficient for her; she would need the centuries-old ritual and the intellectual ballast of Thomas Aquinas and the church fathers. When she came home to America, she began to take instruction from a friend of hers, a simple Polish priest, but he quickly passed her on to Fulton Sheen, understanding full well that Clare Luce would need a priest—as she herself later said—"who had seen the rise and fall of empires."

However pious she could appear, there were still flashes of the old Clare. Like Harry, she was terrified of Communists and believed as fervently as he did in the notion of the American Century, the anthem and the flag, Manifest Destiny, Significant Ideas. When she addressed the Republican National Convention of 1948, Dorothy Kilgallen wrote of her, "Clare was a sight to see as she stood on tiptoe in her black suede flatties and railed against the 'troubadours of trouble' and 'the crooners of catastrophe.'" She called the former vice president Henry Wallace "Stalin's Mortimer Snerd" and Wallace's notions "globaloney."

Clare had always thought in terms of absolute good and evil, and perhaps the Church, with its belief in divine absolution, saved her life. Later she would write in *McCall's* that she had become Catholic "in order to rid myself of my burden of sin." She became convinced that she would meet Ann in the beauty of the afterlife, but however religious she became, the loss of Ann remained a persistent and tragic wound. In her last years, as she was moving from her retreat in Hawaii back to Washington, her friend Cobey Black discovered her in a studio on the grounds of her Kahala estate sobbing uncontrollably. "Never move at this stage in your life, Cobey," she told her. "Throwing away a lifetime of possessions will cause you such pain it will undo you." Nearby, in a trash can, was a small pair of Dutch wooden shoes a servant had thoughtlessly discarded. On the back, in a small, childish hand, was the message "To Mommy, I love you so much, Ann."

But in the 1950s Harry was still alive, chasing Communists and reigning over his empire, and Clare's becoming a devout Catholic had the additional and unexpected benefit of releasing her from feeling sexually rejected by him. She told friends she now had a psychological loophole to save her female vanity as Harry sought the comforts of other women—a fact which was known to their intimates. Clare had been, after all, a divorced woman when she married Harry, and the Church did not recognize her second marriage. If she slept with Harry Luce, as a Catholic convert, she would be committing a mortal sin. And so, she confided to friends, once she became Catholic she and Harry lived together as "brother and sister." Ironically, once the sexual pressure lifted, the Luce marriage went into high gear. They became terrific allies, stronger together than they had ever been in the past. Clare was soon campaigning for Eisenhower, who repaid the compliment by naming her the first woman ambassador to a major country, in this case Italy. "I won't go without Harry," she told him, and Harry agreed to being in Rome with her six months a year. He soon grew used to his wife affecting a huge cross with every outfit she wore, and he tolerated all the priests who now surrounded her. But neither Clare nor Harry could ever go back to Mepkin with a clear heart, and soon after her conversion Clare turned her beloved plantation over to a community of Trappist monks, who to this day happily give visitors a tour of the Luce azalea beds.

She created an image and she stuck with it, living a long life with the same desires which had driven her as a child: she wanted to be taken seriously and she wanted to be a factor in society, even after Harry had retired from *Time* and the Luces had retreated to Phoenix. In one photo, her face is serene, sheathed with the tiniest lines; she holds a rose of such perfection the French flower painter Redouté might have created it. A print shawl is wrapped around her shoulders.

Harry Luce surprised everyone who knew him when he actually retired from *Time* in 1964 and turned the magazine over to his successor, Hedley Donovan. Clare was less willing to slow down and move into another phase of her life. She continued to call Richard Clurman, who was then one of the top editors of *Time,* to suggest story ideas. "Clare used to be fascinated by U.F.O.s, and wanted all kinds of antivivisection stories assigned," he said. It was impossible for her to sit still. In Phoenix, Clare campaigned for Barry Goldwater, wrote articles for *National Review,* and followed the minutiae of politics to such a degree that she could recite the voting records of key Republican senators and congressman. At night, while Harry read, she would sit with him, surrounded by boxes of glue, Styrofoam, velvet, sequins and ribbons, making Christmas ornaments of such professionalism that she sold them to Henri Bendel and donated the money to charity. But in Arizona, surrounded by retirees and shopping malls, Clare began to sag in spirit. She lost interest in her looks, stopped wearing makeup, and cut her hair in a Buster Brown style. She told friends that the worst thing about getting old was that men "no longer want you." "Oh, Harry, you are married to an old, old woman," she once said to her husband, according to Shirley Clurman. "Yes," Luce replied, "but I am married to a beautiful old woman."

Clare continued to be depressed in the desert and longed for the sea. She had fallen in love with Hawaii in 1938, when she had vacationed there with Harry and Ann. She had published her experiences in *Vogue,* with photos of her with her surfing instructor, Captain Hale, and of Ann "surf-riding" at Waikiki. "Here's another secret about Hawaii," she wrote breathlessly, *"how* you'll miss it, miss it *all,* when three thousand miles of the calm Pacific is between it and you! Hawaii, someone once said, is a state of mind."

Harry and Clare made elaborate plans to build a Kahala retreat on the beach on fashionable Diamond Head Road, and once again they chose Edward Durell Stone as their designer. It would be the most expensive house ever constructed in Hawaii up to that time, with a dining room that could accommodate thirty, separate studies for Harry and Clare, and several houses on the grounds for servants and guests—all facing the ocean. They no doubt imagined that a stream of journalists and politicians would make this place a necessary stop on the way to the Far East. Additionally, Harry would be much closer to his beloved China. "This was to be their last house," a friend said, and they were making plans to entertain the local bankers and mayors. "They were so happy," Cobey Black said. "It was to be a new life."

But it was not to be. In Phoenix, a few months before they were to move, Harry Luce began to cough violently. He was hospitalized, but by later in the day he seemed fine, reading his Bible and watching *Perry Mason* on TV. That night he woke up and screamed, "Oh, Jesus!" Nurses came running, but Luce had died instantly of a coronary occlusion. He died so unexpectedly that he had left no burial instructions with either his son Hank or Clare, but Hank remembered that he had once mentioned he would like to be buried at Mepkin next to Ann. The monks made a simple stone to mark the site in a grove of live oaks, and carved Clare's name on it too. After the funeral, the Trappists approached Mrs. Luce. "We have some marble left over that we are planning to use for your tomb," they told her. "Would you like to see it?" "God, no!" she replied.

Curiously, for all their closeness, Harry Luce left Clare "the absolute minimum he could get away with without having the will challenged," according to a close associate. Clare would receive the interest from a trust he set up for her—and nothing else. Upon Clare's death, the trust would revert to the Henry Luce Foundation, which was to be administered not by Clare but by Hank. And so Clare Boothe Luce could not properly enjoy the spoils of power, as Brooke Astor, for example, was able to when her husband Vincent willed her control of the Vincent Astor Foundation. At age sixty-four, Clare became a widow on a fixed income, although an extremely high fixed income. "Why wouldn't Harry Luce have given his wife that power?" I asked a close friend of hers. "In the end, maybe Harry didn't like Clare all that much," the friend said. But perhaps the explanation was more complicated: in death, Harry Luce was finally able to score one on Clare. She might be a better shot, a wittier host, a more sought-after speaker, the one chosen as ambassador, but he was after all the boss, and he knew that his son would carry on his tradition in a manner more to his liking.

Clare instructed Edward Durell Stone to redesign her Hawaiian house as a one-person palace. "I don't want a lot of guests," she said. Friends moved in to supervise the construction. "You better make sure I can see the sunset from my lanai when I'm drinking my evening martini," William Buckley said was one stipulation. Clare's house was "eccentric and nutty," a friend said, with the same immense dining room and entertaining areas that she and Harry had wanted, but now it had only one small guest bedroom. Macaws and parakeets flew free inside. Clare's own bedroom was huge, a vast pastel retreat with a study attached, leading out to private beach paths. Her bathroom had a separate beauty-parlor sink for her hairdresser's daily visit, and six servants changed the house's dozens of arrangements of tropical flowers each day. In her one-person retreat, Clare had three room-size closets, where her dresses hung on rotating electric racks of the sort usually found in dry cleaners'. One entire closet was used to store Louis Vuitton trunks from her days as Mrs. Brokaw. "Clare was a pack rat. She never threw anything away," a friend said. Even Clare's living room had a glass-case coffee table with every medal she had ever won displayed inside. Clare would answer the phone as if she were the housekeeper in order to screen calls: "Hello, Mrs. Luce's residence. Who is calling Mrs. Luce?"

She flourished in Hawaii, swam every day, and started wearing makeup again. She ran her Hawaiian household with a discipline that was often daunting to guests. "We would be told that drinks were served on the lanai at six-thirty P.M. sharp and dinner was to be at seven P.M., because Clare did not want to discommode the servants," the writer Miriam Ungerer said. In the guest room, there was a row of buttons on the telephone that one could use to call for a laundress, a snack, or even a sleeping pill. Clothes left in a heap on a chair would be returned within an hour, beautifully pressed, with hems magically repaired. But women guests soon learned there was a down-side to Clare's hospitality. They found they would be served iced tea while the men received a carafe of white wine. "There was something about Clare that prevented you from ever dreaming of asking if you could have a glass of wine," Miriam Ungerer said.

But Clare was hardly idle in Honolulu. For a long while she served on political committees such as the President's Foreign Intelligence Advisory Board, to which Richard Nixon had appointed her. She prided herself on her role as the grand old lady of the Republican Party; the *Washington Post* was hurled onto her lawn as soon as it hit Honolulu. Her telephone would ring constantly from Washington—politicians seeking advice and favors. Once, she was on the telephone with Edward Kennedy when her neighbor Allan Carr was over. "When Clare hung up, she came onto the lanai and said, 'Teddy is a nice boy, but he has so much to learn.'" Often she would fly to Washington or New York for meetings and dinners, and when Reagan was elected president she made plans to leave Hawaii and sail into Washington for her final years. She didn't understand that the special treatment which she had had in Hawaii was as a novelty act. "She felt like she was going back in triumph, as if she were playing the final scene from *Hello, Dolly!*" Allan Carr said.

Washington, however, would prove a letdown as Clare began to realize that her luster had dimmed. She remained an indifferent hostess, and her apartment at the Watergate was spacious but not grand. Unlike another elder, Averell Harriman, whose accomplishments and prestige were constantly propped up by his tireless wife, Pamela, Clare had no one in Washington to champion her in old age. The grand reception which had always been accorded her when Luce was alive seemed more difficult to come by in a city which cared more for current leverage than history. Her friends appeared to have entered into a tacit conspiracy to allow Clare the illusion that she was still the young and vibrant dynamo. Inevitably, she would say she was working on a new article, or concept, or speech, and she hired public relations consultants to introduce her to the "right" people in town. She still cared so much. Once, when a friend came to visit her, Mrs. Luce pulled up her bedsheet: "Look at those legs. They used to be so gorgeous!" A new group came into her life, notably Edwin J. Feulner, the head of the conservative Heritage Foundation, but also columnists, lobbyists, and young White House speechwriters. Her loyal friend William Buckley was a great help to her in Washington, reminding the Reagans of her presence, for example, and Mrs. Luce was thrilled when, two months before her eightieth birthday, President Reagan awarded her the Medal of Freedom at a luncheon in her honor.

But her last years were not happy; the effort required to keep up the image was too great. Always searching for family, Clare grew especially close to Hank Luce's second wife, Nancy, whom she had known since Nancy was a schoolgirl in Charleston. Clare always said Nancy reminded her of Ann. Although Clare and Hank had had a distant and cold relationship when Hank was young, after Henry Luce died, Clare went to him and apologized for years of neglect. "The reason I have been cold to you all these years is because I never wanted to compete with your mother for your affections," she told him—a bit of flattery he was gracious enough to believe. In fact, Clare needed Hank Luce, and she adored his wife. She was devastated to learn, in 1986, that Nancy, who was fifty-six, had incurable cancer. And so Clare Luce in the last years of her life was paradoxically at her most maternal, traveling to New York almost every weekend to take care of her stepson's wife. Perhaps she reasoned that she would be able to do for Nancy what she had never been able to do for her Ann. Sometimes she would arrive at the shuttle in a wheelchair, telling the friends who accompanied her, "This was what I always dreaded, to be a helpless little old lady."

Once, in New York, however, she was strong enough to take a long walk down Madison Avenue and over to her old neighborhood near Beekman Place. She strolled back to Bergdorf Goodman to look for a dress, but was horrified to see that a new Geoffrey Beene evening dress now cost $3,000. Despite her huge income, she was appalled by this excess, and, like so many old people reared in poverty who become rich, she was consumed with money worries, as if she were still the destitute Clare Booth eating penny rolls in the boardinghouse. That night she seemed overwhelmingly sad. "This is not my town anymore," she said. "I feel lost here."

After Nancy Luce died, Clare slipped into another profound depression, as if she were reliving Ann's death. She began exhibiting disquieting symptoms, such as forgetfulness and halting speech. At first her doctor believed she was suffering from "hysterical depression," a theory supported by most of her remaining friends. Like Harry Luce before her, Clare had driven away many of those friends who had had the potential to truly love her.

"I want to give a farewell party," Clare suddenly told her friends the last summer of her life. She was eighty-four years old, and she had learned that her problem was not psychological. She had a brain tumor. Instead of becoming gloomy, she became extraordinarily cheerful, even smiling when the doctor explained the severity of her condition. "She knew she was at the realization of a conclusion," the Trappist abbot of Mepkin told me. At the memorial service for Grace Kelly in St. Patrick's Cathedral, she had said to William Buckley, "That is how I would like to go out." Even at the end, she was a woman of theater, planning her goodbye party at the Watergate. Shirley Clurman counseled her to do it "properly," with plenty of staff and good food, but Clare had her own ideas. "I want it very simple," she said, "home-style, with lots of children, and bowls of spaghetti on each table, and maybe Dove Bars for dessert." Thirty guests were invited, and Clare sat on a low stool for part of the evening so that her guests had to bend down to talk to her. "Goodbye," she would say weakly, as if she knew that this was the last time she would ever see them.

One month later the abbot of Mepkin drove up through the Blue Ridge Mountains to Washington to see Clare. Although he had not been invited, he knew it was time. Father Christian and Clare had been together on dozens of occasions through the years, as recently as the previous June, when Clare had showed him photographs of Ann in the glory days of Mepkin, on a swing in a grove of Spanish-oak trees, a young girl filled with promise and joy, smiling as the wind caught her hair. "Isn't she a lovely girl?" Clare had said, reverting to the present tense. And now it was autumn and Father Christian had felt compelled to come to Washington again. "When I arrived, I introduced as tactfully as I could the sacrament of reconciliation and the last rites." From her bed, "in a beautiful clear voice," she said to him, "I want everything." And so the abbot of Mepkin administered the rites and spoke with her of the beatific vision, the celebration of eternal life, in which she would once again be united with Ann. As the abbot left Mrs. Luce's bedroom, she said to her housekeeper, "I am so happy now. To think that the father came all the way from South Carolina." Three weeks later, Clare Boothe Luce was dead.

Her funeral at Mepkin was private. A sign went up in front of her former plantation: NO VISITORS. Only about thirty people traveled to South Carolina to mourn one of the women of the century. She was buried in the shadow of an immense white granite cross, in the small grove where she had walked so many times, staring at her daughter's headstone or off into the distance at the Cooper River, where Irish immigrants building a dike had once toiled for twenty-five cents a day. The Trappists performed the ceremony with their characteristic austerity: no organ, just a simple guitar. Mrs. Luce was laid out not in a bronze coffin but in a varnished pine box.

Although by stipulation Clare's money from Harry reverted to the Luce Foundation, Hank Luce was thoughtful enough to allow her to make bequests of her choosing. Her list was, William Buckley said, "eccentric and rather charming, perhaps Clare's way of saying 'Up yours!'" The girl who had never gone to college left fellowships to all the colleges and universities that had honored her with degrees. She left $500,000 to the Heritage Foundation, but not a cent to Buckley's *National Review*, although she had told him that she wanted to leave a grant for summer internships for worthy young journalists.

The week after Clare Luce's death, a memorial service was held at St. Patrick's Cathedral, but that celebration too seemed curiously anticlimactic. In New York, where celebrity funerals are often great social events, Clare Boothe Luce's service was crowded but not stellar, as if there were a recognition in the upper reaches that she had outlived her time. Fifth Avenue was not cordoned off to hold back the curious, as it had been for Averell Harriman's funeral, and neither President Reagan nor Vice President Bush chose to attend. The noontime service on that crisp October day was filled with heavenly rest seekers who seemed startled to have wandered into an ordinary mass conducted by Cardinal O'Connor with William Buckley as eulogist and Richard Nixon and Jerome Zipkin among the mourners. The altar was not banked with Clare's favorite peach-colored roses, and there were no children to mourn her passing and to carry on. "Clare would have been mortified by this service," a friend said as he walked out of the cathedral into the brilliance of the clear autumn day. "But perhaps her life was a cautionary tale." Even as he spoke, a few paparazzi who had gathered on East Fiftieth Street were scanning the crowd for the notables, but their cameras remained mostly at their sides.

MARCH 1988

Luise Rainer

It was always said about Luise Rainer that she was thorny, skittish, and difficult to manage. At the height of her career, in 1938, she shared a luxurious cottage on the MGM lot with Metro's other screen goddesses—Greta Garbo, Joan Crawford, and Norma Shearer. She was "an echo of Europe," Anaïs Nin wrote of her. Seeing her for the first time at a dinner party in October 1940, Nin described her arrival in a "white floating dress." She wore no makeup and had a childlike compulsiveness, combined with "a sadness older than the world."

Rainer came to Hollywood from Vienna in 1935, and her movie career was incandescent and ephemeral. For her, the Hollywood years "are not even a fraction of the picture." Romance and passion have defined her long and dramatic life. Rainer was a superstar, the first performer to win an Oscar for best actress two years in a row, for *The Great Ziegfeld* in 1936 and *The Good Earth* in 1937. And then, inexplicably, her days as a star were over, as if the Oscars had come with a curse. "I felt hunted," Rainer said of that time in her life. "I will never forget those years. . . . I was very unhappy."

After Rainer fled MGM, she encountered Anaïs Nin again. Watching Rainer dress, Nin was struck by how she rejected the "movie-star hats, the movie-star shoes, movie-star furs and bags" and chose "the simplest beige dress," a delicate skullcap with a veil, and "the simplest shoes." In bed, Nin observed, Rainer slept with a blanket pulled over her head, as if she were a child frightened by a nightmare. Nin wrote in her diary of her ethereal nature and unpredictable ways. "Luise's image of herself and the image on the screen do not match. . . . She repudiated the worship, the flowers, the love letters addressed to her, as if the person on the screen were a fraud."

Mention *The Great Ziegfeld* to a movie buff and wait for the Luise Rainer imitation. The telephone scene has become a classic riff: Rainer as the soubrette Anna Held, the abandoned wife of the theater impresario Florenz Ziegfeld, is a quivering bundle of suppressed grief and feigned joy. She has just learned of her ex-husband's marriage.

> *Ooh . . . Hello, Flo . . . I am so happy for you today. I could not help but to call on you and congratulate you. . . . Wonderful, Flo, never better in my whole life! . . . Oh! It is so wonderful. I am so happy. Yes! And I am so happy for you too, yes? . . . It sounds funny for an ex-husband and ex-wife to tell each other how happy they are, oui?*

She hangs up tremulously and, after a beat, collapses sobbing onto a chaise.

Rainer became celebrated for her intuitive acting and emotional range; she was a Method actress years ahead of her time. "I never acted," she said. "I felt everything." Rainer was an anomaly in the studio system: her contrarian, bookish nature set her apart. She did her own hair, and was often seen in white chinos and tennis shoes. "Let's show them that this is a world safe for poets!" she once scribbled on a napkin and gave to her husband-to-be, the playwright Clifford Odets.

In another famous movie scene, as the peasant O-Lan in Sidney Franklin's *The Good Earth,* opposite Paul Muni, Rainer dies memorably, relaxing her feeble grip on two pearls which she treasures. During the filming, she was so overcome that she sat on a curb at Metro, weeping.

"A big limousine comes by and stops—it was Joan Crawford," Rainer told me. "She said, 'Luise, what happened? Why are you crying?' I did not want to sound like a phony about acting, so I told her that I had received terrible news from Europe about my family." After Rainer returned to her house in Brentwood that evening, a large bouquet of flowers from Crawford arrived.

Rainer's disappearance from Hollywood was considered unfathomable, a neurotic quirk, perhaps, of a formidable talent. "My so-called career went sky-high, but my private existence went down to hell."

It was late morning, Eaton Square, London. Luise Rainer lived in an apartment in a Regency building with a legacy: Vivien Leigh lived here at the end of her life. On the telephone, Rainer has been precise, Germanic, bossy, taking my measure. "You will arrive at eleven A.M. It is impossible to come anytime sooner. Impossible!" When I ring the bell, her clear European voice calls through the intercom. "You are here! My torturer has arrived!" A tiny woman peeks out the door. She is all eyes, a Pierrette, with a vamp's seductive come-on and a strategist's cunning. She pulls me to her with both hands. "Come in! Come in! You must have coffee. You must eat something!"

Rainer moves through her apartment like a ballet dancer, but with daunting speed. Her drawing room is fastidious and filled with antiques. "I hate disorder," she says. There is a portrait of the star as a young woman, dun sofas, and a large Ecuadorian religious retablo, which dominates the room. Rainer's posture is that of a girl, and she weighs what she did when she was at Metro, ninety pounds. She wears beige trousers, a matching cashmere sweater, and a silver choker. On the matter of her age, Rainer is succinct: "I am a freak of nature. I am eighty-seven! When you think how old I am! And I am proud of it!" She says, "I want to show you something. I have never had a face-lift! Look!" Her hands dart to her scalp: she flattens her hair. "No scars!"

She hides behind tartness: her conversation is punctuated with synthetic commands, theatrical gestures, and grand sighs. Her drawing room is her stage. "Darling. I have had so much love in my life! How will you be able to capture it all?" she asks me. The expressions on Rainer's face shift quickly; she is by turns excited, imperious, alluring. "My mother should walk around with the little man with the clapboard," says Francesca Bowyer, Rainer's fifty-year-old daughter, who lives in Bel Air. The actress Anne Jackson says, "Every time I am out with Luise, it is like a three-act play by Euripides. Walking her dog can become the end of the world."

Rainer instructs me to follow her to her study and moves toward a wall of bookshelves. Her two Oscars gleam from a high shelf. She very obviously does not call my attention to them. "They mean nothing to me," she says coolly when I point them out. "It was expected that I do my best work . . . Now, darling, *this* is what is important!" she says firmly, presenting me with a Penguin edition of interviews with luminaries: Trotsky, F. Scott Fitzgerald, Mark Twain. "It is a very difficult thing to do a proper interview." Of earlier stories about her, she says, "Darling love, all of these things are bullshit. and therefore I don't want you to write bullshit. I would come personally over and kill you." Later she says, "My life has been so full. To come to the essence of one's existence, one must speak of things that are both true and not true. . . . For every statement, there is a counterstatement. . . . You will never be able to write about my life! There is too much."

I have come to London to see her because, for the first time in more than fifty years, she is in a movie, filmed in Hungary, of Dostoyevsky's *The Gambler,* starring the English actor Michael Gambon as the novelist. Her decision to play the part seems of a piece with her personality: the imp of the perverse. "Everyone thinks I am dead!" she tells me. "They all say, 'Luise Rainer, she can't be still alive!'" Rainer's fifteen-minute appearance is high-camp relief in the ponderous film. Carried in on a sedan chair, wearing a black dress and feathers, she plays an aristocratic matriarch in a world of croupiers. "Did you think I vould send a telegram?" she asks with bravura, after surprising her son, a gambling addict. Rainer's face, gloriously lined and filled with intrigue, shines from the poster at the theater on Shaftesbury Avenue.

One afternoon Rainer tells me that she is flying alone to Africa in December on the eve of her 88th birthday. My obvious surprise makes her snappish: "If you were my daughter, you would try to lock me up in a cell to prevent me from going, but I must be free! . . . If I am killed, I've had an extraordinary life. You will not be able to prevent me from going! I must live!"

Rainer once told Odets that she was "a seven-month child, and I am missing those two months and I want them back." Her life has been an ongoing rebellion against any form of domination. She was reared in a well-to-do family in Hamburg, Germany. Rainer's father, Henry, orphaned at seven, had been sent to Dallas, Texas, to be raised by a prosperous uncle in the import-export business. He had crossed the Atlantic on a schooner, and two decades later, in 1907, returned to Europe. While in Dallas, Henry Rainer had become an American citizen, which would save his life during World War II. In Essen on business, he saw a beautiful young girl on a swing at a carnival. That night he was invited to dinner to meet with a local industrialist. The hostess's sister, who was also at the dinner, turned out to be the girl on the swing, Emily Königsberg, a gifted pianist. Henry Rainer's future in-laws were assimilated Jewish *hauts bourgeois* who lived in a world of privilege, with lady's maids, daily visits from the *coiffeur*, embroidered trousseaux, and holidays at the seashore.

Rainer ruled Emily and their three children like a tyrant, Francesca Bowyer says. She believed that her mother felt diminished by her father's harsh ways. "The family was terrified of him," she tells me. "My mother had to spend so much time proving how intelligent she was." Rainer recalls moving from city to city when she was a child, as her father expanded his oil-and-soybean import-export business. "I changed school eight times," she says. "I lived in Munich during the terrible flu epidemic . . . and then we went to Switzerland," where, she says, "I skied to school." The family settled in Hamburg in 1922.

Rainer, her father's favorite, viewed him as "a tragic figure," a sort of Don Quixote with a dim sense of reality. He often made "terrible scenes. . . . He would leave the house." When she announced to her parents that she intended to be an actress, she says, her father "implied I was a whore. He said, 'It is a low and vulgar profession.' . . . I was thrown out of my house at age sixteen or seventeen, and I had to live on apples and eggs!"

Often, with Rainer, I felt that I was observing her through scrim, taking down a narrative of her life not unaffected by illusion. "I'm going to tell you everything," she had said melodramatically on our first afternoon, and I occasionally imagined that I was an audience of one, lost in a world of vanished splendor, which Rainer had neatly shaped into perfect scenes. As a teenager living with her grandparents outside Düsseldorf, she told me in the plummy tone of an ingenue, she appeared one day at the door of an important theater belonging to Louise Dumont, a well-known theater owner of the era. She was sixteen years old, with a perfect, heart-shaped face and a fragile beauty. "I presented myself to the secretary and said something completely idiotic, like, 'I would like to have a job for next season.'" Granted an audience, she did a scene from Schiller's *Joan of Arc*.

In her first months at the Schauspiel Haus in Düsseldorf, she took the lead in Frank Wedekind's sexually frank *Spring Awakening*. Soon Rainer was sent for by the great director Max Reinhardt. She eventually joined his Vienna company and became part of the impressionistic acting tradition which emphasized Reinhardt's rejection of naturalistic style.

Rainer flourished in this atmosphere, although she also acted elsewhere, starring in an adaptation of Theodore Dreiser's *An American Tragedy* and Shakespeare's *Measure for Measure*. Reinhardt's company was part of an insular culture, protected, they believed, from the Fascism that was sweeping Germany.

All around them, however, were signs of the inevitable. In 1933, while Rainer was in Berlin performing in a French play, *Sardine Fisherman*, she was called to a meeting with producer Victor Barnovsky, who wanted to cast her as Cleopatra. Sitting in his office, Rainer looked out the window. She later wrote in her unpublished memoirs:

> *I saw . . . first a cloud of smoke and flames, high flames licking the sky. . . . It was light, then dark. The Reichstag went up in flames. How could I tell what Barnovsky was talking about? Adolf Hitler was to declare my race had "poisoned blood." . . . Barnovsky, his back to the window, was angered by my total inattention. "Don't stare out the window. Whatever this is, think of your work and nothing else. This all has nothing to do with you."*

Later, Rainer was apolitical; caught up in her life as a young star, she was driven by emotion. On the morning after her first sexual experience, she twirled across the stage exclaiming, "I've lost my virginity!" The expressionist playwright Ernst Toller was in love with her, and she became enamored of a well-known director. "There were so many men," she told me. In Vienna she collected encomium after encomium. "How do you do that?" Max Reinhardt himself asked her after one performance. The company had the feeling almost of a religious cult, equals plying their art and being paid almost nothing for it. The growing tensions in the world outside were but a blip.

Soon Rainer began to worry about her parents. "This fellow Hitler is nothing, he's a housepainter," her father said. Henry Rainer published vigorous letters attacking Hitler. Rainer did not believe in religion; he had turned against it as a boy, and now convinced himself that the Nazis were unaware of his wife's Jewish origins, which were never discussed in the house. The Rainers had the deep ambivalence about their religion which was integral to the life of the German upper middle class. All of the children were reared "wild, with no religion at all," Luise Rainer said. She used Goethe's word *Wahlverwandtschaft*—elective affinity, meaning, for her, choosing one's own relatives—to describe her ties. Scorned by her father, she had made the theater her family.

Rainer was very aware of her history. "I never made a secret about it," she said. "This whole thing about being Jewish . . . it's a very American thing. In Europe, on the Continent, people of the upper class never talked about Jewishness or not Jewishness. . . . Then came Hitler. *Then* this became an issue."

Rainer was besieged by admirers, who filled her dressing room with flowers. She had a rich girl's willfulness; she gave the impression of being entitled and oblivious, a dangerous set of traits. In Frankfurt, soldiers worked as stagehands at the theater, wearing brown shirts and heavy boots. "I said to them, 'Would you do me a great favor? Get rid of those blasted boots and put on slippers, as stagehands normally do!" Another time, as part of the play she was in, she asked the young actress who played the maid to bring her flowers onstage so that the audience could see them. The Gestapo visited the theater and accosted her. "I was told that I had told the stagehands to strip their uniforms! And that I had asked a talented young actress to bring me flowers, as a page boy to a queen!" Because of her status as a star, however, Rainer had been given a special title: Honorary Aryan.

She was soon offered an escape from the growing chaos in Frankfurt—a European tour with Reinhardt's production of Pirandello's *Six Characters in Search of an Author.* The playwright accompanied the tour, and Rainer recalls him as "a birdlike little man, pixilated." In Vienna one night at the theater, she met a young, rich Dutchman, who later arranged a party so that he could see her again. They fell deeply in love. He pursued her everywhere, flying her in his two-seater plane over the Dutch tulip fields. "He was everything to me," she said.

In Vienna, a scout from MGM saw her perform and asked her to go to London to read for the film version of Hemingway's *A Farewell to Arms.* The Dutchman insisted on flying her there for her screen test. As Rainer unpacked, she realized she had brought two left silk shoes. She became upset because she could not afford new ones, and she would not allow her lover to buy them for her. "Shoes from a man! I would never have accepted," she said. He gallantly crossed the Channel to Amsterdam, where her luggage was with friends, and returned to present her with her right shoe in a basket. Within months, he would be killed when his plane crashed in Africa.

Rainer was invited to Hollywood in 1935. Mourning her lost love, she had fallen into an affair with his brother, who physically resembled him. "I had mixed them up in my mind," she told me, "but they were not at all alike." She crossed on the *Ile-de-France* and celebrated her 25th birthday on the ship. The violinist Mischa Elman serenaded her in the dining room. During the trip she discovered she was pregnant. "It was a romantic, idiotic thing! I thought that the child would be like [her dead lover]. . . . It was a young foolishness." Walking Johnny, her Scottish terrier, on deck, she realized she could never have both the baby and her career.

"Darling, don't make me a tragedienne," Rainer said of this period. "When I went to America I thought they would take one look at me and send me home again. . . . I never dreamed of becoming a movie actress, never. My father always talked about America. I could see that America that I'd always heard of."

After arriving in New York, Rainer took the train to Los Angeles. She was taken from the train station to the Beverly Wilshire Hotel, and at the desk she spotted Gary Cooper. "I nearly fainted," she said. She then went for a walk through Beverly Hills. "There were flowers all over! I couldn't believe all of the windows were open, and the lights were on, and it was like a theater. You could see what the people were doing!"

She was invited to a party at the singer Jeanette MacDonald's, where she met MGM's then reigning star, Norma Shearer, and her husband, producer Irving Thalberg, as well as the émigré director Ernst Lubitsch. Soon she was sent for by Louis B. Mayer's closest studio aide, Eddie Mannix. Rainer had no sense of American slang. "They had me read, then they slapped me on the back and said, 'See you later!'" She thought she had been invited to a party. Next they drove her around the lot at Metro, through the back streets and onto a set where Johnny Weissmuller was filming a Tarzan movie. The drive continued. At one point Luise asked the driver what set they were on now. Beverly Hills, he said.

She was given a small house in Santa Monica, down the beach from Shearer and Thalberg. Rainer took long walks with her dog and studied English. One day she met the writer Anita Loos, who asked her, "Aren't you that girl who just came from abroad? The studio is looking all over the world for a woman to take over Myrna Loy's role in *Escapade.* You should call the studio." With calm hauteur, Rainer told Loos, "I'll wait until they come to me." They did. She was cast in *Escapade,* a turn-of-the-century Viennese romance, opposite William Powell, who was so impressed with her that he badgered Louis B. Mayer about her billing. "'You have to star that girl or I look like an idiot,' he said," Rainer recalled. "That is how I became a star!"

From the start, the studio played up Rainer's waiflike appeal. In stories from the period, there is no mention of the fact that her family owned a large import-export company or that she was German; to avoid growing anti-German sentiment, the studio called her Viennese. MGM made plans to typecast her as the abandoned wife, the woman scorned.

After *Escapade,* she was again paired with William Powell, in Robert Leonard's elaborate film biography, *The Great Ziegfeld,* which featured cameos by vaudeville stars Ray Bolger and Fanny Brice.

According to Rainer, "Louis B. Mayer did not want me to do that part. Suddenly I was a new star, and they had not expected that! . . . The producer Hunt Stromberg said to me, 'Please go to Mayer and tell him that you would like to do it.'"

"I was very unsophisticated! They had written the telephone scene. It was nothing. I said, 'Can I write that scene?' . . . And I went to Louis B. and said, 'Look, I very much want to do this film. There is a scene . . . I might be able to make something out of it!' He was very annoyed. He thought I was wrong! He said, 'You're out after the film is halfway over!' I said, 'I don't care how long the part is!'" Rainer had seen Cocteau's one-act play *La Voix Humaine,* a monologue of a woman talking on the phone. She imitated it, she said, and instructed Leonard, "Do it in one take."

When *The Great Ziegfeld* turned out to be more than four hours long, Mayer famously insisted that Rainer's "dreary" telephone scene had to go. Stromberg fought to save the scene. It stayed in, and won Rainer her first Academy Award. At the ceremony, held at the Biltmore Hotel, she wore a charming white suit and posed smiling between Paul Muni, who won the best-actor award, for *The Story of Louis Pasteur,* and Frank Capra, who won as best director, for *Mr. Deeds Goes to Town.* On the night she accepted the Oscar, she said, she had no sense of what an Academy Award meant. "Darling, in Europe we did not need these accolades. It was a blur to me." For film critic and author Molly Haskell, "Rainer's Oscar represented Hollywood rewarding high culture with a capital *C.* It was a reward for theater art and a sign that Hollywood still did not take itself seriously." The award, however, allowed Rainer to demand better movies. "I was an enigma to them. They did not know how to handle me. I would say, 'I don't care about money.' And they would say how 'shrewd' I was. I didn't even know what the word 'shrewd' meant. It was so crazy!"

Rainer chafed under the studio system; lacking the political skills of Joan Crawford or the grit of Bette Davis, she was soon on a collision course with Mayer. "Mayer used to say to us, 'Just give me a good-looker and I will make her an actress.'" A 1936 *Collier's* profile of her, titled "The Girl Who Hates Movies," reported that her very name caused arguments all over town. She was either "a talented young woman who does as she pleases" or "a shrewd, phony, fake temperamental lady with big eyes and an exaggerated opinion of herself." Rainer made no secret of her feelings about the movies. "This is not acting," she told *Collier's*, adding that she would love to return to Vienna and her life as a stage star.

Rainer arrived at MGM when it was a feudal system ruled by a despot and nicknamed "Mayer's-Ganz-Mispochen," Yiddish for "Mayer's whole family." Louis B. Mayer wanted stars to be obedient and docile. Crossing him was like asking to be run out of town. The atmosphere was doggedly provincial. When Hunt Stromberg took Emlyn Williams's play *Night Must Fall,* which would become one of the first psychological mystery films, to Mayer, the studio chief said, "We make pretty pictures." Rainer's Mitteleuropa sophistication was protected from Mayer's orders solely by Irving Thalberg.

Mayer appeared baffled by Rainer, who was taken up by the European-exile community and developed friendships with the novelists Thomas Mann and Erich Remarque, the composers George Gershwin and Harold Arlen, the lyricist E.Y. "Yip" Harburg, and the architect Richard Neutra. She criticized Mayer publicly, as if her talent could protect her. "They call me a Frankenstein that will destroy the studio," she told *Modern Screen.* "It is more important to me to be a human being than to be an actress."

On the first morning we are together, I raise the subject of fame. How could Rainer have so easily walked away from what most actresses spend a lifetime trying to achieve? "I was never aware that I was anybody," she says dramatically. "Do you want to hear what I wrote about this?" she asks. She retreats to her study and emerges with a sheaf of papers from her 240 pages of unpublished memoirs. Softly she begins to read about a dinner that would alter her life. It was the autumn of 1936, and Rainer was at the Brown Derby with George Gershwin and Harold Arlen:

A hush came over the restaurant. Someone had entered. I did not know him. Heads turned. Most others seemed to know him. . . . His eyes came to rest on our table. Slowly he came towards us. He spoke to Gershwin and to Harold Arlen, and they asked him to sit down. I was introduced. "Clifford Odets, our new Chekhov." I had never heard of him. Tall, well-built, with large gray-green eyes, his light hair brushed back from his high forehead. He somehow reminded one of a Disciple. He did not address me with a single word. During conversation and questions concerning his last play, which, as I heard, was the rave of New York's critics, he answered in a quiet, low voice. I felt strange. What was that? There was something flamelike about this man, attractive, warming, burning as well. As though to protect myself, I moved my chair a little away. And he noticed it and looked at me. Our eyes met.

Two weeks later, Rainer was invited to a party at the home of Dorothy Parker:

Except for Ginger Rogers, most guests were unknown to me. On the far side of the room, surrounded by people who seemed to lap up his words, stood Clifford Odets. Over the crowd I felt him looking at me. I left early; I had to be up at six o'clock in the morning to get to the studio by seven A.M. . . . A few days later while on location, I was called to the telephone. It was a man's voice: Clifford Odets. "Can one ever see you alone?" he asked. Two evenings later he collected me and took me out to dinner. We went to a restaurant at the end of the long Santa Monica pier. Afterwards we went for a walk along the beach. To my horror, it was littered with lifeless fish. Something in the water had poisoned them. I trembled. Clifford Odets took me back to my house. That night started for me the wildest, the most compelling and frenetic, the most tragic relationship. It changed the flight and rhythm of my life.

Rainer stops and looks up. "You see," she says, "I used to fly. I had wings inside. And suddenly I could no longer fly."

Brilliant and tormented, the creator of an American theater of protest, Philadelphia-born Clifford Odets would soon be on the cover of *Time*. *Awake and Sing!* and *Waiting for Lefty* had brought a new realism to the stage. His plays were performed by the Group Theatre, a New York company devoted to the acting method of Stanislavski, whose members included Harold Clurman, Elia Kazan, Lee J. Cobb, and Stella Adler. In the summer, the Group would adjourn to Lake Grove in upstate New York to work on its next season. Like many of the young intellectuals of the era, some of them were strongly left-wing, sympathetic to the Loyalists fighting in the Spanish Civil War.

When Rainer talks about her three-year marriage to Odets, she quotes Oscar Wilde: "Each man kills the thing he loves." "He devoured me," she says. Rainer calls Odets "the passion of my life," but she says he was constantly torn between his commitment to the Group and his desire for intimacy.

At one point, she brings out a binder filled with hundreds of Odets's letters to her. They are carefully preserved, each page in a plastic cover. Because Odets was forced to remain in New York for much of their courtship and subsequent marriage, his letters were prolix, discursive, filled with longing and dread. He sometimes wrote three times a day. Of a weekend they spent together, he wrote,

> *very good, nourishing and I . . . [am] better and happier than I've been for a long time. . . . It would be terrible if something happened, if in the end we went different ways. . . . I give you Beethoven's Seventh because it is most like what I feel for you, not forgetting the slow movement. How terrible and wonderful this feeling. . . . How wonderful our last night together.*

Odets's passion for Rainer intrigued the press and nettled Odets's Group Theatre comrades. He was their leftist hero, son of a Jewish printer, all hard edges and nasal accent, and he was dazzled by Rainer's beauty and delicate *grand bourgeois* manners. "Clifford was a poet," Rainer says. She did not disguise her resentment of director Harold Clurman's influence over Odets, which resembled Mayer's domination of her. She told Odets that Clurman was "fattening on him," according to Odets's biographer Margaret Brenman-Gibson, and sixty years later Rainer still says Clurman "behaved very badly. He was very possessive of Odets, and I was of course in the way."

She was filming *The Good Earth* during the first months of their romance, and the production appeared "jinxed and interminable," according to Brenman-Gibson. It took years to complete. George Hill, the first director, committed suicide; the next director, Victor Fleming, fell ill. Sidney Franklin, who finished the picture, and Irving Thalberg had to pacify Chiang Kai-shek, who thought the film would concentrate on the suffering in China.

Rainer again fought her bosses. "The makeup man wanted to make a complete mask." She insisted on playing the part with almost no makeup. "I became Chinese," she says. "I came one day when they tested people for mass scenes. There were many Chinese people—cooks, waiters, servants. . . . And my pocketbook under my arm fell. As I bent down, one of the little Chinese women also bent down. Our heads hit, and she looked at me. . . . She was O-Lan."

The scale of the production was immense; Franklin orchestrated swarms of peasants, a revolution, even a plague of locusts. Paul Muni's wife sat on the set every day in a deck chair, Rainer recalls peevishly, instructing the cameraman on the best angles for her husband. Rainer's performance was a tour de force. Ironically, the strong-willed Rainer was lauded twice for performances in which she acted walking two steps behind a powerful husband. In the front office, meanwhile, Mayer feuded with Thalberg, her champion, over the making of quality movies.

In September 1936 when he learned of Thalberg's sudden death at thirty-seven from pneumonia, Odets wept. He identified with the creative genius cut down by philistines. He wrote to Luise:

> *To have a harrowing sense of what can happen to anyone . . . well, it sickens one at the heart. . . . For what is work and effort without a friend, a lover, a mother and father and brother and sister all rolled into one? Darling, let me be all those things for you (and you for me). . . . For the present, Luise, I send you my softest, most ten-*

der self and the strength of my arms and mouth, all of which are very
much in love with you.

For Rainer, the death of Thalberg, her protector, was ominous. Mayer
now turned against all executives with "highbrow interests." He was angry
that it was too late to recut *The Good Earth* into one of his "happy pictures about happy people." "What is revolution?" O-Lan asks during a
famine, then answers herself, "A revolution makes food." Rainer, trapped
in a seven-year contract, could not control her resentment. She wrote
Odets that she felt like "a bolt in their machinery." She would be
destroyed as an artist if she had no say in the choice of script or director.
In one letter, Odets advised, "I urge you to let [Myron] Selznick work for
you and to make him feel that you respect him as an agent."

Nervous about marriage to the high-strung Rainer, Odets consulted
a famous graphologist, Lucia Eastman, using false names to camouflage
their identities, according to biographer Brenman-Gibson, who found
the reports in his files. The young woman, Eastman wrote of Luise, was
charming but had had some "deep hurt in her youthful days." She was
mistrustful and had an "inverted vanity." A marriage would have to be
"properly managed," because "Mr. Von Delf," as Odets had called himself, was "still very much of the small boy—sensitive and imaginative."
He would need her to be both "wife and mother. . . . She will [have] to
remember that a hurt child is often apt to try to hurt the mother he
loves."

Odets was not the only nervous party. His relationship with Clurman,
stormy and intense at best, was strained in anticipation of the upcoming
marriage. Clurman did not want the playwright's attention distracted
from the Group. Odets ignored Clurman and went ahead with the marriage. The January 1937 ceremony at Luise's Brentwood house was inter-
rupted when a swarm of photographers rushed through the door. The
couple took off for a hotel in Ensenada, Mexico, empty in the off-season
except for a group of midgets. Odets stuck to his work schedule—midnight to dawn. "I was alone with the dwarfs downstairs," Luise said.

On the beach the next morning, Rainer saw Odets walking alone.
She rushed to him to jump into his arms. "He moved away," she said.

Luise soon began to see a pattern in his behavior. Later she would tell Anaïs Nin:

> *He was always abandoning me. He used to leave at night after we made love, when I wanted him to sleep with me. When I was in Hollywood, he would come from New York with a small valise, and I would look first of all at the small valise and think, He is already planning not to stay long. And I felt deserted as soon as he arrived.*

Rainer's life became defined by intense work and the strain of a difficult marriage. "I made eight films in three and a half years, and in the same period I had to shoot *The Great Waltz* twice, because Louis B. Mayer did not like the director's first cut. . . . I would come home exhausted, change into something pretty, and have dinner with Clifford, who usually just wanted to be with me alone."

Rainer grew to detest Harold Clurman and also actor Elia Kazan, who, among others from the Group, would stay for weeks with the newlyweds in Los Angeles, working on Group Theatre productions. "It was terrible," she recalled. "They would eat everything and drink everything. I used to have to walk in the hills to get away from them." They could be boorish and rude. When Kazan saw the opening of *The Good Earth,* Rainer was anxious to hear what he thought. "He never mentioned it to me," she said.

In February 1938, she was nominated for best actress for that film, as was Greta Garbo for *Camille,* and Garbo was favored to win. Driving back to Los Angeles the day of Oscar night following a two-week holiday with Odets in San Francisco, Rainer called home from Santa Barbara. "My maid was frantic. 'Miss Rainer, Miss Rainer, you must come immediately! The newspapers are calling. Tonight is the Academy Awards. They expect you to be there!'" Rainer had a quarrel with Odets, who was jealous of the attention she was receiving. She wanted to attend the ceremony alone. "He wanted to go with me, but I didn't want him to come," she said. "He made me so unhappy. He made me cry all of the time." Rainer rushed home to change. Then, still arguing, they circled the Biltmore Hotel three times before she dashed in to accept her award. The story has become part of Oscar lore.

Despite her two Academy Awards, Rainer was mired in a sinkhole of despair. Once, gazing out her dressing-room window, she saw Greta Garbo walking alone toward her set. "Ah, she's getting old," an MGM producer said to Luise. At the time, Garbo was thirty.

Odets's obsession with his wife could also be unnerving; he often wrote down her remarks. "He once said a terrible thing. He said, 'Darling, if ever you want to commit suicide, do it in my arms.' If I had been dead, he would have had me forever. . . . I was like a slave with him, and yet he never had me."

The fights with Odets became increasingly frequent. Once, after a Sunday buffet at their house, according to Neal Gabler's book *An Empire of Their Own: How the Jews Invented Hollywood,* Odets screamed at Rainer because she had not hired servants to wait on the table. In Hollywood one had servants, the leftist playwright told his wife; otherwise why come here? When he was angry, he was monstrous, Rainer recalled. "The biggest thing was he used to say, 'Your instinct stinks.'" Forced by the studio to appear in such B movies as *The Emperor's Candlesticks, Dramatic School,* and *The Toy Wife,* a bathetic drama in which she plays Frou Frou, a coquette disregarded by her conventional husband, played by Melvyn Douglas, Rainer could not get away—in her life or her career—from the role of the long-suffering victim. "They used to say, 'She can play a Chinese peasant or Ziegfeld's wife, so she is hard to cast,'" Rainer said. Odets would fly into rages at Rainer, breaking furniture and, once, "every plate in the house." Rainer recalled feeling "constantly diminished," as she had with her father. "Clifford would say, 'You want sugar, sugar, sugar all the time!'" she said. "Look at this picture," Rainer told me one day in London. "This was the story of our marriage." The photograph was startling. In it Rainer was surrounded by photographers. In the background Odets looked dazed and unhappy. "He was so jealous," she said.

As Rainer lobbied for better scripts, she was unaware of a crisis in the film industry. Movie grosses slumped during the recession of 1938. WAKE UP! HOLLYWOOD PRODUCERS, read a full-page advertisement in *The Hollywood Reporter* that spring. "Practically all of the major studios are burdened with stars—whose public appeal is negligible." As theater owners pressured the studios to stop turning out prestige films, which made little money, Greta Garbo, Katharine Hepburn, and Marlene Dietrich were labeled box-office poison. The theater owners demanded lighter fare—Westerns, Charlie Chan movies, Andy Hardy.

In May 1938, Rainer discovered that she was pregnant. When Odets received the news coldly, Luise made another fast decision. "This love was so incredible. And I aborted his child. But it was his fault. Because he was terrible. . . . I knew it was not possible. He would have killed me." Later, Margaret Brenman-Gibson would discover in Odets's papers a wire he never sent to Luise. In it, he expressed pleasure at the news of the coming baby and urged her to run away from Metro and live with him in the country, where they could raise their child. Rainer told the biographer sadly that if she had received that telegram she would have done exactly that.

That summer, Odets left for Lake Grove with the Group to work on *Rocket to the Moon*. The Group's finances were faltering, and they were three years from disbanding. Drinking heavily, Odets began a wildly romantic affair with the blond actress Frances Farmer, who had been in his play *Golden Boy*. In the 1982 film *Frances* Jessica Lange and Jeffrey DeMunn recreated the affair—including his throwing rose petals on the bed before they made love for the first time.

"Nineteen thirty-eight was very, very hard," Rainer said. "In my private life, devastating. I was exhausted." Separated from Odets for five months, under pressure at the studio, Rainer vented her rage on her makeup woman, saying, "I don't want to make films anymore. I don't want to see this camera anymore. I can't stand myself on the screen! I don't want it anymore!" Soon after, she was summoned to Mayer's office. He was furious at her for her disloyalty, but he might have been placated by a display of humility. It was not to be. "Mr. Mayer, I cannot work anymore. It simply is that my source has dried out. I have to go away, I have to rest."

Rainer recalled his icy response: "What do you need a source for? Don't you have a director?" At the core of their argument was a clash not only of temperaments but also of class resentments. Mayer needed to dominate the snobbish German star. "If you can't release me from my contract, at least give me a leave of absence," she said.

"Luise, we've made you, and we're going to kill you," he told her.

That moment changed Rainer's career forever. Instead of groveling, she told her tormentor, "Mr. Mayer, you did not buy a cat in the sack. . . . I was already a star on the stage before I came here. I shall tell you something. All of your great actresses in this country are between their early forties and fifties—Katharine Cornell, Helen Hayes, Gertrude Lawrence, Laurette Taylor. I am in my mid-twenties. . . . In twenty years you will be dead. That is when I am starting to live!"

They never spoke again.

Breaking her contract, Rainer left Hollywood to rejoin Odets in New York. LUISE RAINER AND CLIFFORD ODETS RECONCILED AND SHE WANTS WORLD TOLD IN BIG HEADLINES, one paper bannered. It did not last. There was constant jockeying for power, which created an inexorable tension between them. Rainer wanted "security and peace," and Odets could never provide them. Increasingly sensitive to the coming war, Rainer was soon caught up in the events in Europe. She had long since made peace with her parents, but she could not get them to leave Hamburg. When Jewish neighborhoods were destroyed by Nazi storm troopers during Kristallnacht ("night of the broken glass"), she wired her husband in New York: "Am sick over happenings in Germany. Many friends . . . newly imprisoned." She begged him in a letter to write "a new anti-Nazi play." By then Rainer had brought her two brothers to America, but, she recalled, "my father was impossible." For months he refused to move to Brussels.

When the Germans marched into Paris, Rainer learned that her father had been arrested in Brussels and sent to a camp as a political enemy of the Reich. Frantic, she approached William Bullitt, the U.S. ambassador to France, to pressure the State Department into rescuing him. Near death from starvation when he was released, Henry Rainer then had to cross the Pyrenees on foot. His arrival in New York was noted in the press. Luise was described as looking wan and exhausted, as if the complexities of her life had suddenly overwhelmed her.

Earlier, in 1937, Albert Einstein had received Rainer and Odets at a rented cottage in Peconic, Long Island. Rainer asked him to help rescue European refugees. A famous photograph was taken of them in a rowboat on Long Island Sound. Rainer wore her trademark white pants. "He was very normal," she said of Einstein. "He played the violin and did not talk about the Theory of Relativity." Odets became so jealous of Einstein's attention to Rainer that he later cut off the scientist's head in the photograph of them together.

Rainer and Odets lived in Greenwich Village, at One University Place. He insisted that she be a hausfrau, deferring to his need to write with music playing at full volume and keeping the refrigerator stocked with his favorite foods. She sometimes took refuge at the Waldorf or with friends. She confided in the photographer Alfred Stieglitz, who wrote her long romantic letters. The fights with Odets became more and more violent. Once, she said, "we were walking along Fifth Avenue, and he was screaming at me. We went into a taxi, and he was screaming. At one point the taxi stopped, and he got out of the taxi, and the driver looked at me and said, 'Get rid of that bastard.'"

In 1939, after two years of marriage, Rainer wrote her husband a sad farewell letter. "So many beautiful words had come all ready from you, so little had been done to realize them, and horrible words . . . and you didn't realize what you had said or done and were surprised or disturbed when I was broken into pieces."

When she left Odets, she told me, "he tried to kill himself. He went to Mexico and he ran into a tree! It was all crazy. . . . I just left! . . . Probably if he had said something, he would have said, 'Go!'"

In her London apartment, Rainer has a highly organized filing system. There are drawers full of meticulously preserved papers and a master list that reads "People Who Have Corresponded with Luise Rainer." These include Pearl Buck, Bertolt Brecht, Eleanora Duse, Chiang Kai-shek, George Gershwin, Lillian Hellman, Luchino Visconti, Vivien Leigh, Tennessee Williams, Lotte Lenya, and Alfred Stieglitz. In the rare interviews she has given over the past sixty years, Rainer mostly talks about a period that was over by the end of World War II, when she was only thirty-five. A year after Odets's death, in 1963, she recalled him in her memoirs: "His lack of ever relying on anything but himself was the source of his restlessness and self-destruction."

While Odets was carrying on with Frances Farmer, Rainer stayed in England for a year, appearing in a West End production of a romantic comedy, *Behold the Bride,* and fell in love with a British aristocrat. Jealous and possessive, Odets broke off with Farmer and attempted to win his wife back. But it was over. Rainer and Odets tried unsuccessfully to reconcile one more time after their divorce in 1940, but soon after that, Rainer discovered Odets with a young actress, Bette Grayson, whom he had met through Harold Clurman.

Rainer made one more movie in Hollywood, for Paramount. The film was *Hostages,* a 1943 wartime melodrama, which she once told an interviewer had been such "a horrendous experience" that she had never seen it. She returned to New York to sell war bonds and then toured Europe for Mrs. Roosevelt. By then Mayer had blacklisted her. Rainer wanted the role of Maria in Sam Wood's *For Whom the Bell Tolls* opposite Gary Cooper, but she wasn't ever asked to audition, and the part went to Ingrid Bergman. Bertolt Brecht approached her and said, "I must write a play for you." She suggested an adaptation of A.H. Klabund's novel *The Chalk Circle.* She even went to a close friend who was a producer and had him bankroll the playwright. Months later, Brecht had written only two pages of what would ultimately become *The Caucasian Chalk Circle,* one of his plays with Chinese settings. Rainer recalls, "I told him I thought his behavior was outrageous!" To which Brecht replied, "Another actress would be on her knees to play this part." Rainer said angrily, "I don't want anything more to do with you."

Near the end of the war, at a party in Manhattan, Rainer met a young Swiss publishing executive, Robert Knittel, who worked in New York. The son of the wealthy Swiss novelist John Knittel, he shared Luise's love of music and the cerebral life. "I am going to marry her," he told a friend at the party. Each morning on his way to work he would push a love poem under the door of her room at the Plaza. "He worshipped her," their daughter, Francesca Bowyer, says. Knittel was quietly uxorious. "Cliff was my passion, Robert was my home," Rainer says. By then Odets had married Bette Grayson, with whom he would have two children.

After their marriage in 1945, Rainer and Knittel lived in a town house on Sutton Place and later in an 18th-century farmhouse in Stamford, Connecticut. By 1950 she had moved to London, where Knittel had a job at the publishing firm Jonathan Cape. He later became the editorial director of William Collins. After Knittel retired in 1979, the couple moved to Vico Morcote, a village outside Lugano in Switzerland, where Rainer painted and worked on her memoirs until her husband's death in 1989.

One afternoon after lunch, Rainer turns to me. "I am a little bit tired," she says. "Come with me to my bedroom, and we will both lie down. I will close my eyes, and then you can continue the psychoanalysis." I follow her to her airy pink bedroom, which is filled with photographs of her daughter Francesca, who resembles Ali MacGraw, and her two beautiful granddaughters.

Rainer arranges herself on the pillows and closes her eyes. "You may continue," she says softly. "What can it mean to be an artist and not have done serious, meaningful work for the last fifty years?" I ask. Rainer suddenly leaps up on the bed and exclaims, "I am a great talent, yes! . . . I would say it is my greatest achievement to have come out of that. . . . It would be a lie to say that I did not think much of myself! Because I thought enough of myself. I would have loved to give out! . . . One wants to be the best one can be, and I suppressed it!" Her voice fills the room, tears well in her eyes, and for once there is no performance. "I lived like a nun!" she says sadly. Later she says, "It was me who withdrew. I got a reputation that I did not want to work. And I did not counteract that."

She retreated into the pleasures of a happy marriage; she painted, made collages, and lived beautifully in London, in a large house in Eaton Mews. Sometimes, in the dead of night, she would cry to Robert about the loss of her career. From time to time there were offers, but Rainer's energies had shifted: she had grown tired of "the baloney and nonsense," as she called it. Rainer appeared sporadically in the theater, in New York in 1952 in *The Lady from the Sea* and later in *The Little Foxes* in Vienna, but she was often impatient and querulous. She refused to compromise, routinely taking refuge in her family life.

In 1958, when Federico Fellini was planning *La Dolce Vita,* he approached Rainer and said, "I need your poetic face!" He sent her an early script, which she told him was "absolutely terrible! . . . Pure non-sense!" She was to play a single scene, opposite Marcello Mastroianni, a comeback that could have revived her movie career. Mastroianni plays a foolish Lothario, and Rainer would have none of it. She insisted on rewriting their scene. During that torrid summer in Rome, she and Fellini argued. "I love what you wrote," Fellini said, "but you must fuck Marcello Mastroianni!" Rainer responded, "I want to go back home to my husband! I do not want to sweat my summer away! We must talk about my scene." They reached an impasse, and Rainer said she would do it her way or not at all. She recalls, "Fellini got down on his knees and said, 'You cannot leave!' and I said, 'Leave me alone!'" Later she sued the production company, holding up *La Dolce Vita*'s release until she was paid.

At the end of our interviews, I discovered an oddity. I was on the telephone with Francesca, and the subject of her mother's religion came up. "I did not know she was Jewish. Do you know something I don't know?" her daughter said lightly. Although she had read her mother's memoirs, she insisted that she had no idea her grandfather had been in a concentration camp. "You did not know that your mother was listed as a prominent Jewish actress in the *Encyclopaedia Judaica?*" I asked. "Really?" Francesca said. Later she said, "There were a lot of people who were in concentration camps who weren't Jewish."

When I interviewed one of Rainer's closest friends of forty years, Ingeborg ten Haeff, an artist who lives in New York, I experienced a similar moment. "I didn't know," she said when speaking of Luise's Jewish heritage.

Two days later, Rainer called me from London. "Why are you tormenting Francesca?" she asked. "I've been thinking about your obsession. It's mad, racist. It's just as racist as how Hitler felt about being Aryan. I personally do not believe in religion. It's a man-made formula." I asked Rainer to explain: how can she appear in the *Encyclopaedia Judaica,* yet with her daughter and her close friend never mention her religion?

During our talks, Rainer had alluded to a drama that undercut her marriage to Robert Knittel, but had dismissed it with, "Once again, it is a big story." On the telephone she chose again to be vague saying, "Why should I burden my child?" She finally explained. Before meeting her, Robert Knittel had attended Oxford and the University of Virginia. He was eager to volunteer for the Royal Air Force, but as a Swiss citizen he was not legally allowed to join. Knittel's parents remained in Switzerland during the war, and when Robert and Luise got married, he phoned to tell them the news. His mother responded negatively in a letter: "We read about Luise Rainer, and if she had to leave Austria for political reasons it would be the death of your father." Mrs. Knittel's "political reasons" was clearly a euphemism for Rainer's Jewish heritage. Although Rainer had been reared in a family that was not observant, she was outraged at this insult. To her horror, she came to realize that her in-laws were Nazi sympathizers. The hostility was palpable. "One day I was taking a bath, and my mother-in-law walked in and saw me naked," Rainer told me. "She said, 'The family has different breasts from you.'

"When Francesca was ten weeks old, Robert, the nurse, and I and the baby left for Switzerland to visit," she told me. "My nurse came to me one day and said, 'Mrs. Knittel, I was walking behind your mother-in-law and I heard her say to your father-in-law, "Luise thinks you are a Nazi."' It was like suddenly being at Berchtesgaden, in Hitler's country retreat." However ambivalent she may have been about her own background, she now told Robert that she wanted a divorce. "I cannot come between the man I love and his family," she told him.

She moved into the Savoy in London. "Robert was miserable," she said and they soon reconciled. When news of John Knittel's sympathies leaked out after the war, his popularity as a writer waned in Switzerland. Rainer's mother-in-law, whom Rainer did not see until shortly before she died, asked her to appear with him at interviews. "I would not do it," she said. However much she despised her husband's family, she made a decision: Francesca would be shielded at all costs. "I've written it all down for her, what really happened, and someday she will read it," Rainer told me.

On our last afternoon together, Rainer returned the conversation to the essential fact of her life. "Look, darling, I'll tell you something. As you look around at other actresses who are [still] working now, are any as healthy as I am?" She stood and made a tiny bow. "And, darling, look at me!"

From Africa, Rainer sent me a joyous postcard describing a night she had spent in the bush under the stars, after a long train ride from Cape Town to Victoria Falls. Back in London, she telephoned and, her voice brimming, read me a description of her trip. "The horizon so very far, the sky unending, floating clouds, higher, higher, more voluminous than I have ever seen . . . no artifice." She hesitated. "Darling love, you just don't know the beauty of it."

APRIL 1998

Pamela Harriman

I met her for the first time in 1984. I was invited to her house for one of her famous Election Night parties. The TV commentators had been using phrases like "Reagan landslide" and "decisive Republican victory" that make Democrats cringe. Pamela Harriman was standing in the Georgetown crowd. Television screens seemed to be everywhere, and around each one a cluster of somber faces. Next to Mrs. Harriman was Edmund Muskie, the former Democratic presidential candidate, in tears. Nearby was the former defense secretary, Clark Clifford, his face a slate of despair. Clifford traced his government service all the way back to the Truman years, and he seemed as much a fixture in the Harriman living room as the Chinese porcelains. Here was a world that few people ever see, the closed world of hidden Georgetown, a society where people use their private "green books," the Washington social register, to get phone numbers, and where most of the richest and the brightest favor old tennis shoes, good pearls, and New Deal politics. On this Election Night, with four more years of the Reagans to contemplate, there was no election celebration at the Harrimans'. Pamela Harriman took Muskie's arm, a

gesture of caretaking for a politician whose world was crumbling. She was surprisingly calm, supreme in her timeless salon with the Matisse, the Van Gogh roses, the muted chintz sofas, and a field of family photographs in silver frames. Her husband, Averell Harriman, the distinguished statesman, ninety-two years old, had long since gone to bed, but Mrs. Harriman radiated confidence in her future. "We will not be defeated," she said to Muskie, adding, in a tone that sounded eerily like her former father-in-law Winston Churchill's, "Next time we will win!"

April 1988. Washington, springtime. In the crowded ballroom of Loews L'Enfant Plaza Hotel, for the first time it seemed Mrs. Harriman might have been right that dismal Election Night four long years ago. The Senate was now run by the Democrats, and real Democratic presidential hopes were evident as the rhetoric that was in the air. "If Dukakis chooses Gore . . ." "The White House will be ours next year!" "On to Atlanta!" "We need your help to win in '88!" These quintessentially American pronouncements were all spoken in that cool, upper-crust British voice.

She had organized this evening with her usual attention to detail, and had seen to it that all the proper players gathered. Senators, congressmen, and governors swirled among liberals in English pinstripes and lobbyists and labor leaders in polyesters. "I need you!" she would say as they moved up the receiving line to meet her, and her tone was as crisp as fine silver clinking against good crystal.

Watching Mrs. Harriman, it was easy to imagine how she had enchanted the men in her past—Edward R. Murrow, Elie de Rothschild, Jock Whitney, Gianni Agnelli, and Aly Khan, as well as her three glamorous husbands. Her first was Winston Churchill's son, Randolph, whom she divorced after the war. Next, the producer Leland Hayward. And finally, Averell Harriman, with whom she had first fallen in love thirty years earlier.

If some of her men viewed her as frivolous, Mrs. Harriman knew better, even then. "I was always very serious," she said. "We used to say about Pamela that if you put a blindfold on her in a crowded room, she could smell out the powerful man," a close friend said, with admiration in her voice.

Pamela Digby Churchill Hayward Harriman had risen to prominence in Washington, a man's town, in a tough and traditionally closed male profession: political fund-raising. In recent years she had made an unofficial fact-finding trip to China to confer on Sino-Soviet policy and several semiofficial trips to Russia. During the Washington summit conference, the Soviets returned the compliment by asking her to invite Raisa Gorbachev for tea—much to Nancy Reagan's annoyance, it is said—and this certified Pamela Harriman as "one of a handful of people who have direct access to the Gorbachevs," according to Richard Holbrooke, the future U.N. ambassador. She had studied her briefing books, given foreign policy speeches, written about American-Turkish foreign policy, masterminded several Senate races, and raised over $7 million for Democratic candidates. Substantial credit goes to her for helping the Democrats regain the Senate in 1986. She succeeded to such an extent, indeed, that she was referred to in Washington, unkiddingly, as "the empress of the Democratic Party."

The receiving line snaked toward the newsstand of the Loews lobby, and hundreds of dark suits with faces familiar from TV waited patiently to clutch the hand of the daughter of the eleventh Baron Digby of Dorset, who had become a widow since Averell Harriman's death at the age of ninety-four. "Marrying Pamela was the best decision I ever made," he once told his friend Clark Clifford, and he willed her over $75 million, much to the consternation of several members of his family.

Her interest in American politics started long before she married Harriman. "You see, I was always a Democrat. When I was in London during the war, Kathleen Kennedy was my closest friend. For me, the Tory Party and the Democratic Party were very much alike. You took care of people and you were compassionate. There was never any doubt in my mind I would be a Democrat," she said. When she first married Harriman, her friends say, she began studying American politics with such a vengeance that she would lecture on the subject at dinner parties to friends like Evangeline Bruce and Katharine Graham, who were already Washington experts. "Finally, I had to tell her gently not to do that anymore," one friend said.

At times, standing in the receiving line, Mrs. Harriman seemed as girlish as a county debutante smiling out from a Gainsborough portrait. She was dressed in a lovely red silk gown, very feminine yet simple, a column of scarlet set off with ropes of Indian diamonds, pearls, and emeralds to the waist, the only obvious sign of her wealth. Her auburn hair had become muted, but her skin was still almost as flawless as a piece of her Spode. She had always been famous for her skin and for her voluptuous shoulders.

For each senator, governor, and friend, she had the right word—"What about the I.N.F. treaty?" "My favorite senator!"—and she never repeated herself. She showed no signs of boredom or restlessness as she shook these hundreds of hands—far from it. She seemed to thrive on it. She had come full circle in her life, back into the inner sanctum of high-level political gossip and maneuvers where she had started at age nineteen, newly arrived in London as the bride of a Churchill. It was easy to imagine the girl she must have been in that wartime London, presiding over Isaiah Berlin's speeches and Edith Sitwell's poetry readings at the Churchill Club, or listening with similar optimistic and rapt attention as American and British generals poured their plans for strategic bombing. "I don't think you think about much of anything when you're nineteen years old," she told me that night in Washington, "but I learned a great deal in London then, and there were many good times and terrible times and we never knew how any of it was going to turn out. . . ."

"It never entered my head that she was ambitious," a dear friend who met her after the war said about her. But she was, from the time she was a child. "My sister Pamela decided early on she was going to turn herself into a very glamorous person. She had a lot of ambition," her younger sister Sheila Digby Moore said. The Digbys were nowhere near as powerful or rich as the Marlboroughs, but their title was good; they were part of the "very few," as Churchill called their world, even if there wasn't a lot of family cash. Although Mrs. Harriman was reared during the

Depression, the Digbys didn't suffer much, but they were often called on "to take baskets to those of the townspeople who had lost everything," Sheila Moore said. Pamela, the firstborn, and her sisters and brother grew up in a stately home called Minterne, she says, as "country bumpkins," riding ponies, hunting, learning French from their governesses. "You know how the English are—we rarely even saw our parents," Mrs. Harriman told a friend. Lord Digby served for a time in the consulate in Australia, and when the family returned to England, Pamela, who was then four, was already winning hearts and minds and was named "best baby" on the ship. "The Digbys were almost cartoon peers who seemed to come from the pages of *Punch,*" said William Walton, who covered the top command in England for Time-Life during World War II. Lord Digby owned a large dairy farm, and was nicknamed "the milkman" in the press, but he was also a passionate horticulturist who cultivated rhododendrons. Lady Digby, "a very forceful and somewhat difficult character," according to Sheila Moore, doted on her husband and also on her gorgeous red-haired oldest daughter. She would never say a critical word about her. "When our parents would have people to tea and dinner, it was Pamela who always begged to be allowed to sit at the table, while I was so shy I hid in the nursery," Sheila Moore recalled with amusement. Despite mastery of country skills such as riding and hunting, Pamela Digby couldn't wait to live life in a wider realm. "I used to go up in the hills with my dogs and say, 'When I am grown up I will leave this place . . . and I will live in a city,'" she told Diane Sawyer.

Her ambition may have been inspired by her nineteenth-century ancestor Lady Jane Digby, who was celebrated in *The Wilder Shores of Love,* Lesley Blanch's 1954 study of great courtesans. In her day, Jane Digby not only titillated Balzac but also stirred up "torrents of scandal," a contemporary once wrote, until she was denounced in the House of Lords as an adulteress and left England. She later went to Arabia, where she happily spent the rest of her life riding in the desert and washing the feet of her Bedouin prince. "Our aunts couldn't hear it when we would discuss Jane Digby," Sheila Moore said, "but Pamela was always intrigued by her," so much so that she still has a bracelet that belonged to her famous relative, and has been known to read aloud from *The Wilder Shores of Love* during country weekends when the conversation flags.

The Digbys were strict. "If our mother told us to do something, we wouldn't have dreamed of defying her," Sheila Moore said, a fact which may have inspired Mrs. Harriman's own later cool maternal style. Like other members of their class, they did not believe that women should be formally educated, but they did allow Pamela to attend finishing school in Germany. There, in 1938, she was invited to tea with Adolf Hitler, by her friend Unity Mitford, the Nazi sympathizer. "He was a cardboard figure," Mrs. Harriman later said. "It was a frightening experience." When she arrived back in London she was nineteen, and Germany had first invaded Poland. The English were desperately starting to mobilize for war, and soon the world would go crazy. Yet up to then Pamela Digby had been so sheltered that she had never been allowed to eat lunch alone with a man.

October 1939. Randolph Churchill, the callow, twenty-eight-year-old son of the First Lord of the Admiralty, was home on leave, wandering through the Ritz in search of a date. He ran into a friend, Lady Mary Dunn, who told him to call "Pamela Digby, who has just arrived from Dorset." And so, according to his cousin's memoirs, he did. "What do you look like?" Randolph said when Pamela Digby answered the phone. "Redheaded and rather fat, but Mummy says that puppy fat disappears," she answered. After three dates, the girl who had never been allowed to be alone with a man was engaged to be married.

That was the moment when she believes her political life really began, but she paid dearly for it, with a hasty and bad marriage. What could Pamela Digby have understood about men at nineteen? Fresh from the country, she was filled with ambition but innocent of the ways of the spoiled sons of famous fathers. Her clothes, she said, "were not as luxurious as my friends'," and she was so self-conscious and concerned about not being able to keep up appearances with other, worldlier debutantes that once during a country weekend she insisted on playing poker with the men and lost, and lost big, "then cried all night until the debt was forgiven," Lord Harlech used to tell friends. "She could have been down on her uppers in that swank London world," another friend posited. If marrying Churchill had seemed the ideal solution to her, she soon found her husband to be a gambler, a drinker, and a second-rate journalist and politician, who, not surprisingly, had a complicated relationship with his father.

Within months of her wedding at Admiralty House, she became pregnant and her father-in-law became the prime minister. She moved into 10 Downing Street during her pregnancy, but not, as commonly believed, for the entire war. "She had a joke during the Blitz and the bombings, when she and Winston had to spend so much time in the shelter's bunk beds," William Walton recalled. "She would laugh and say, 'I have one Churchill on top of me and one inside me.'" Her only child, Winston II, was born and christened a few weeks before the bleak English Christmas of 1940, with Max Beaverbrook, the British press lord, and Virginia Cowles, an American journalist, serving as godparents. When the prime minister proposed a toast to his new grandson, Lady Diana Cooper noticed that he was weeping. She too was overcome, then she suddenly heard the roar of R.A.F. training planes overhead, maneuvering to ward off what everyone was convinced was the German invasion.

Pamela Harriman's detractors inevitably point to the war years when they try to explain her cold-blooded streak. She was thrust into a world where she learned about every possible coming disaster directly from the prime minister himself. Once Sir Winston took her to an underground air station to watch the entire English air force dispatched against the Germans. "Its display of light bulbs told us which squadrons were in combat, in the air, on the ground, or heading home. . . . The bulbs began to glow, and in ten more minutes it was clear that a massive attack was under way. . . . Within five minutes all our planes were on the ground, unprotected as they were refueled and rearmed. If another wave of German bombers had come in . . . all of England's air defenses could have been wiped out," she wrote.

Her husband was so unpopular that when he asked for a transfer his commanding officer was pleased to tell him how much his regiment loathed him, and that they could hardly wait to get rid of him. Two months after that dismal Christmas of 1940, he was gone to Egypt, where he irritated everyone by reading out loud in an arrogant tone his famous father's letters. Even Evelyn Waugh noticed the tension between Pamela and Randolph. "Panto hates him so much that she can't sit in a room with him," Waugh once wrote to his wife.

Like many other society women of that era, Pamela Churchill set up a salon to entertain the men—rarely the women—and General Eisenhower, Bill Paley, Jock Whitney, and all the best reporters in town often stopped by. Soon her reputation as "the fixer" spread. "She was the girl you called if you wanted anything—a flat, theater tickets, cars, restaurants. She always had that extraordinary command for detail," William Walton said. She took a job typing at the Foreign Office, and in 1941 she appeared with her infant son, photographed by Cecil Beaton, on the cover of *Life*. As the star of young London society, Pamela Churchill spent her days taking care of the men who frequented the Churchill Club, a highbrow service club in Westminster which offered a variety of seminars, lectures, and films. "The titled women were running the place, and they could get anyone to talk! The information you could pick up there! Rank was abandoned at the door, and the room would be filled with generals, captains, and majors, all of whom were mad for Pamela," Walton recalled. At night after a lecture, the young Mrs. Churchill would often make her way through the London blackness to dinners at the White Tower or to dances at the Four Hundred.

The atmosphere was hardly frivolous, though. After the United States got into the war, the British and the Americans disagreed about bombing strategies. The British believed in area bombing, the Americans in precision bombing—concentrating on certain key targets and supply points. It was commonly believed in London that Winston Churchill used his daughter-in-law to try and probe the minds of important Americans, such as General Ira Eaker, to whom she was close. Conversely, Lord Beaverbrook, Pamela Churchill's closest friend, used her "to plant ideas on Winston," a logical and wise move. "Pam and I traded information all the time," Walton recalled, "because there were so few people you could trust." By the time she was twenty-one she was at the very pinnacle, knew everything and everybody, and surely luxuriated in the knowledge that her father-in-law, whom she called Papa, was so fond of her that often in the middle of the night he could call her at her flat and ask her to come and play bezique with him because he couldn't sleep. "We would be sitting around after dinner," William Walton recalled, "and the phone would ring and Pamela would come in and say, 'I have to go. He's calling me now.'"

Of all the Americans who arrived that year, few were more commanding than Averell Harriman, Roosevelt's emissary who was there to organize the American aid program, Lend-Lease. The distinguished heir to the Union Pacific Railroad fortune, a man who had been trained from Groton and Yale on to serve the public, he represented the very best of America. The war was raging, life was lived for the moment, and, as Mrs. Harriman often said, "he was the best-looking man I had ever seen." He was forty-nine years old, and Pamela Churchill was twenty and a friend of his daughter Kathleen.

When Harriman left London to become the American ambassador to Moscow, he reportedly allowed Pamela Churchill, by then unofficially separated from Randolph, to take over his Grosvenor Square flat. His wife, Marie, a salty society girl who had chosen to stay in New York, soon heard of the relationship. "Give her up," she cabled her husband in Moscow, according to a Harriman family tale. He didn't, not then anyway, and Pamela Churchill wrote him letters about the terrors of living through the Blitz. "I was awoke by siren and gunfire. I ran to the window just in time to see a black monster with a flaming tail roar past at the height of my window. . . . It went on all day. . . . It really is very bloody, not frightening, just uncanny and sadistic," she wrote. "Pamela was the only person in London to receive three letters from three separate participants at Yalta, including Harriman," Walton said. "She kept them all in a vault."

Actually, her real love during the war was American Edward R. Murrow, the great CBS radio reporter, whose voice would come to symbolize his country during the era. Like Harriman, Murrow was married, and his wife, Janet, was with him in London. She was formidable in her own right, not only as a friend of Pamela's mother-in-law, Clementine, but as a member of the American ambassador's liaison board. If she wasn't glamorous, she was certainly sensible enough to see what was going on and to take off for America, hoping the affair would run its course.

When Paris was liberated in the autumn of 1944, it was at the time of her affair with Murrow. She hitched a ride to Paris. Anything must have seemed possible to her then. Paris was free, the Ritz bar was open, and she was all of twenty-four years old, away from the bombs of London. She must have hoped she would be able to escape from her foolish and unlucky marriage to Randolph as well.

But it was not to be. Murrow was puritanical and guilt-ridden. As months went by and Janet wisely didn't write him, his letters home became abject. He once wrote Janet that he had been at a dinner thrown by "little P," where much of the talk was about the departed Janet, and the guest of honor, the chief of the English air staff, Sir Charles Portal, was "particularly enthusiastic . . . didn't go so well with the hostess . . . think probably the saturnine flyer is marked down as next victim." Soon after, Murrow wrote his wife again. "It might be that I am still in love with you . . . let's renew the contract." Murrow flew home, and the following spring Janet Murrow, at age thirty-five, after years of trying to have a baby, discovered she was pregnant.

If Pamela Churchill had wanted to get away by marrying Averell Harriman, that too became an impossibility. However smitten he was, he was also very much a Harriman, and disliked scandal. Highly ambitious, he was then considering making a run for the White House, which would have been inconceivable, in 1945, for a divorced man. At the end of the war, Pamela, free of Randolph at last, left for a four-month trip to New York. In the style of the era, she parked her son Winston and his nurse in London with her family.

Paris, 1952. "I can remember meeting the most enchanting redheaded Italian girl at a party and thinking how wonderful Italy must be if the girls were this nice. Imagine my surprise when I discovered her last name was Churchill!" an English journalist said, remembering Pamela Harriman in her gay Paris years. She had set up in a grand corner flat near the Rue Président Wilson. Like Jane Digby, she appeared determined not to be constrained by bourgeois conventions, and had taken up with the very rich but controversial Gianni Agnelli, the head of Fiat. She had adapted herself so completely to him that she even spoke English with an Italian accent when she was in his company. Rumors flew around Paris then, especially one about Pamela's having prevailed on Winston Churchill to exert influence on the government to ignore Fiat's business doings during the war. Her reputation as a hostess grew; her parties were said to be extraordinary, her salon incomparable. Having survived the war years and her tumultuous marriage, she was ready to experience the youth she never had. "When I got to Paris, it was years of laughter and fun," she told a friend. "I was still very much growing up."

A friend from that period, Susan Mary Alsop, told of Pamela's problems bringing up a son while looking for a husband. She would have the boy delivered to friends if she went on trips, and when he visited her in Paris as a boy of twelve or thirteen, she would take him to Maxim's, "which was considered a fairly tacky thing to do," another friend said. In those days, the stuffy British ambassador may have had to be prevailed upon to receive the now notorious Pamela Churchill, but there was no question that she was having a fabulous time.

The Duke and Duchess of Windsor, Arturo Lopez, Frank Sinatra, Cecil Beaton, Nancy Mitford, the Duff Coopers, and Daisy Fellowes gathered in Pamela Churchill's salon. Once, on a visit to his daughter, Lord Digby was picked up and taken to the races in her Rolls. He later remarked admiringly to a friend, "Isn't it marvelous how my Pam can make the tiny allowance I give her stretch so nicely! What a good housekeeper she is!" "My mother was very disturbed by the way Pamela was living in Paris," her sister told me, "but of course she wouldn't have dreamed of criticizing her."

The horrors and deprivations of the war were now almost forgotten, and Paris was reawakening to luxury. Dior reigned. Mrs. Churchill was known for sending new acquaintances elaborate gifts, such as gold Cartier cigarette cases. Although the country was Catholic, there was a fine appreciation of the European concept of the mistress in aristocratic life, who lived in almost ostentatious splendor and had a special genius for creating "an atmosphere," as one person put it.

Paris was Churchill's real finishing school. She studied furniture and worked with the interior decorator Georges Geoffroy. She radiated an aura of effortless refinement; "Women who had this ability could surround themselves with furniture that was exquisite, but was never discussed. After all, a chair was to sit on, not to brag about! They knew literature, languages, every political reference. Their tables were seated with genius, and the arrangement of their linens and porcelains was highly original as well as lavish. To live like this was an art form," Reinaldo Herrera said.

One night Agnelli was in a car crash. "Who was he with?" was reportedly Pamela Churchill's first question to movie studio head Jules Stein when he called to tell her the news. She had been madly in love with Agnelli, her friends say, but was so dignified when he married his elegant wife, Marella, that they remained friends.

Her close associates often compared Pamela to Nancy Langhorne Astor, who went from a Virginia farm through the vehicle of a brilliant marriage to conquer Parliament as the famous Lady Astor. She possessed neither sublime looks nor a perfect figure, neither a commanding intellect nor a devastating wit. What she did have was ineffable, "an ability to make a man feel supreme," in one male friend's words. "If you squinted in the sun, without her even asking you, a hat or an umbrella would appear magically to shade you. If you squirmed on a sofa, there would be a pillow." Once at lunch with the editor Clay Felker, she sensed something was wrong. "Pamela packed me off to the hospital, stayed with me while I was diagnosed as having pneumonia, then moved me into her apartment so she could take care of me," he said. Diana Vreeland once called her "the greatest nanny of all time."

In Paris in the 1950s, as the consort of Gianni Agnelli, besides speaking with an Italian accent, she converted to Catholicism. When she attracted Elie de Rothschild, she became an expert on furniture, especially the period of Louis XVI.

New York, 1959. "The first night Father told me he had fallen in love with her, it was like he was telling me a fabulous story. It was my twenty-second birthday and this was the night I realized men—or maybe just my father—were crazy. He knew I loved my stepmother, and he began to tell me about Pamela as if he were selling a movie script to a studio. I asked if she was beautiful, and he said no. But he said she was close to Max Beaverbrook, and that she had had famous love affairs with Edward R. Murrow and Gianni Agnelli and Elie de Rothschild. He said that she had an extraordinary attention span and wonderful lily-white skin, and that her apartment in Paris was known for its fabulous Louis Seize furniture. He talked about her incredible jewels, and said that Somerset Maugham had told her it was time for her to marry. He talked to me for hours about wartime London and Churchill, and I came away from the table realizing that Father felt completely validated, as if he were entering a kind of golden circle through his association with her."

Brooke Hayward was talking about her late father, the flamboyantly elegant agent Leland Hayward, producer of such Broadway shows as *Mister Roberts, Gypsy,* and *The Sound of Music.* His second wife was Brooke's mother, the actress Margaret Sullavan, and he was at this point in his life married to another great beauty, Nancy, the ex-wife of movie director Howard Hawks, known to all those close to her as Slim.

Pamela Churchill and Slim Hayward hardly knew each other when Mrs. Churchill, divorced and perhaps tired by then of the jaded mannerisms of Paris society, came to New York in search of air. She stayed with Betsey Whitney. She had been through several more exciting but dead-end relationships, with Aly Khan, Jock Whitney, and Frank Sinatra. Slim Hayward had left Leland for several months to travel to Paris, to Russia, and to the spa, Maine Chance. *Slim is not watching her knitting,* the New York ladies said at that time. The story goes that before Slim left, the ladies had gotten her permission. "Do you mind if we borrow Leland for a theater date?" "I don't want to go to the theater with an Englishwoman," Hayward had said. "I find them all amoral." But he went anyway, to *A Raisin in the Sun,* and that night Pamela Churchill wore a brown taffeta coat over a simple dress. "She looked ravishing," Leonora Hornblow said. "I was there." And so was Truman Capote, who couldn't wait to put it on the circuit that Pamela Churchill and Leland Hayward had vanished at the intermission.

Pamela Churchill quickly moved her home to New York, and, as Brooke Hayward recalled, "what was going to be a six-week stay became three months and then six months, and suddenly we were seeing plans for apartments and where the priceless furniture would go." A scandal ensued. The phones did not stop. Pamela Churchill was taking on a difficult and extremely unsympathetic group. Slim was popular, and the endlessly circling New York ladies were not at first enthralled to have a glamorous, foreign newcomer in their midst. But in Paris Pamela Churchill had learned to keep her own counsel, and she knew how to stay close to her man. "I was the first person to invite them for dinner, because Leland and my husband were the closest of friends," said Leonora Hornblow. "Babe Paley called me on the phone and said, 'Leonora, how did they behave?' I had adored Pamela, and was so annoyed at Babe's tone that I said, 'Babe, when she and Leland came in, they made love on my floor in front of everyone!'"

Marriage to the great Leland Hayward "legitimized" Pamela Churchill, and the woman of Paris now began to study *Variety* and to inhale every aspect of show business. At age forty she went from "knowing absolutely nothing about Broadway to being able to quote box office grosses in about two weeks," Hayward's daughter Brooke said. "My mother is a chameleon," Winston Churchill II once said. She also began to entertain "brilliantly," as Kitty Carlisle Hart recalled. She invited Leland's friends to their new apartment at 1020 Fifth Avenue. The Haywards also settled into Haywire, a country estate near Bedford, New York, named for Hayward's cable address, and there the new Mrs. Hayward spent days on a tractor cutting paths through the brambles and the poison ivy, while friends commented that Leland had always loathed the country.

"She was madly in love with Leland," Leonora Hornblow said, so much so that she even made the unthinkable sacrifice of going on the road with him during tension-filled out-of-town tryouts, cooking for him on a hotel hot plate because Leland would eat only "white food"— vichyssoise, mashed potatoes, and a special version of chicken hash. If a script conference lasted until two A.M., she stayed, happy to be a devoted wife. And when Hayward suffered flops, she was also there, "a girl very much for the bad weather as well as the good," Hornblow said. Her style as a wife was daunting. "Father's whole routine changed," said Brooke

Hayward. "He used to have lunch at the Colony with his cronies, and now he was suddenly going home for intimate lunches on Fifth Avenue. The masseuse would be there, or maybe a manicurist. His home became a paradise, all controlled by Pam." She even won over Babe Paley, who finally said of her, "I can see that Leland has fallen into a tub of butter."

Soon the newspapers were full of her fashion show appearances. It had taken her to the age of forty to achieve domestic tranquility, but there was a flaw in this idyll. Hayward's three children were not quite adults when their father met Pamela and they liked Slim. "My sister has never been maternal," Sheila Digby Moore told me, and certainly she was not maternal enough to know how to neutralize these very bright but complex characters she had inherited. She got very little guidance from her husband, who was himself fairly cavalier about his children's well-being. As a woman who did not understand the potential hazards common to children who feel shut out, her cool mien caused tensions that never healed.

In the beginning, however, she made an effort. "When Pamela met me for the very first time, she said, 'How nice to meet you!' and placed a lavish jeweled blackamoor pin on a suit I was wearing and said, 'Don't ever sell this,'" Brooke Hayward recalled wryly. Although most twenty-two-year-olds would have been delighted with such a gift, Hayward was unsettled by it. "Pamela was trying too hard to become my new stepmother." Early on, she began issuing dicta about who was "appropriate" for Brooke to date, and when Hayward married Dennis Hopper, "Pamela and Father banished me from the house for seven years." Brooke also resented that it was Pamela who broke the news to her not only of her mother's possible suicide but also, later, of her sister Bridget's. If Pamela Hayward believed she was doing the right thing by stepping in for her husband, or if out of weakness he had asked her to, her action solidified the resentment from her stepdaughter.

She also got off on the wrong foot with Bill Hayward, Brooke's brother, a young man who had been unfairly placed in the Menninger Clinic by his father when he was a troubled teenager, but who had pulled himself together and joined the paratroopers. "I was in the army in Germany, and I was meeting Pamela and Dad for my twenty-first birthday. Suddenly, I was called in to headquarters and told I was the subject of an investigation. They asked me if I was Winston Churchill's grandson. I called my father and asked him what was going on, and he said he knew nothing about it. Later, with some mortification, he told me that Pam loathed my new girlfriend and did not want her tagging along to meet them for my birthday. She had told some of the generals she had been friends with during the war to run a dossier on me and my girlfriend to see if anything untoward was going on. That was how Pam liked to do things. But she did make my father happy—that much I have to say."

"We all began to hear about these 'dreadful Hayward children,'" a close friend said, "and certainly Pamela's coldness to them was quite astonishing." It was especially so when Leland Hayward died, after months of grueling illness, during which he was tended beautifully by his wife, who hardly ever left his hospital room. Pamela's son, Winston, flew in for the funeral, and Brooke and Bill Hayward were told that Winston, and not they, would deliver the eulogy. "Pamela was trying to tell us, *You do not exist,*" Brooke Hayward said. When Hayward's will was read, there was another scene; he had stuck with the provisions of his 1948 will, which gave his children half of his estate. "Pamela's face turned ashen," Brooke Hayward recalled, "and later that day she flew into a terrible rage—the first time I had ever seen her lose her temper completely. She actually said to me, 'How could I have been married for so many years to a man who would leave me so little?'"

A few months before Leland Hayward died, Averell Harriman's wife, Marie, died too. Although Harriman had not seen Pamela since the war, she would often ask Peter Duchin about him. Duchin, whose mother died when he was a baby, had been reared by the Harrimans, because his own father, the pianist Eddy Duchin, was always on the road with his orchestra. When Eddy Duchin died, Averell Harriman became Peter's official guardian. "Ave and I were like a father and son," he said. All this was long before Peter Duchin married Brooke Hayward.

After his wife died Harriman went into a deep depression. "He could not pull himself out of his sadness," his friend Clayton Fritchey said. "He had always seemed thirty years younger than he was," his former assistant told me. "He was still skiing in his seventies." But after Marie's death he seemed to age quickly. Peter Duchin and his then wife, Cheray, moved their children to Hobe Sound and later to Sands Point, Harriman's summer home, so that they could be near him, and Harriman's granddaughters, Pam and Alida Morgan, "practically moved into his house." "We didn't want him to be lonely," Pam Morgan said.

It was Leonora Hornblow who saw Harriman at a funeral in New York and said to her husband, "Pamela for Averell!" When Katharine Graham invited Harriman to a party, and he told her he didn't feel like going out, Graham's response according to Clark Clifford was to tell him, "Pamela Hayward is coming from New York." "When we saw each other, we began to reminisce about London, and it was as if no time had passed," Pamela Harriman later said.

A glorious picture in *The New York Times* announced their engagement. Pamela Hayward, radiant, with a jaunty silk scarf around her neck, holding Harriman's arm. As for their age difference, "it mattered to him, but it didn't matter to me," she told Diane Sawyer. They were married in September 1971, and Ethel Kennedy was their witness. When they moved into his large Federal-style house on N Street in Washington, a friend said, "she made it completely wonderful." The pillows were re-downed, new chintzes were brought in, and the famous Harriman pictures, including the Van Gogh roses, were hung.

In 1977, just before Brooke Hayward's searing memoir, *Haywire,* was published she received a phone call from her former stepmother, whom she hadn't spoken to since her father died. "What is your book called?" her stepmother asked her. *"Haywire,"* she answered. "Why would you call it that?" Mrs. Harriman asked her. "Because that was Father's cable address," Hayward answered evenly, "and it also refers to the fact that everyone in our family was crazy." Within days of the book's publication, a neighbor remembers, "every sign, every matchbook, every napkin that said 'Haywire' at their country house had vanished, and were replaced by ones bearing the house's new name, Birchgrove."

Haywire became a best-seller, and the portrait of Mrs. Harriman as a cold and unfeeling stepmother in it infuriated her. "I think it's a terrible violation of privacy to write about your parents when they're dead," she told Diane Sawyer. "It offended me rather than hurt me."

Slowly, her new husband's relationships with some of his own relatives began to change. "Before, we could just go to Grandfather's house anytime, and he would be thrilled to see us and say to the butler, 'Thin the soup,'" one grandchild reported. "But when Pam married Ave, everything was different. We had to schedule appointments, and when we got there, there were new butlers who didn't know us, and my perception is that we were never allowed to be with our grandfather alone again." Peter Duchin also felt shut out. "One Christmas after they first married, I can remember we were all together, and when it came time to open the presents, it was quite humorous," he said with a laugh, "because Pamela's son, Winston, got an airplane, and I got a tie." When he learned that Pamela wanted to sell the Harriman property in Hobe Sound, he reminded her that Averell had given him an adjoining acre and that he had plans to build a house on it. "Do you have that in writing?" he said she asked him. "Are you kidding?" Duchin said; "Ave gave it to me." "Well, if it's not in writing, I see no reason to honor it," was her response, according to Duchin, who added that he wouldn't have dreamed of going to Averell about it.

"Perhaps this is a profound sense of possessiveness that borders on an affliction," Pamela's friend Clayton Fritchey says of her behavior toward some of her husbands' children. "I can only say that if these stories are true, and I have no reason to believe they are not, Pamela might have felt threatened and wanted to hold all the power." There were, however, members of her new family that she appeared fond of. David Mortimer, her old friend Kathleen's son and Averell Harriman's grandson, for example, she asked to accompany her on a fact-finding trip to China. "I think when Pam married, she had the idea she was marrying the husbands, not the children," a close friend said. "And the men she married cared less about their own children and more about *her*, so they truly didn't notice, or didn't mind."

The new Mrs. Harriman filled her husband's house with diplomats and politicians, a group his late wife had loathed. And his new wife was there to enjoy it as well. Her husband had been an expert on Soviet-American affairs, and he was impressed, he told friends, with "what good questions Pam asks." On another trip to Russia in 1983, he even took her to a meeting with President Andropov. It was a symbolic gesture. Harriman was notoriously impatient of extraneous presences in important meetings. Peter Swiers, Harriman's former assistant at the State Department, who was at the meeting, remembered that Harriman said to Andropov, "I am grateful to my wife, Pam, for coming with me. I hope she will continue my work when I am no longer able to."

Mrs. Harriman's salon was "not a lot of laughs," as one Washingtonian put it, but maybe she had had enough frivolity in her life; she was ready to move into another sphere, where being considered serious was high tribute. "There was so much despair and hand wringing on the Election Night of 1980," Sandy Berger, then Mrs. Harriman's longtime advisor, told me. "It was Pam's instinct not to give in to the gloom, but to start the process back." She was a public woman now, and not only did she have a powerful and extremely prestigious last name behind her, she had a cause. That year she announced the formation of Democrats for the '80s, the political fund-raising group, which was at first laughed at in Washington and called "PamPAC."

In the first eighteen months she raised $1.1 million and gave Maryland senator Paul Sarbanes the idea and the financing to fight off a conservative attack. Georgetown began to take "Pammy's PAC" seriously. Her notes to governors, senators, and congressman, on distinctive green-and-white stationery, were sent all over the country. "Keep up the good work and keep running those fine campaigns," she would scribble to Democratic politicians, and she would often enclose a check in five figures. Her years around powerful men had taught her the benefits of controlling vast sums, and with her PamPAC she now became a woman who could please not just a rich husband but an entire political party. Her days often started before eight o'clock—giving speeches on the Hill and going to meetings, fund-raisers, and seminars—and ended late at night. Guest bedrooms on N Street were turned into offices, and visitors to Middleburg would return and say, "All weekend long, all they talked was politics, brokered conventions, congressional races!" For a woman who, as William Walton phrased it, "was never interested in figuring out what motivated her to lead this romantic, adventurous life," she had finally found the ideal occupation. She could concentrate on the detail work of the here and now; current affairs that might have bored a more intro-spective or cynical personality clearly enthralled her. Mrs. Harriman brought labor leaders together with businessmen, and her office began to put out press releases about what would be discussed at the "issues nights," which featured guests such as Richard Gephart, Albert Gore (whom Mrs. Harriman endorsed early on for president), Jesse Jackson, and Paul Simon. "This is really Pam's evening," Averell Harriman would say before turning everything over to his wife.

While Harriman was alive, he thrived in this political bazaar. When he began to weaken, the care Pamela Harriman took with an ailing husband was unceasing. "Averell was part of every dinner and every lunch," an intimate said. "He could hardly hear and he couldn't see, but Pamela would carry on exactly as if he could, including him in every word of the conversation, saying things like, 'Yes, Averell agrees with you completely,' and then turning to Averell and saying things like, 'Senator so-and-so has just made the very good point that . . .' and then she would turn back to the table and say, 'Averell would also like to add that . . .'" He did not like her to be out of his presence. He could hear only her voice, which she had trained into a middle register, and he would shout, "Pamela, Pamela!" if she wasn't in the room. "Another wife would have been driven mad by this," Kitty Hart said, but Pamela Harriman rarely, if ever, complained. "With Pam, a deal is a deal," Leonora Hornblow said.

When Averell Harriman died, Fifth Avenue was cordoned off for his funeral. Afterward, in a procession of twenty-eight limousines, with state police lining the highways, the family went to their estate in Arden, New York, for his burial. Bishop Paul Moore officiated at the ceremony in the family cemetery, and Harriman's coffin, piled with flowers, rested twenty feet away from the grave of his former wife, Marie. At lunch, later in the day, one of Harriman's daughters told the other members of his family that he in fact would not be buried at that grave site, but three miles away, near a lake, a fact which Pamela Harriman had not informed them of. "If she had told us herself, we wouldn't have cared," a family member said, "but the way we found it out was so peculiar." The story was reported in *The Washington Post*.

When Harriman's will was read, just about everything went to his

widow, it is said, much to his daughters' shock. There were a few interesting surprises; for instance, however icy Mrs. Harriman's relationship
with her stepson Bill Hayward had been, she had arranged for a small
trust from Harriman's estate to go to Leland Hayward's son. A few weeks
after the family funeral Mrs. Harriman organized a memorial service in
Washington, at the National Cathedral. All two thousand seats were filled
as Washington's diplomatic corps turned out to honor the great statesman. Mrs. Harriman had personally arranged the seating in the roped-off
section, leaving, as always, nothing to chance. She walked up the stone
steps of the cathedral wearing a chic black suit and a small diamond pin
in perfect taste, on the arm of her son, Winston, now a Tory MP.

JULY 1988

By the time I interviewed Pamela Harriman, she had retreated into the role
of the powerful Sibyl, protected by a cluster of bright and hungry young
men. I was vetted by Richard Holbrooke. Speaking of Mrs. Harriman,
Holbrooke used the reverent tones one might if discussing a head of state.
Mrs. Harriman had learned and observed the strategems of opportunity
from the inside, taught by her lovers William Paley, Edward R. Murrow,
Gianni Agnelli, and Averell Harriman. She understood the power
bestowed by image and inaccessibility, the implicit linkage of celebrity.
Harriman was a stealth operator who kept her eye on the prize. Cast in the
first act as an ambitious bimbo, the second act complications led to
the joyous third act. She trumped her detractors, racing through high society in London, Paris, New York, and Washington to become President
Clinton's ambassador to France, an end-of-the-century Lily Bart. She was
awarded Paris by another bright and hungry young man whose own urgent
ambitions she had furthered as he furthered hers. "Today I am here in no
small measure because she was there," President Clinton said tartly in his
eulogy celebrating her life at a mobbed National Cathedral. It was, Liz
Smith reported, "Washington's big social occasion of the year."

In February of 1997, while swimming laps at the Paris Ritz, the
Ambassador to France suffered a cerebral hemorrhage. France's President

Jacques Chirac posthumously awarded her the Grand Cross of the Legion of Honor in tribute, laying the medal on her coffin. "I regret infinitely that this ceremony takes the form of a final adieu. . . . She was elegance in itself; she was grace." At her funeral, R.W. Apple of the *Times* noted that her honorary pallbearers were the young men whose careers she had helped advance and who were her fiercest protectors—Richard Holbrooke, Samuel Berger, and Vernon Jordan. The fact that Brooke Hayward, her stepdaughter through Leland Hayward, and Peter Duchin, her former honorary stepson through Averell Harriman, were not present made the *Times* eulogy as well. The oblique reference in the *Times* was as close as the newspaper of record could come to conveying the darker aspects of her personality.

Her sexual cunning made her a vector for anger from other women. A twenty-eight-year-old, unfamiliar with her history, read this manuscript and sent me a terse note: "I understand Pamela Harriman's significance as an historical figure, but I reject her as any sort of role model. Here's a woman who chose her spouses very carefully, from very early—marrying up was her career. . . . Yes, she gave wonderful parties and was attractive and charming, but are those worthwhile talents? All of her sophistication and glamour doesn't erase the fact that she was an adulteress, a bad mother (to her own children and stepchildren), and basically slept her way to the top. It's hard for me to even see her as a loving, devoted wife because of how upset she was that Hayward didn't leave her much in his will. . . . All that being said, she was a formidable woman, with amazing political connections and influence. It's interesting to me that all the shortcomings I perceive in her character translated into acceptance, advancement, and, even reverence in the upper echelons of politics and society."

She had always chosen her lovers and husbands from the haut establishment, and by the time she was a septugenarian—she still had creamy shoulders—the establishment embraced her as its own.

If Harriman yearned for respectability, she was never able to neutralize her critics. Money defined her life from the time she was a young bride in London and accepting a monthly stipend from her lover Averell Harriman. That stipend continued for the next thirty years. When they finally married in the 1970s, Harriman's accountant is said to have asked him, "Does this mean I can discontinue the allowance to Mrs. Harriman?"

Even when she was old and had money of her own, it continued to be the central issue of her life. She raised fourteen million dollars for the Democratic party, but through poor investment advice lost a considerable amount of the Harriman fortune and wound up being sued by his heirs. Paintings she had promised to the National Gallery had to be auctioned to pay off her debts.

Thelma Brenner

Well, darling, I have something to tell you . . . I think this is it for me. Curtains," my mother tells me on the telephone. Her voice is casual. She sounds like a deb, very Boston, as if she were coming home from a dance. Her frequent calls from San Antonio to New York were a fixed part of our routine. Over the years these conversations had tabled the unfinished business between us; we had the luxury of being cavalier. "So, the news isn't great," she said, "but doctors are often wrong. What is the matter with the medical establishment?" I began to hear the terror underneath the party tone.

Two days later she was in New York. The entire family gathered at Sloan-Kettering in the office of a brand-name surgeon—the "greatest in America," a "top man," people said. Mother was late from the airport. Her brother and sister waited for her in the examining room. There was much looking at watches, grim faces, a concern among her siblings that perhaps they wouldn't have time to straighten out the years of misunderstandings and complications between them. We strained for civility, but I think we all knew that this would be one of our last times together.

"Hello, everybody!" she said as she breezed through the door in a linen suit the color of lemon pie. Her stride was bold and festive. Head high, she was playing it for grandeur and appeared to be in supreme command. "You look great!" she said, her inevitable greeting, even to the butcher. As always, her auburn hair was brushed in a pageboy, but she was much thinner than she had been only a few weeks earlier when she had been with me in New York.

She hid panic with whimsy, asked questions of others as camouflage. How were her nieces and nephews? "Marie darling, what are you working on?" She was eager to tell us all about a woman she had sat next to on the plane. We could have been at a dinner party. Mother looked more beautiful than I had ever seen her. I thought: Not yet, please. She was only sixty-six.

"You have to hear my list," she said. "What list?" I asked. "Women I want your father to go out with after I am dead." She opened her purse with theatrical flourish and pulled out a legal pad. "I am serious," she said, adjusting her gaze to approximate world-weariness. "One needs plans, *n'est-ce pas?* So . . . how about this idea?" She paused. "Number One: Louise Michelson! She'd be a fabulous stepmother. And she'd make your father laugh . . . Number Two: Jane Dreyfus. I don't know her that well, but she's attractive, don't you think?" Mother looked at me for approval; both women were friends of many years. "But here's my best idea: Marion Oppenheimer!" She repeated her name again, in case I hadn't heard it. "Why Marion Oppenheimer?" I asked, seeing in my mind the artistic matriarch of a local clan. "It's perfect," she said. "Herbert Oppenheimer was impossible. Your father will look like a prince in comparison."

Then everyone laughed and the ferocity in the room temporarily vanished. Did her sister and brother understand the immense effort she had put into every gesture and word? Her performance was a triumph. Soon she would be gone, impossible for me to reach.

I learned to ask questions by watching my mother with her friends. My mother had an ability to project interest without certitude, to allow a monologue to flow. Mother was at her most vibrant then; she had real power in her circle for her gifts as an interviewer. Her friends later told me that they believed that she "oozed empathy." Certainly her friends oozed experience, and she allowed them to let it rip. She was a sponge for confessions and confidences traded at tea. I would come home from school to discover Mother curled up on a white love seat in "the game room," as she called our den, although no one actually played cards or shot pool here. A Texas hodge-podge, crammed with skins and heads. The walls were decorated with actual game: mounted heads of record-book kudu, Cape buffalo, and eland. I can hear her voice so clearly. *And then what happened? And then what did she say?*

The ladies gathered in the late afternoon. I often perched on the sofa and listened to the stories of glamorous exiles on the lam from bad marriages. Mother seemed to vanish into the dramas of her friends; her true self was hidden in the role of witness to bolder lives. Sometimes I would make notes in my diary: "Mother's friend Barbara over this afternoon. She ran away from a creep—some relative of a Mexican president. Her son is in Mexico City and she is all upset. She cried."

My mother's friends wore denim prairie skirts to the ankle, stockings, Delman shoes, and carried a status symbol of the time: the Collins of Texas wooden box handbag with its leather strap. Those were early Texana—roadrunners in rhinestones, armadillos of faux pearls, Texas flags with metallic gilt—and these women were linguistic pioneers, the first to convert the noun "accessory" into a verb: "How would you accessorize that outfit?"

We lived at a time and in a place when it seemed to us our South Texas suburban enclave, Olmos Park, was the center of the universe. Lyndon Johnson was in the White House for the entire length of my high school years. Johnson's rise to power was part of our daily conversations at the houses of our friends. Many of the local *jefes* had cut the inside deals. We felt as involved as the courtiers at Versailles. As teenagers we knew by heart the shadowy history of Johnson's past, narrated over drinks by our parents—who he had cheated financially and politically, who he had paid off to stuff the ballot box. I knew that Johnson's first call to his daughter Luci after the Kennedy assassination was to tell her to "get her hair done so she looked good for the cameras." We had inside information; we knew before it was reported in the papers that Johnson sold grain from the elevators of his former partner, Billy Sol Estes, and shipped it to Viet Nam. Warrie Lynn Smith, our neighbor's daughter, moved to Washington to room with Lynda Byrd Johnson at the White House. My father's tailor, Eddie, went to the Johnson ranch many weekends to work on the President's suits. He reported that they kept a can of Ajax, not hidden in a cabinet, but by the kitchen sink. Ajax! My mother was dismayed that the Johnsons did not hide their cleaning supplies.

From time to time, the White House helicopter would land in front of the white Spanish mansion at the top of our hill. My friend Judy's father, Morris Jaffe, was a partner of the President. Morris Jaffe then resembled the actor Tyrone Power and traveled around San Antonio in a limousine. At home, he was surrounded with business partners and associates, men in suits speaking in low voices, smoking cigarettes. He rarely ventured from his library, paneled in Spanish wood with portraits of seventeenth-century Mexican saints. At cocktail time, Judy's mother, Jeanette, filled conch shells with bushels of Texas shrimp on ice. Floating by us in an embroidered caftan and a cloud of Chanel No. 5, she smiled. "Are y'all having fun?" Did she dye her hair to match her platinum blond Cadillac, or was the car painted to match her hair? There were five Jaffe children, seven servants, and a vast house filled with baroque furniture and with no adult supervision of any kind. We tried to overhear Morris's conversations, got drunk in the basement chapel decorated with Spanish tapestries and 18th-century Italian putti and religious art. We would hear Morris bellow repeatedly into the telephone: "Senator," "President," "Son of a bitch!" When the governor came for dinner, Judy and I wandered through in our cutoffs and thong sandals, pretending to be unimpressed. In those days John Connally's hair was arranged in a silver pompadour. "Hi, y'all," he said in his deep Texas accent, suggestive of sex and inside deals.

We lived down the hill from the Jaffes on Contour Drive, a winding road with Tudor houses and impressive mansions of local limestone. In comparison, our house was small—"modest by design," my mother always said quickly. Our neighbors were bankers and lawyers, cattle barons and sports kings, the daughter of a man who paved the highways of Viet Nam for Lyndon Johnson, a Texas air-conditioning giant who kept his Palominos in the forest across the street. From my bedroom window I watched the pale horses running in the moonlight. Around the corner lived Pola Negri, vamp queen of the silent movies and inamorata of Rudolf Valentino. Swathed in leopard print chiffon scarves and dark glasses, tight capri pants, she glided through our quiet streets in her pink Cadillac.

My mother taught me to view the panorama of personalities of Olmos Park as if they were events—the bare bones of what narrative is about. "To understand history you must understand people," she said. It took me years to understand what she meant. Mother listened to my stories, questioned me. She made me feel that my impressions mattered; she had aspirations for me.

Mercilessly, we analyzed behavior, feelings, and appearance. She was an amateur sculptress and had a keen eye for body image. Mother defined fat as anyone who weighed over 135 pounds. "People treat you better if you look good," she often told me. "Looking good" was a euphemism; she had me on Metrecal at age twelve, Dexedrine by thirteen. I wrote in my diary: "I will lose two pounds by the end of the day." She was five feet five inches tall and the ideal weight for her size: 135 pounds. She wrote to me, "My trouble is that since I was 23 or so, I've been 10 pounds overweight and then I was only 125 for a short period of time, just long enough to land your father . . ." Weight and diet was a theme in our letters and in my pink leather Barbie diary with its tiny key. "I've lost 4 pounds since you've been in New York," I wrote my father when I was twelve. "Mommy starves me when you're gone." She also bribed me with offers of trips to Europe, clothes from DePinna in New York if I would lose six pounds.

Like Clare Boothe Luce, Mother kept her eye on the prize. She talked in terms of résumés and bona fides. She used colleges and ranks as adjectives; she was courted by a "Harvard-trained" doctor and a "tenured" Yale professor. During the war she worked at the OSS. Meeting my father at an officers' dance at the Jewish Community Center in Washington, she checked out his background and even had a prosperous uncle look up the family business in Dun & Bradstreet's financial rating books. He was a lieutenant colonel, a Wharton School grad, thirty-two years old and in charge of the finance division of the Air Transport Command. His picture was often in the papers. My mother kept all the clippings. FINANCE CHIEF VISITS POST, December 9, 1944. "Colonel Brenner just completed a 40,000 mile inspection tour of Air Transport Command bases around the world." She had a file of his statements to the press: "We find everything at the 556th in excellent condition with the finance office operating in an extremely efficient manner."

She confided in her sister Roz that she was worried he had "a mean streak," but she ignored her intuition. She bragged to Roz that Milton sent "planes around the world with troops and even Fala," Roosevelt's dog. With meat rationed, Mother had steak dinners with C.R. Smith, the crusty founder of American Airlines. The illusion of power suited her, quieted her envious nature. She hid her ambitions behind her questions; she was convinced her ability to listen attracted my father in wartime Washington. They married quickly, and Mother, who had been reared in Boston, found herself in the small town of San Antonio, surprisingly lonely and out of sorts with a fractious new family in the heat of postwar years.

How did my mother think her life would turn out when she arrived as a bride in the San Antonio of 1945? She had met my father when he was on the crest; he sent her dozens of romantic letters with rows of X's for kisses. He told her "to answer the phone at his apartment and tell everyone that she was Mrs. B." He swept her up, called her "my dearest little baby." "I hope by the time I get back to Washington you will have decided to become Mrs. Milton Conrad Brenner." The letters arrived on impressive stationery: Headquarters Air Transport Command. The beginning of their life together must have been absolutely wonderful.

Mother would have been oblivious to the rolling underboil in the Brenner family, the hole in the center of my father's life. "My father is the most difficult man I have ever met," he wrote my mother during the war. "I will never understand him. I think I don't even like him very much. I am coming to believe that my own father does not know the difference between right and wrong."

The Brenner family was part of an extensive social history of Jews in the South who were defined by their stores. In all the towns and cities of Texas, "trade" was what many Jews did. It was one of the few professions open to them. Medicine and law were still restricted, as were the quotas of Jewish students permitted to enroll in college. Open for business at the end of the flu epidemic in 1919, the first Solo-Serve used the former county jail site on the San Antonio River—shoe boxes were warehoused in the cells. By then, the Joske family owned the fancy local department store, the Franks were in men's wear, the Kallisons owned the ranch supplies.

My grandfather, Isidor Brenner, arrived in Texas at the end of the nineteenth century and moved to Mexico. He was reared in Kurland, a Baltic duchy. It was said in the family that at his best moments he had a powerful charisma: he was a raconteur, but he could be boastful, and after he left Mexico he did not correct people when they called him "Don Isidor." My aunts believed he had a tendency to mythologize his contribution to Texas retailing, bragging to his family that Solo-Serve was the first discount store in the state. The women of the family reported that he could inflate the smallest act, even the moment when he thought of a catchy name for self-service—"Solo-Serve"—while strolling on a beach near Galveston during the Woodrow Wilson administration. The truth was he had started as a peddler on a bicycle and was scrambling to make a dollar. He had prospered in Mexico and had to start over in San Antonio. My grandmother used to plant cuttings in discarded coffee cans to sell at the new store. In those days, Solo-Serve unloaded anything my grandfather could deliver: tamales, plants, designer dresses, whiskey, groceries. He marketed a form of crepe fabric that you could clean with a sprayer: Crepe Zuki.

In the 1920s, Solo-Serve had a roof garden theater which ran Saturday night movies for the Mexicans and Sunday tea dances for the Anglos. The Solo-Serve Sale of Progress in the 1930s attracted swarms of early-morning customers; the sheriff would sometimes close off the block. Some years later, Solo-Serve was the kind of place that had tables of tangerine patent leather shoes fashionable in the days of the *pachuco*, fancy dresses for the country club set, velvets and satins for the costumes for the yearly Fiesta queens.

Like Louis B. Mayer or Harry Cohn, my grandfather had a large vision, but appeared to lack a moral censor. My mother-in-law would later tell me that the gossip in the San Antonio Jewish community of her girlhood was that he frequented the red light district, carried on with the Mexican cashiers. He seemed to have no interest in how the community or his family viewed his behavior. While my father was off sending troops and planes around the world, my grandfather married his secretary. He was by then in his seventies and his new wife in her twenties. Before my father left for Washington, he confronted his father about his behavior. Dad had been out riding that day and he lost his temper; he took after his father with his braided leather crop. It was 1941. My father was thirty years old and his father had him arrested by the sheriff—the story made the local papers. They did not speak for the entire length of the war.

Why did he go home? In later years, I often asked my father this question; he could never answer me. It is my belief that he wanted to understand his father's contradictions and sought his affection. "I.B.," as he was known, was a commanding figure in the community: the president of the synagogue, a man who sat on various charity boards. It was difficult, my father told me, for him to forgive his father's harshness within the family. "I tried to be as different from him as I possibly could," Dad admitted to me when he was in his eighties. I admired my father's attempts to seek clarity about this vexed relationship; he never brushed away my questions. It was said in the family that my father had been his mother's favorite child, and as a grown man he doted on her, Surely, he must have gone back to Sam Antonio because he felt protective of his mother, and believed that Solo-Serve was his rightful patrimony. Of his five brothers and sisters, he was the only one who had business skill. He turned down offers from Macy's and American Airlines to battle a private war.

"You're not like other mothers," I told my mother when I was ten. I had come home from school in the May heat of Texas to discover her standing on her head. "Have I ever told you the importance of reversing the blood flow? Gaylord Hauser recommends it! Marvelous beauty treatment! It gives you such élan vital and joie de vivre!" "Joie de vivre" and "élan vital" were the pillars of her maternal wisdom, but this was the first time I had heard either phrase. In this upside-down position, she carried on a running commentary. There was often an urgency in her manner, an agitation underneath her quiet voice with its whiff of her native Boston. "How was school? What did you have for lunch? Let's go to the store and see if there is anything new in the warehouse. They might have a smashing new dress for you or the shipment of Don Sophisticates from New York." My mother's feet pressed lightly on a white wall of our living room, her plaid pedal pushers bagging, her face flushed.

She was often playful and unconventional. "I don't believe school should get in the way of your education," she said, and she occasionally appeared in my classrooms to spirit me away to attend a movie or meet an interesting visitor from out of town. Mother had a policy against attending PTA meetings, and for that matter had no interest in pep squads, cheerleaders, football, Fiesta princesses—the activities that other San Antonio mothers felt were crucial to their children's success in life. "Why waste your time with callow youth?" she said. "Read a book instead."

My mother taught me not to be lonely by myself, and to this day I rarely am. "Only boring people get bored," she told me, a bromide I have repeated to my own daughter, Casey. I could pass hours then exploring the Solo-Serve warehouse full of Easter bunnies and Christmas trees used by the window dresser, Salvador, or watching the paste-up ritual of the ad man who produced six pages of coupon specials twice a week for the local paper. The Solo-Serve price tags were stamped "Look for Defects." I would spy on the dressing rooms, on the housewives who carpooled to San Antonio from Austin or Seguin to work the racks. "Daddy said today a movie star came into the store. She was wearing an orchad," I wrote in my diary when I was seven years old.

In my childhood there was tension about money; my father had gone into debt to expand to the suburbs. It was risky business in 1958. President Eisenhower was in the White House. My father was convinced that the downtown retail areas of this country were doomed. By then, his own father was long dead and the siblings were warring about the terms of his will. My father's brother and two of his sisters fought his ambitions. I remember my father's oppressive moods, his inability to joke or laugh. My mother warned me not to ask too many questions about Aunt Anita or Aunt Leah. It would set him off. At night, he would drive us in the station wagon to what seemed to be the country. There in the moonlight was Robert Hall, a men's clothing store, the first to open so far out of town. The area was thick with mesquite trees. Within the decade, it would be covered with strip centers and gleaming malls. But in those days you could have been in the Texas hill country, it felt that rural and remote. My father's anxieties were palpable in the car. He would tell us what he had been told by a descendent of Sam Houston who ran the Alamo National Bank. "I would give you money for anything, Milton." He was pumping himself up, terrified he would lose it all. In the parking lot of Robert Hall, my older brother, Carl, and I would count the cars, to see if they were "doing any business" at this hour of the night. "Fifteen, Daddy!" I would shout. "Twenty-two," Carl would say. Then, my father, convinced of the rightness of his decision, would take us to the nearby Howard Johnson's for ice cream. Mother always ordered mocha chip and seemed filled with hope as we drove home, her sneakers on the dashboard, as if she knew she would soon be on easy street.

Soon there were Solo-Serves in a few locations all over town. The company expanded to Austin, then acquired tracts of land for malls. None of this success made my mother any less ambivalent about her life. The subject of money unnerved her. There was no consistency in her attitude: Mother bought a Raphael Soyer painting and bid on Matisse lithographs at auctions, but she never got over the reversal of fortune she had experienced when her father lost his money. Financial anxiety hung on her like kudzu.

My father wanted to expand our lives. He began to talk about moving to another house. My mother appeared to go along with this idea and took me looking at real estate in the neighborhood until we found a charming and larger house around the corner. It was pink, I remember, with balconies and verandas, black wrought-iron French provincial trim.

Not a mansion, but more spacious than our ranch house. Several days before the closing, I found my mother sobbing. "Get in the car," she said, and drove me through the quiet streets of Olmos Park near the new house. She parked in front of a magnolia tree, blooming in the May heat. I remember vividly her hysteria, the stories of her childhood terror as her father lost his money and they were forced to move to smaller and smaller apartments. "I cannot move," she said. "Every time we moved when I was a child, it meant my father was even poorer." I moved to the driver's seat and took her home. "Thelma, you are acting crazy," my father said, then mashed a few Miltowns in a scotch and soda and cancelled the contract.

Instead, Mother began to build sprawling rooms onto the ranch house. The game room with its cathedral ceilings, an airy master bedroom suite. There were painters and carpenters adding windows, pushing out walls. It must have cost my father more than the new house would have, but the additions did not set off my mother's demons. I observed him becoming more and more irritated by the contradictions of her character—the flossy upper-middle-class ambitions and her panic attacks. "You will never know what my childhood was like. My father lost everything. *Everything,*" she said. Her father had once owned three jewelry stores in Boston and had been comfortable enough to send his own sister to Radcliffe. In moments of extreme self-pity, my mother played her childhood as if she were Madame Ranevskaya in *The Cherry Orchard.* "We used to have to scrape the gold off my father's watches to pay the rent," she said, berating me for my freewheeling ways.

Mother glided around San Antonio with no money in her wallet. Like royalty, she rarely carried more than five dollars in cash. She would announce airily at the grocery store, "I'm Mrs. Brenner. My husband owns the Solo-Serve," and then turn the phrase into a question, as if she did not quite believe it. She was never comfortable with cash. Once I started working, she rarely picked up a check when we had lunch or dinner out. She expected that I would take care of her; she envied my independence. There were always comments about money issues. "A family of four could live on the amount of change you leave on the mantel," she would say. I kept angry manifestos from my high school days when I would rail against these accusations of my irresponsibility. "Even Granny thinks I am mature and I deserve an allowance to pay all my expenses of $100 a month." I submitted lists of monthly proposed budgets and they were small, even in 1967 dollars: "$5 for gas, $15 for clothes." Long after I was married, I would come home when my mother was visiting to see that every piece of silver was laid out in my dining room. "I'm writing down exactly how many forks and spoons you have," she said, "You are so hopeless, you would have no sense of when anyone is stealing from you."

My brother and father often spent weekends on fishing and hunting trips. We were as divided as a Balkan nation. My mother joked about it: "The boys against the girls." Out of necessity, my mother and I became a club with two members. I think it would have been impossible for either of us to define our relationship with any clarity. We shifted roles subtly and frequently; we were confidantes and antagonists, teacher and pupil, Scarlett O'Hara and Butterfly McQueen. It was clear that my brother and I shared a desire for the attention of the opposite parent, and we squabbled constantly as kids. Did my parents not understand the minefield they were setting up? It took years for my brother and me to view each other as if we actually shared the same childhood. Neither of us was consulted about the arrangements. My father once tried to explain his inattention to me as my mother's plan, but it became obvious to me later that there was some understanding between the two of them. Maybe they knew they were better off spending a lot of time apart.

Like the tsarinas, mother issued imperial *ukases,* tricks and strategies for all life situations, but her most urgent campaign focused on the need for me to make a rapid marriage. The letters with my mother's schemes arrived weekly from San Antonio. When I was twenty-four and trying to earn my stripes as a reporter in New York, she suggested that I write a "Where the Men Are" guide that would have had me searching through several cities. "Think of all the girls who would love to read a book about the availability of *real men* in Texas. With taped interviews—you could get loads of interesting material—limiting your investigation to perhaps three cities, Atlanta, Chicago, and Houston. . . . Along the road you would be in the propitious situation of finding yourself a great husband which then would be a Two-fer. It could be a gold mine! Just on the tennis courts alone . . . visiting the coffee shops in the splendid legal buildings where there are only the best law firms, investment houses, etc."

She wrote: "Always take an elevator going down, never up. First, you need the exercise climbing stairs. Most important, if you are on an elevator going up and someone handsome gets on, you get out on your floor and that's it. He has vanished out of your life forever. But if you meet him going down, he will take one look at you and say, 'Let's go for coffee.'"

The words sounded useless and empty to me even then; it was difficult for me to see any poetry in the house my parents shared. It was a dwelling without irony. The atmosphere was never harmonious, although my mother would try to jolly my father into affection. She used to joke that the only way to gather the Brenners in one room was with subpoenas. We were a family with tightly drawn borders. My father was a difficult man, outer-directed, cut off from anything that had to do with an inner life. The war with his sisters over control of the family business continued to pervade the house. He had a euphemism—"the trouble"— to describe the financial cataclysm that had left him bloodied but victorious against three of his siblings. Aunts, uncles, and cousins disappeared from our life as if they had fallen down a rabbit hole. My mother was left to lighten the gloom, but she was powerless, unable to penetrate the "Brennerian granite," as my sister-in-law later called it, the misanthropic braying, the closed-off hearts.

Mother never seemed peaceful in her marriage; she yearned for intimacy. "He has no idea who I am," she told her friend Louise; but she was a woman of her era and held to the belief that men were needed for the ascent. She had fidelity and loyalty, but scant affection. My mother's sister holds the belief that mother was my father's prisoner, Nora in *The Doll's House*. I disagree. He gave her a sense of power that was crucial to her.

For years, she dismissed the concerns of my generation. Her bookshelves held more books such as *Women and Psychoanalysis, Women's Urge to Achieve*. She sent me scores of letters, filled with harsh judgments and opinions on my life. "You must admit to yourself that your urge to work is a sublimation of not having the right man in your life," she wrote to me when I was starting out. Envy made her angry; she lashed out. If she saw Gloria Steinem on television, she would call me. "That young woman is not happy. The tension in her face is terrible. I don't understand how such a pretty girl can be so furious! Why are all of you so angry?"

When I was twenty-seven and working in London, I fell in love with a forty-two-year-old reporter. A telegram arrived from San Antonio: "Forty plus man usually not marriage minded. Let head rule heart. I love you, Mother." It took years for her to let up, but as time passed she got tired of her struggles. "You are as stubborn as the rest of the Brenners and it is too exhausting and (dare I say) frightening to take you on sometimes," she wrote. I think she began to change. "Never let anyone order you around," she told me years later. "That was my problem. I wasn't independent enough. You young women are lucky. You have so many options. I never felt I had many options."

In the absence of his family, my father turned his energy to the world. "Make your life about something," he told me frequently. At times, it seemed that he was a one-man district attorney's office, marshaled against local corruption. He saved a historic but modest Mexican-American neighborhood from being destroyed by greedy local developers. He tangled with the Federal Trade Commission. I can remember the phone calls and his booming voice through the house. "This city is so god damn corrupt."

The cashiers' stands at Solo-Serve were his bully pulpit. He printed thousands of handbills as stuffers on every issue that concerned him. This began even before the war. "Do You Want Price Dictatorship in Texas?" one handbill opposing price-fixing bannered in July of 1939. "Do you feel yourself 'flush' enough to help Eastern manufacturers pay for their yachts and European jaunts?" The ad man had drawn a swastika and a hammer and sickle on the page, in case anyone missed the point. TAX TRUTH! headlined another of many campaigns. He reprinted a speech he had given to the City Council in the summer of 1975. "My son, Carl, and I listed for your investigation 12 specific properties that are under-assessed a total of about $25 million. We think this doesn't even scratch the surface . . ." The "surface" in this case was the status of the San Antonio Country Club, the preserve of my school friends. It appeared that the club was underassessed $6 million—my father had hired private surveyors to help do the math. "This means that about 790,000 people who don't belong to the club are partially paying for the pleasures of about 1,000 paying members," it said.

"Attention shoppers! Attention shoppers!" My father is speaking on the PA system in the downtown Solo-Serve in the summer of 1966. I was spending my summer before 11th grade bagging dresses in the store. We were busy that day. I remember Dad walking the floors greeting customers by name. A Sale of Progress promotion was going on, the lines at the cashier were ten deep. My father's office was behind a glass wall on the second floor. I could see him sometimes during the day swiveling in his green leather chair. He kept a glass wall plaque on view: SELL AND REPENT. That day, in the afternoon, I looked up to see him as he walked to the microphone. "Shoppers," he said, in his deep Texas drawl, a puckish smile on his broad features, "there is a celebrity in our midst! The famous Leonard Lauder, the son of the great Estee Lauder of *Noo* York has flown all the way to San Antonio to try to find out how we can sell our Estee Lauder cosmetics at such a tremendous discount! He is here to see how Solo-Serve undersells Frost Brothers and Neiman Marcus! And he is right now in our cosmetics department checking out our merchandise! I want y'all to walk over to the cosmetics department and shake hands with Mr. Leonard Lauder of New York!" I recall my father's pleasure that night at dinner, his head thrown back laughing; *he had shown him!* "I bet that son of a bitch went right back to New York," he said.

My father was convinced of the rightness of his battles, no matter that it meant he would later be isolated socially within the intimate confines of the community. He took on crooked local mayors; he offered large cash rewards for whistleblowers. In the midst of one of his campaigns there was excitement around him, a feeling of possibility. He was just secure enough to stick his finger in the eyes of the authorities and not fear that any harm could come to him. I think my parents' best moments were when he was riding a hobbyhorse and she could listen as he worked the phones. The largeness of his personality defused her anxieties that they would be shunned; in fact, she never was. She seemed then particularly girlish, appreciative of his spirit.

But sometimes I would find her wandering in the hallway in the middle of the night, distracted and melancholy. "What is it, Mother?" I would ask. "Oh, nothing. Everything is fine," she would say, unconvincingly. She refused to lift the curtain and let us see what was in the darkness. I understand now that she was adrift in a marriage which had given her security and fidelity, but that wasn't enough. Mother was a woman of smoke and mirrors, she deflected us by explaining that she was worried about how she was perceived. Sensitive to slights of all kinds, she would puzzle over ambiguous remarks. What did this mean? Why did someone say this to her?

Oddities of behavior would play out as hypochondria—she kept files of clippings on nitrates in processed meats, carcinogenic substances, contagions found on toilet seats. It feels to me now that she was looking for a catch-all for her anxieties, but her coping mechanism was motion, a trait she has passed on to me. Sleeping late was unheard-of in our house. She set the standard—up at sunrise in full maquillage, ready to set off on her day. The silver Buick would zoom down Contour Drive heading for the University of Texas seminars, tennis games, conversations about Martin Buber, assignments to teach the history of the Holocaust in the local schools. She began to quote Abraham Maslow on the "fear of non-being" and put up signs in my room with telling remarks from Hannah Arendt: "We must think about what we are doing." In parenthesis, she had added, "In case you are interested, that comes from *The Muses Flee Hitler,* page 132." She went back to college and earned one degree and then another in psychology, but she had a fear of analysis of any kind. "I know more than these shrinks do," she told me, and later was contemptuous of my belief in the beneficial quality of psychoanalysis. "Do hope you are seeing results from the 6 to 9 month period you have been going—not that I am as intolerant as Fritz Perls (the Gestaltist) who thinks that talking to a psychoanalyst in free association is a schizoid exercise by its very nature and does not impart authentic insight." Perls was concerned, she wrote, that in psychoanalysis, "Something must be wrong if it takes many years and decades to get nowhere."

At night she read from the dictionary, quizzing me with words— "tautology," "hegemony," "loquacious." She mastered French and often used phrases: *"Ma vie!" "Il faut que nous partions!"* That coping mechanism had a flair. "It's good that you too are taking French," she wrote. "As Pascal said, 'When all else is gone, knowledge remains.'"

Mother's attraction to that sentiment was real. She had her first cancer at forty-six. She lost a breast, but she was on the tennis court two weeks after surgery. That first performance must have been excruciating for her. She confided that if she lost ten pounds, finished her master's degree in psychology, or perhaps had a spectacular party, her marriage could be "transformed," but she spent many nights believing that the cancer had come back and she would die.

Soon there were fewer visits from the flutey ladies. Mother began to see the futility in idle conversation and trying to penetrate my father's isolation. She used the expression "climbing up a glass wall" and he would stare at her blankly, impervious to insult. She continued to serve my father dinners that would often feature myriad uses of Stouffer's frozen spinach soufflé. He never once got up or learned to cook or help himself. I found that disturbing too. "Why can't he serve himself?" I would snap. She never had an answer. Mother would eat only dry-roasted peanuts. Later she discovered they were laden with the carcinogens she was so terrified of.

It could not be coincidence that she became obsessed with the rights of victims of all kinds. She underlined Hannah Arendt with a shocking pink marking pen. The shelves in the game room filled with new books, Elie Wiesel and William Shirer, memoirs of survivors. It was crucial, she believed, to know every fact, every date, and she started to teach the history of the Holocaust to high school students. They were mostly Hispanic and there were those who could hardly read. What did they care about Treblinka? "I must teach them the perils of demagogues," she said as I drove with her to hear her speak. We passed the Delicious Tamale Factory on South Zazamora Street. The air suddenly was filled with the smell of chiles and frying corn and beans. In her zeal that day, she got all tangled up on the dates of Treblinka and Bergen-Belsen. She was upset on the way home in the car, as if she had let them down. On Zazamora Street again, I was desperate for those bean tamales, but my mother was too agitated to stop. "You don't need all that grease," she said.

She began to feel she had limited time to accomplish something important in her life. Mother saw oppression and darkness around her; she spent hours counseling child victims of "sick and perverted" families, a phrase she often used in her work as an advocate for CASA, the volunteers who took on child welfare cases in family court. I found it hard to listen to her descriptions of the children's lives.

This was a difficult time. I was in my twenties, and Mother came to believe I was her doppelganger, perhaps because she was finally alone in her marriage. My father would rarely travel or go to parties with her. They lived separate lives, but they were loyal to each other. She persisted in trying to crack his code. It was clear to her friends that this yearning was the essence of her life. She more and more talked about her carefree days in wartime Washington where she had been surrounded by beaux at the OSS. Mother would describe being bused to dances somewhere near Langley, Virginia, the curtains drawn for security reasons. She wrote odd and melancholy letters to me. "There is no one role we are destined for but we act as the situation demands. That is why we can never know who we are. We are not just a mother or wife or artist or sweetheart or teacher or friend or competitive sports player or businesswoman—but a person with versatility. The best thing we can do for ourselves is to act with fair play and integrity in all we do—remembering Kant's Categorical Imperative. . . . When we affirm what is good in ourselves (and in others), we lose the habit of self-pity, which can keep us everlastingly sick and neurotic."

She believed, however, that a deal was a deal. Once at a dinner in San Antonio, an acquaintance of my new husband insulted my father. "You married the Brenner girl? The daughter of that impossible man?" "We have to think of a way to respond to these people," my mother said the next morning when we told her what had happened. "How about this? The next time someone insults Milton to you, just look them straight in the eye and say, 'A peasant never understands an aristocrat.' That is a line of Diderot."

I see myself with my mother in the summer of 1967. I am soon to leave San Antonio to attend college in the East. I will never live in South Texas again, but I don't know that yet. I am at the beginning of the beginning of a long journey. I am gathering clothes to take in my trunk to Penn. I tie pastel yarns in my new fall, the thick hairpiece that was a Texas wardrobe necessity. I have matching Pappagallo loafers in pink and green. For this summer, I wear white shoes, lime green miniskirts. My mother has convinced me that the sky is the limit: I have picked up her interior panic but I keep it hidden underneath an odious teenage superiority.

I know everything. I will never have her life of bourgeois convention, I tell her and myself. Your friends are phonies, I tell her, although I truly love the women who gather around her and luxuriate in a warm bath of classic Texas female hyperbole. *You look good. I don't. Ewe look good.* You've lost some weight. I haven't. Well, I love your hair. Who is doing it? Your skin! The texture is like a pearl.

They were smart women with college degrees; they had opinions on events and organized against the Viet Nam war in a claque called San Antonio Mothers for Peace. That summer, when Robert McNamara came to San Antonio to lecture, they forced their way into his room at the St. Anthony Hotel. He was on the telephone, my mother told me, and he was baffled by this cluster of society matrons in their linen suits and color-coordinated shoes. Everyone knew them at the hotel—their husbands were powerful men—so the bellman had let them up.

It was difficult for me to see how serious she was, determined to keep the game going, no matter what. She often stayed up past midnight typing papers for her college courses. At the breakfast table, she would read them to us: "Two Philosophical Concepts in 'La Vida Es Sueno' by Calderon de la Barca." She wrote toadying notes to her professors: "Dear Dr. Benavides: All the work done on this paper has been original, based on thoughtful reading of the text combined with lecture notes which have enriched my analysis. Have a nice summer vacation! As usual, I have

enjoyed and benefited from being in your class and am looking forward
to seeing you in the fall."

She was an anomaly, a housewife among the nineteen-year-old students, and could annoy her professors with her high-flown phrases and
opinions, culled from my father's tirades and *The New York Times*. I recall
that in 1963 she was asked to leave her economics class at San Antonio
College. Something about a fight that had to do with price-fixing on
General Electric's discounting appliances. I'm sure my father was the
ventriloquist, and delighted in making a fool of the teacher, oblivious to
how he was harming her. My mother wrote a furious six-page letter and
copied it to the dean.

> *You are not doing the student justice when you teach a negative
> approach to capitalism . . . I believe that the core of our problem
> revolved around the fact that you did not like my frankly liberal-
> capitalistic approach and that I was not afraid to question your
> socialist slant on our economic system. Certainly, if I had agreed with
> your notions, you would not be in the position of having axed
> me. . . . On the contrary, it would have occurred to you what a
> delightful person Mrs. Brenner is: You might have thought, "She
> doesn't talk up enough."*

My last summer living at home I belittled her for trading recipes for
King Ranch casseroles and mango mold. I did a mean imitation of her
conversations with her friend Louise: "That mold will never gel unless
you go to the *mercado* and get the Jacques Clementes canned mangos
that come from Mexico." "I add sour cream," Louise said. "What an
interesting idea? Do you use apricot or lemon Jell-O as your base?" I was
merciless, determined to cut the ties. The more petulant I became, the
less she seemed to notice. She would make a joke about it. "I'm counting the days!" she said. She became ferocious about my virginity. I parked
my car by the local boys' school and made out with my boyfriend for
hours. My mother knew where to find me. She would drive up in her silver Buick and shout at the fogged windows of my red Opal Cadet: "You

are acting like a whore! Remember who you are!" I drank Black Russians and whiskey sours until I was woozy and smuggled vodka bottles into the dorms for my beau at the Texas Military Institute.

Did she intuit I was taking off for the world? She appeared desperate for me to finish my education. She saved her best lesson for the day I was leaving. "Remember, always ask anyone you meet fifteen questions in the first fifteen minutes you meet them. Fifteen questions. They will like you better and the answers might teach you things."

"You don't need me any more," my mother said to me, as I wept outside a doctor's office on Park Avenue shortly before she died. It was the summer of 1989. We had been to see another miracle man who told her that her rare cancer could be cured with coffee enemas and his regime of fifty vitamins a day. My mother wasn't buying; she had an unerring instinct for a phony. "Please, Mother, try it," I said. "Do this for me." She would have none of it. "You are independent. My work is done." She had been well enough to travel by herself back to San Antonio, but she was soon too weak even to venture much from her bed. She insisted that she wanted to be at home in the large airy bedroom decorated with Japanese woodblocks.

"Please don't wear black to my funeral," she said. "The color has never suited you. Stick to jewel tones. A rich true red. Vibrant yellow. Royal blue." I see my mother so vividly in her bedroom that day. She was in fine spirits, issuing orders. She was by then ravaged by her cancer, but had somehow managed to retain the essence of her looks. She was propped up on pillows, wearing a lace gown. On the bed beside her were lists, always lists. She was at last the grand Texas lady. She dictated lengthy instructions about her funeral, as if she were planning a dinner party. "Keep the red roses and 'awful' flowers like gladiolas out of the Temple. Try to find bougainvillea and oleander. Tell the rabbi not to go on and on. You know I can't stand sentimentality."

The room sparkled. Her house sparkled. On one wall were the signed engravings, the flowers and tea gardens, warriors and city scenes. She insisted that I go through her closets. Her blouses were hung by color; her good shoes were in plastic boxes or neatly arranged in racks. In the kitchen, the recipes were sorted in categories: "Desserts and Dessert Sauces," "Salads and Dressings," "Main Course, One Dish."

I wrote about this on my first Mother's Day without her. I was still angry that she determined to die exactly as she lived; she never dropped the pose. Now, I view her last moments as an act of supreme courage. She was a class act: I tried to distract her with talk of parties, a coming hoedown in New York. Mother was slipping into a coma. The nurse was alarmed and was frantic to call the doctor. My mother looked up. Her timing was as good as it got. "Do you know where Marie can get a pair of red lizard cowboy boots?" My mother saw my tears. *"Quel* hassle, *cherie,"* she said weakly. She was losing strength, the pages slipped off the bed. "Please, darling," she said. "Don't lose your looks over this."

I've thought about my mother's last line to me for years. My friends all laugh when I tell the story, but I am haunted by the subtext of her words. Her message was strength and fortitude: she had the mettle of a pioneer woman and had carved out an interior private world all her own. For my mother, image was a version of a tribal mask, the outer layer of the hidden self. Mother had havens of thought, arcs of silence, moments of deep retreat that were hers alone to guard fiercely, especially from me. She left no diaries and made no revelations on her deathbed except once when she whispered: I've had a wonderful life.

In the years since she has been gone, I have made it a policy not to visit her grave. My avoidance of the cemetery seems selfish to my father and I have tried to explain my reasons: my mother may be dead, but I don't have to believe it if I don't want to. My father's answer is characteristic: "That is ridiculous." For several years, he sent me a photograph of her grave, an impressive gray marble tomb surrounded by azaleas. I could easily read the carving of her name: Thelma Brenner 1924–1989. I keep the pictures in my desk drawer in their original envelopes.

I couldn't escape her if I wanted to; the idea of my mother continues to live. I carry her with me every day. "What if your mother did float around above you big as a barrage balloon blocking out the light?" asks the poet Liz Lochhead. And even as I type Lochhead's line, I can hear my mother taking me to task: "What do you mean, 'blocking out the light?'" She is nettled at my need to hurl a spear at her. She thinks I have an inability to savor her legacy, but of course I do. When I was a child I believed that I could tell her anything and she would listen. It felt then that her love was soft and emotive. If she wanted a man with a parallel soft and emotive heart, she never got one. She learned to be an independent thinker, to seek out friends and women to admire. I learned as well to read the roiling feelings that hid beneath the well-crafted patina of her surface. She never let down the side. And in the end, mystery surrounded her and unexpressed desires, and did it really matter? She was tender and imperfect and striving. My mother was the best of the breed—a great dame with tenacity. She persevered.

OCTOBER 1999

Acknowledgments

Peggy Noonan once wrote that books are pushed along with the gentle help of an invisible cast. Wonderful women—and plenty of great men—have helped me along the way. At Crown, my editor Betty Prashker has been unstintingly generous with her time and advice. Tina Brown first thought to assign me to write about these remarkable women and sent me out in search of the life stories of Clare Boothe Luce, Pamela Harriman, Marietta Tree, Kitty Hart, and Constance Barker Motley. Graydon Carter had the fine idea to assign me to write about Kay Thompson and Luise Rainer. At *Vanity Fair,* my peerless editor Wayne Lawson has been a steadfast and elegant presence in my life. At *Vogue,* Anna Wintour and William Norwich asked me to write about Jacqueline Kennedy Onassis's life soon after she died. I am especially grateful to my friends Jane Hitchcock and Peggy Noonan for inspiring the title of this collection. Fond thanks to my agent Amanda Urban for our long alliance and her friendship, support, and candor.

I have written two new chapters on Diana Trilling and my mother, Thelma Brenner. The portrait of my mother could not have been written without the help of Dr. Ellen Hollander, whose perception and deep empathy illuminated for me many elusive aspects of my family. Warmest thanks for their memories of Diana Trilling and my mother to Jeanette Longoria, Judy Barnes, Carl Brenner, Patti Kenner, Patricia Bosworth,

Peter Manso, Roz Udow, and Louise Michelson. For Nancy Nicolas, a special thanks. And to my researcher Miranda Tollman for her enthusiasm and zest for seeking out hidden facts. Wesley Mittman, Jenna Lamond, and Audrey Costadina provided last-minute editorial assistance. For years of sharing profound friendship, special love and appreciation to Annie Arensberg and Jonathan Schwartz. Warm thanks as well to a platoon of great dames who have helped me to write about the women of this book: Liz Smith, Peggy Noonan, Jane Hitchcock, Virginia Cannon, Joelle Shefts, Carla Carlisle, Nancy Novogrod, Lesley Stahl, Joan Ganz Cooney, Lisa Weinstein, Alexandra Penney, Betsy Gotbaum, Naomi Shihab Nye, Elinor Renfield, Valerie Wade, Eleanor Lambert, Jackie Leo, Delia Ephron, Wendy Wasserstein, Suzanne Goodson, Helen Bransford, Sarah Lewis, and Elise O'Shaughnessy. For their herculean patience, to my husband, Ernie Pomerantz, and my daughter, Casey Schwartz, my unending dear love and gratitude.